Classical Christianity and Rabbinic Judaism

Comparing Theologies

Classical Christianity and Rabbinic Judaism

Comparing Theologies

Bruce D. Chilton
and
Jacob Neusner

Baker Academic
Grand Rapids, Michigan

©2004 by Bruce D. Chilton and Jacob Neusner

Published by Baker Academic
a division of Baker Publishing Group
P.O. Box 6287, Grand Rapids, MI 49516-6287
www.bakeracademic.com

Printed in the United States of America

Library of Congress Cataloging-in-Publication Data

Chilton, Bruce.
    Classical Christianity and Rabbinic Judaism : comparing theologies / Bruce D. Chilton and Jacob Neusner.
        p.   cm.
    Includes bibliographical references and index.
    ISBN 0-8010-2787-X (pbk.)
    1. Judaism—Relations—Christianity. 2. Christianity and other religions—Judaism. 3. Judaism—Doctrines—Comparative studies. 4. Theology, Doctrinal—Comparative studies I. Neusner, Jacob, 1932– II. Title.
BM535.C5157 2004
261.2′6—dc22   2004016943

Contents

Preface

Judaism and Christianity, among all the world's religions, relate to each other in a unique way, because they share a common origin and tell a single story. They share revealed Scriptures that tell them that story, the tale of man from creation to the end of time. Both originate—by their own word—in the Hebrew Scriptures of ancient Israel. These writings Judaism calls "the Torah" or "the written [part of the] Torah," and Christianity, "the Old Testament" and so the first half of "the Bible." So they differ even concerning that on which they concur.

They differ also on the contents of the revelation, part of which they share. By "the Torah" Judaism means not only the Five Books of Moses (Genesis, Exodus, Leviticus, Numbers, Deuteronomy) but the whole of the Hebrew Scriptures, encompassing also the Prophets (Joshua through Kings, Isaiah, Jeremiah, Ezekiel, and the Twelve Minor Prophets) and the Writings (Psalms, Proverbs, Job, Song of Songs, Ruth, Lamentations, Ecclesiastes, Esther, Daniel, Ezra, Nehemiah, Chronicles). And beyond those authoritative writings, Judaism assigns a place in the Torah revealed at Sinai to an oral tradition, ultimately written down by the rabbinic sages of the first six centuries of the Common Era. Christianity, for its part, includes in its Bible not only the Old Testament but also the New Testament. But the story set forth by ancient Israel's Scriptures, and the knowledge of God conveyed therein, form a common heritage and a shared foundation. That narrative, with its insistence on the omnipotence and justice of the one and only God of all creation (or so both parties read the story), imposes its own logic and tensions. Accordingly, while each goes its own way, each builds on that common foundation a theological structure, and the two structures at critical junctures prove symmetrical.

The two religions respond to the logic of the common story by shaping corresponding category-formations. Both tell the story of man—beginning with creation in God's image, after God's likeness, and continuing through middle and end—in relationship to God.[1] They both therefore speak about many of the same things in much the same way—for example, God and man, creation, revelation, redemption, sin and atonement—but within the resulting shared framework they construct corresponding sets of conflicting propositions. This unique relationship between Christianity and Judaism imparts an intense and vivid character to the theological debate (a confrontation over two millennia, really) precipitated by Christianity's alternative reading of Judaic Scripture.[2] That debate, made possible by common convictions, began in Christian representations of the person and teaching of Jesus Christ,[3] which right from the start took issue with the convictions of those later on identified as obstacles to Christianity. These are called "scribes, Pharisees, hypocrites," or "the Jews" in the Gospels and "Israel after the flesh" or "the law" in Paul's letters—and so on into the long, dismal future.

At issue was a sequence of self-definitions. First, Christianity early on defined itself not only by what it taught, but also by what it did not teach: Christianity, not "Judaism" (whatever "Judaism" meant). And, second, among the diverse Judaisms of antiquity, one system would emerge to take over the category "Judaism," using the language of "the Torah" to counter "Jesus Christ" with "Moses our Rabbi."[4] For their

1. By "man" in these pages we mean mankind: all humanity, both sexes.

2. Islam bears a different relationship to Christianity and to Judaism from the relationship between Christianity and Judaism, but its category-formations in important ways correspond to those of the other two monotheisms. See Jacob Neusner and Tamara Sonn, *Comparing Religions through Law: Judaism and Islam* (London: Routledge, 1999). In the interfaith dialogue among the monotheisms, such as it has been and now is, Islam deals with its predecessors by claiming to affirm and now to absorb their truth, Christianity explains itself by inventing what it then labels as its predecessor, and Judaism finds itself required to account for phenomena for which it bears no responsibility whatsoever—an odd trialogue of three monologues. But that is not our problem here. See also Jacob Neusner, Bruce Chilton, and William Graham, *Three Faiths, One God: The Formative Faith and Practice of Judaism, Christianity, and Islam* (Boston: Brill, 2002).

3. In this work of theological discourse, we freely use the language and native categories of the two faiths, thus, in speaking of Christianity, "Christ" rather than simply "Jesus," and, in speaking of Judaism, "Moses our Rabbi" and "Torah" rather than simply "rabbinic tradition" and "rabbinic Judaism." Those more neutral terms can function as circumlocutions meant to avoid affirming what the speaker does not hold.

4. Rabbinic Judaism reached full definition in the fourth century: the legalization and later establishment of Christianity as official religion of the Roman Empire, joined

part, the advocates of the Torah of Moses our Rabbi rarely conceded the existence of Christianity, which it held to be comprised of people who knew the Torah but did not follow it. For Judaism, Scripture set the limits: God or idolatry. The Judaic sages' world was divided into those who knew and worshiped the one and only God, who made himself known in the Torah at Sinai and in the oral traditions beginning there, and those who did not. By "Israel," therefore, rabbinic Judaism meant those who adopted for themselves Scripture's account of God's people by accepting the Torah of Sinai and so hoping for life beyond the grave. It defied all comprehension that others should make a competing claim to possess and interpret that revelation and its promise of eternal life or to know one true God made manifest in it. So while Christianity invented the Judaism that it would reject and supersede, on its good days conceding "the Jews" the position of "elder brothers in faith" but never allowing "the Jews" to constitute the "Israel" to whom God revealed himself in the Torah, Judaism for its part ignored Christianity for ten centuries and more, declining to engage it except under duress, and then with contempt.

We need hardly rehearse the events of the twentieth century that changed Judeo-Christian engagement from the old pattern of aggressive confrontation met by an implacable act of ignoring to the recent benevolent pattern. But we do stand on firm ground in alleging that goodwill has yet to nurture theological engagement, much less actual dialogic argument. Only seldom have significant theologians of Judaism addressed the crucial claim in Christ's behalf that animates Christianity—all Christianities.[5] And Christian theologies of "Israel," while full of goodwill, rarely step beyond the limits initially defined by Paul's reflections in Romans—if, indeed, they even recapitulate what Paul was prepared to concede to "Israel after the flesh." Supersessionism—the doctrine that Christianity superseded Judaism, replacing it entirely and turning it into a relic and a fossil—takes many forms but competes with no other Christian theory of Judaism. And, it goes without saying, no Christian theology of Judaism has known how to cope with the claim of the Torah, written and oral, to convey God's will for that part of mankind that wishes to know God.

---

with the dramatic failure of the Emperor Julian's plan to embarrass the Christians by allowing the Jews to rebuild the Temple (360–361), necessitated a systematic response to the Christian agenda. In this connection see Jacob Neusner, *Judaism and Christianity in the Age of Constantine: Issues of the Initial Confrontation* (Chicago: University of Chicago Press, 1987).

5. Franz Rosenzweig and Eugene Borowitz are the only significant names, Borowitz's *Contemporary Christologies: A Jewish Response* (New York: Paulist Press, 1980) being exemplary.

In that context of remorse and recrimination—the Christians unable to transcend the evangelical motivation of old and frame a dialogue with holy Israel (a.k.a. "Judaism"), the Judaic participants unwilling to grant much more than grudging recognition that Christianity, after two thousand years, really does exist—theological debate has hardly flourished. Indeed, insofar as theological debate requires more than a mere trading of information, each informing the other about the basics of his particular faith, intellectually substantive debate has been rare.

That is not to suggest that religious—as distinct from theological— dialogue has languished even in such a favorable age as the last half century. Judeo-Christian dialogue on issues of social concern and even religious sensibility has not only flourished but even attained a high level of institutionalization. Indeed, it has come of age with the advent of numerous associations and organizations, publications, and professorships in Europe and the United States under ecclesiastical sponsorship (for Christianity) and rabbinical and secular supervision (for Judaism). But religious dialogue seldom acknowledges that in the formative age of Christianity and rabbinic Judaism, the first six centuries CE, Christianity and Judaism parted company for substantive, theological reasons, disagreeing not only violently and politically, but also rationally and with solid reason. The parting of the ways finds its explanation in history, sociology, even politics, but rarely in intellect. And that misconstruction defies the fact that the parties to the quarrel were not generals, administrators of institutions, or politicians, but, all of them, engaged by ideas and issues of thought. In their writings about one another they argued logically from what they advanced as common premises and shared logic—intellectuals one and all. And the theological confrontation necessary for spelling out the issues and clarifying the logic that precipitated schism between the two within the shared premise of Scripture has scarcely come to realization. The crushing burden of Christian guilt and Judaic suspicion, many thought (and with good reason), would only grow weightier should confrontation define the next step of the fragile dialogue. And at stake, to begin with, was Judaic and Christian collaboration.

A second consideration has raised still higher the barrier to substantive theological dialogue about religious truth deriving from shared Scriptures and agreed-upon logic. Theology itself, in the classical, disciplined form embodied in such works as Moses Maimonides' paired *Mishneh Torah*, a philosophical law code, and *Guide to the Perplexed*, a work of theology and philosophy of religion, has known better times than these. Judaism has made its disproportionate contribution to the walling out of theological discourse between kindred faiths. Two distinct parties have helped raise the barrier. First, practitioners of the classical faith of the written and oral Torah have followed theologians who have (quite logically) recapitulated the received conviction that Christianity is not to be afforded recognition of any kind. No theological engagement, let alone dialogue, should take place. Second, secular Jews, commanding the institutions of what they call "the Jewish community," have misconstrued what is at stake and have from the start considered theological issues vacuous. They have insisted that Judaism has no theology anyway.

Meanwhile, Christian theologians, when dealing with Judaism at all, have persisted in the pattern established in the first Christian century. As did the founders, so also the contemporary continuators have invented a Judaism for dialogue and fabricated an engagement with that Judaism. The result has proved suspiciously similar to the Christian theologies of Judaism of the first four Christian centuries (through Chrysostom), which taken together formed little more than explosions of exasperation with the perfidious Jews. Stated more simply: the theology of Judaism that Christians brought to the conference table never engaged with the truth-claims of the Torah as set forth by "our sages of blessed memory"—the rabbis of the Mishnah, Talmuds, and Midrash—who defined the classical statement of the Torah (a.k.a. Judaism). That is because the Christian dialogue partners defined "Judaism" principally in relationship to Christianity. So the animating question has been, "Why are you not what you are not?" rather than, "Why are you what you are?"[6] From the first Christian century forward, Christianity quite naturally defined the agenda for Christianity—then found puzzling the indifference of potential dialogue partners.

For reasons we spell out in chapter 1, the joint authors of this book believe that comparative theology bears promise for both parties to the comparison. Each has a heavy stake in its success. That is why we take what we hope will prove the first steps, however shaky, toward theological comparison. The work is simply defined. In chapter 1 we define the work of theology, explain the basis for our representation of the theology of Judaism and Christianity, and then spell out the shared topics: the story told in common, the chapters of each religion that bear the same title as those of the other. In chapters 2 through 7 we identify six corresponding and critical components of Christian and Judaic theology and show how they intersect and collide. We suggest in aggregate that

6. At a Judeo-Christian "dialogue" at Harvard Divinity School in the mid-1960s the German theologian Wolfhart Pannenberg shocked the Judaic participants by his paper, which stated in so many words, "The only question of Judeo-Christian dialogue is why you Jews don't accept Jesus Christ."

theological confrontation defines the task of interfaith dialogue for the twenty-first Christian century. In our selection of topics that are pivotal within each of the two religious systems under discussion, we offer productive pathways into that confrontation without pretending to know where it might lead.

Our goal is therefore indicated without being fully reached in these pages. We wish simply to engage in the dialogue to which we feel our faiths call us: the productive argument and dialogue on what is true that is treasured in German theology under the name *Auseinandersetzung,* which lacks a precise counterpart in English-speaking discussion. We hope the path we explore will lead in due course to a renewal of the theological confrontation not undertaken in the first three Christian centuries, then begun but abruptly broken off at the moment of engagement in the fourth. By theological confrontation, not just comparison, we mean the systematic sorting out of truth-claims and the advocacy of one position over another on the basis of common Scriptures, common premises, and shared reason.

Why insist on the language of "confrontation"? Because Judaic and Christian theologies make truth-claims about, in part, a single program of propositions and base these claims on a shared corpus of revealed truth: Judaism's (written) Torah, Christianity's Old Testament. Since, as we argue in the opening chapter, theology means to think philosophically about religious truth, we mean to point out the conflict that characterizes the two faiths' theological intersections—and to underscore the rationality of the opposed positions. For in theology there can be no dialogue without confrontation, and difference of position (not merely "opinion") demands not negotiation but serious consideration. Serious consideration entails reasoned argument based on agreed-upon rules of rationality and shared evidence and conforming to common rules of rhetoric and logic. Put briefly: we identify critical, fundamental theological issues on which classical Christianity and formative Judaism intersect and differ.

We take as our task the exposition of theological confrontation. We hope that after all these centuries both parties have attained to that maturity of confidence that permits engagement with difference concerning a common agenda. The present work is meant to make possible theological debate about questions of religious truth that, in our conviction, only Christianity and Judaism, among all the religions of the world, can truly undertake.

It remains to call attention to books of ours that have engaged in different kinds of Judeo-Christian comparative studies, besides the theological ones of the present work. These have taken up historical, religious, and literary problems. Our comparative history is in the following:

Trading Places: The Intersecting Histories of Christianity and Rabbinic Judaism. Cleveland: Pilgrim, 1996. Repr. Eugene, Ore.: Wipf & Stock, 2004.

Trading Places Sourcebook: Readings in the Intersecting Histories of Christianity and Rabbinic Judaism. Cleveland: Pilgrim, 1997.

We conducted comparative studies on questions of religious literature and intellect in the four-part work:

Jewish and Christian Doctrines: The Classics Compared. London: Routledge, 2000.

Judaism in the New Testament: Practices and Beliefs. London: Routledge, 1995.

Types of Authority in Formative Christianity and Judaism. London: Routledge, 1999.

The Intellectual Foundations of Christian and Jewish Discourse: The Philosophy of Religious Argument. London: Routledge, 1997.

Most important, on what basis do we identify a common set of theological category-formations? We established the commonality of Judaic and Christian religious category-formations in these works:

Christianity and Judaism: The Formative Categories. Vol. 1, *Revelation: The Torah and the Bible.* Valley Forge, Pa.: Trinity Press International, 1995.

Christianity and Judaism: The Formative Categories. Vol. 2, *The Body of Faith: Israel and Church.* Valley Forge, Pa.: Trinity Press International, 1996.

Christianity and Judaism: The Formative Categories. Vol. 3, *God in the World.* Harrisburg, Pa.: Trinity Press International, 1997.

Jewish-Christian Debates: God, Kingdom, Messiah. Minneapolis: Fortress, 1998.

These books have enjoyed wide readership, so we are confident that we are not alone in the conviction the theological comparison is now possible, and confrontation in civil discourse plausible as well.

The authors express their gratitude to Bard College, where both hold professorships; our joint efforts are greatly facilitated by our common academic situation. We express special thanks to Bard's president, Leon Botstein, who has taken a benevolent interest in nurturing the productive intellectual and scholarly partnership that we have established.

Translations of primary texts in the following chapters, except where otherwise noted, are our own. Some biblical quotations are adapted from the Revised Standard Version.

1

Theology, Judaic and Christian

＊

To do theology is to think philosophically about the revealed truth that
a religion puts forth. To think philosophically is to address systematic
questions of definition, logic, cogency, coherence, and proportion. A
theological system emerges from the answers to those questions. An
analogy then presents itself: theology is to religion as language is to experience and perception. Theology constitutes the language of religious
faith, knowledge, and experience, defining its vocabulary (category-
formations), laying out its grammar, setting forth its syntax.[1] Just as
language turns inchoate experience into propositions subject to general
intelligibility in public discourse, so theology expresses in appropriate
language the attitudes and feelings and intangible but very real percep-
tions of religion. It puts them into intellectually accessible terms and
categories, subject to generalization and systematization. Transforming
what is private and inherently individual into something that is public
and intentionally shared, theology does for religion what language does
for experience and perception.

1. These matters are spelled out in Jacob Neusner, *The Theological Grammar of the
Oral Torah* (Oakdale, N.Y.: Dowling College Press, 1998). Volume 1 is *Vocabulary: Native
Categories;* vol. 2, *Syntax: Connections and Constructions;* vol. 3, *Semantics: Models of
Analysis, Explanation and Anticipation.*

15

To treat theology as the language of religion, we must learn how to elaborate the vocabulary, grammar, and syntax of this language as it is spoken (i.e., of the religion as it is lived). The task of describing the theology of a religion—in the present case, of a privileged collection of religious writings, deemed continuous with one another and held to form a cogent statement—is to discover the generative grammar that dictates the flow of thought and imposes form upon it. That generative grammar of theology renders public and accessible to shared discourse the religious faith and encounter of those who value and privilege the selected writings. In these pages we mean to uncover a common theological grammar shared between Judaism and Christianity—the grammar that makes possible shared religious discourse—and to investigate the way in which two distinct and conflicting theological realms of speech can communicate through a universal grammar. We attempt this by comparing and contrasting category-formations native to both religions by reason of their common origin in Scripture.

In the religions of Western civilization, which is founded on the Greek philosophical tradition, namely, Judaism, Christianity, and Islam, "theology" stands for logical thinking about God, or, more broadly put, thinking philosophically about religious truth. By "religious truth" we mean the attitudes and emotions, beliefs and opinions, stories and convictions that form the worldview of a religious community and heritage. Speaking within the faith, religious truth derives from revelation. The record of revelation, in the nature of things, may produce conflict. God may demand in one passage of Scripture what in another passage God forbids. That is where theology—philosophical thinking about religious truth—enters in. Philosophy in the Western tradition insists upon rigorous and critical examination of all claims to speak truth. In the setting of religious thought and discourse, philosophical thinking about claims to state religious truth is called theology. Theology seeks the logic (*logos*) implicit in what reason and revelation alike allege about God (*theos*) and, therefore, about what God wants of us.

When religions examine critically their opinions, attitudes, and emotions, seeking to form them into a proportionate and coherent statement, they think philosophically—rationally—about religion. To think philosophically in the tradition of Plato and Aristotle means to think systematically, rigorously, and critically, and to argue on the basis of shared reasoning and commonly acknowledged evidence. In the tradition of Western thought, both Judaic and Christian (though in different modes), that is what people do when they undertake theological reflection. Faced with conflicting evidence, such as verses of Scripture that assign conflicting traits to God, religious thinkers may accept the paradox, but theologians confront a challenge. They ask critical questions and produce reasoned, systematic responses. And that is as it should be. Still more to the point, they pronounce their conclusions and invite public discussion within shared canons of rationality.

In broader terms, to move from opinion into philosophy is to transform reflection or meditation into a public event, the intent being not only to exchange information or set forth a viewpoint "to whom it may concern" but to change the mind of the listening, responsive other. What marks writing as philosophical is the claim that what is said confronts and withstands contrary opinion, enjoys the validation of argument and evidence, and enters into the competition of truth. The other—reader or listener—is invited to participate, indeed treated as judge of the process. And the thinker becomes a philosopher in the setting of classical philosophy when he acknowledges that his concept competes with some other. That takes place when he assumes the burden not only of announcing his view but also of examining evidence acknowledged by all sides and conducting an argument of advocacy and analysis in accord with modes of argument shared by both (or all) parties. Whoever wishes to claim to have the best explanation, the most adequate theory, must register that claim in the public forum of open debate and universally accessible argument. So theology commonly takes the form of an argument—a dispute, a debate, a dialogue.

Philosophical dialogue concerning religious truth entails the contention of engaged minds, competing as equals in standing and judgment, and holding forth quite contrary positions on the same question. In rhetorical terms too, the presentation of thought for both classical philosophy and the Talmud takes place in public and in the context of contention. The rhetoric of dispute and debate matches the logic of philosophical contention concerning what is the better explanation or the more compelling and useful definition. What is at stake in philosophy in the Western heritage? The great classicist G. E. R. Lloyd describes this matter in language that serves equally well for the Judaic and Christian thought that we shall examine in these pages:

> The Egyptians . . . had various beliefs about the way the sky is held up. One idea was that it is supported on posts, another that it is held up by a god, a third that it rests on walls, a fourth that it is a cow or a goddess. . . . But a story-teller recounting any one such myth need pay no attention to other beliefs about the sky, and he would hardly have been troubled by any inconsistency between them. Nor, one may assume, did he feel that his own account was in competition with any other in the sense that

it might be more or less correct or have better or worse grounds for its support than some other belief.[2]

If we examine the two creation myths of Genesis, or the two stories of the flood, we see how readily conflicting stories might be joined together, and how little credence was given the possibility that one version might be correct and the other wrong. We search in vain through the entire heritage of Israelite Scriptures (with a stated exception given presently) and through all extra-scriptural writings of various Judaic systems for any example of articulated and elaborated dispute and debate. But the character of postscriptural Judaic and Christian thought in antiquity, properly construed, shows a different picture.

In the tradition of Greek philosophy, the rabbinic sages and the Christian theologians confronted difference and proposed not to harmonize conflicting positions but to determine which was right, which wrong. They articulately faced the possibility that differing opinion competed and that the thinker must advocate the claim that his theory was right, the other's wrong. Conflicting principles both cannot be right, and merely announcing an opinion without considering alternatives and proposing to falsify them does not suffice for intellectual endeavor. And with the recognition of that possibility of not only opinion but argument, Greek philosophy engaged in debate:

> When we turn to the early Greek philosophers, there is a fundamental difference. Many of them tackle the same problems and investigate the same natural phenomena [as Egyptian and other science], but it is tacitly assumed that the various theories and explanations they propose are directly competing with one another. The urge is towards finding the best explanation, the most adequate theory, and they are then forced to consider the grounds for their ideas, the evidence and arguments in their favor, as well as the weak points in their opponents' theories.[3]

And what was true of science pertained to civilization in all aspects:

> In their very different spheres of activity, the philosopher Thales and the law-giver Solon may be said to have had at least two things in common. First, both disclaimed any supernatural authority for their own ideas, and, secondly, both accepted the principles of free debate and of public access to the information on which a person or an idea should be judged. The essence of the Milesians' contribution was to introduce a new critical spirit into man's attitude to the world of nature, but this should be seen

2. G. E. R. Lloyd, *Early Greek Science* (New York: W. W. Norton, 1970), 11–12.
3. Ibid., 12.

as a counterpart to, and offshoot of, the contemporary development of the practice of free debate and open discussion in the context of politics and law throughout the Greek world.[4]

The phenomenon of debate brings us to the rules of engagement that dictate where and how philosophy takes place.

For classical philosophy, learning takes place (or at least is imagined to take place) in person, in public, and through universally accessible debate. The same evidence and arguments must appeal to all parties, and the same principles of rational inquiry govern everyone. That is why the ideal circumstances for philosophizing occur in collective argument, conducted (at least in theory and intent) orally, through exchange; or in public exposition in lecture form of well-considered knowledge. Plato's dialogues, Aristotle's lectures, define the norm, even though other contexts of philosophical speech are attested. The public circumstance—dialogue through debate or lecture—defines the rhetorical premise and even dictates the form. Arguments conducted for all concerned parties, aimed at showing a wide audience the reasons for sound convictions, form the wherewithal of rigorous and effective thought. These convictions form the basis of Western intellectual life at its origins, with Plato and Aristotle, and, as we shall see, they are shared by the framers of the classics of rabbinic Judaism and the principal church fathers, whether they wrote in Greek, Latin, or Syriac.

Why Compare Theological Systems?

By "theological systems" we mean systematic, intellectual structures that accommodate and form a coherent statement of religious convictions, attitudes, sentiments, emotions, myths, rites, practices, creeds, and dogmas. That is, theology systematizes, in propositions about God (and consequently everything else), an understanding of the entire heritage of a faith. Like philosophical systems and theories of economics, politics, literature, and art, theological systems display the logic that forms the chosen data into a single cogent and coherent statement. Comparing theological systems requires comparing the logic and rationality of one such system against those of another—a considerable enterprise of description, analysis, and interpretation.

What makes comparison and contrast so urgent in the setting of competing theological systems, the Judaic and the Christian, resting on the same Scripture and comprising some of the same category-

4. Ibid., 15.

formations? When it comes to religion, the theory supporting comparison and contrast is simple. If we hope to understand religions, the work of comparing one with another affords perspective on the choices represented by each. If we need to make sense of many things, it is often by looking for what they have in common, the traits of the whole that govern the parts. In the present context, that means trying to generalize about *religion* out of the study of *religions*. Armed with such generalizations, we take up new cases and test them. That is to say, we ask: if we know this set of facts, what else do we know? This question—"what else?"—aims at logical consequences: it means, fundamentally, "so what?" Comparing religious traditions, then, opens the way to generalizing on some cases in quest of understanding about many more cases. Comparison and contrast open the way to answering the question "so what"?

That quest for generalization about religion cannot be postponed, because religions—we cannot overstress—form a principal part of public life and culture in many, though not all, of the regions and nations of the world. What people think about a given religion will therefore shape the attitudes of nations toward one another. Conflicts loom. People make judgments. We do best to confront difference in the benign setting of the academy before we must face conflicts we cannot understand, let alone avoid. To the work of sorting out difference, especially in religions, this labor of comparison and contrast therefore is essential. That means identifying what religions have in common, where they differ, and how to make sense of both.

It is easy to explain why we must compare religions' theological systems. Comparison and contrast define the work that must be done if interfaith dialogue is to address issues not just of social utility but of religious truth. If religions are going to move beyond superficial civility and undertake substantive conversation about deeply held convictions, they are going to have to take seriously the conflicting allegations of different religions regarding the character of God, the validity of revelation, and the rationality of the godly way of life. Since religions make statements about God that they allege are true, and these statements often conflict (for example, is God one or many?), conflict necessarily characterizes encounter between religions. But how are we to conduct theological dialogue when each religion appears to be pursuing its own particular agenda, and each agenda has little in common with any other? This is the utility of theological comparison and contrast. Without some orderly system we cannot lay the foundation for productive debate about matters of truth because each party may simply speak of its own topic, ignoring issues important to the other. Then even when the same language surfaces—"God" is a good case in point—we quickly perceive that what the one means by that language bears no relationship with what the other has in mind. Facts out of context confuse and rarely signify much beyond themselves. But facts formed into a coherent system, thought framed systematically, in harmony and proportion—that is another matter. In one way or another all religions shape a system and appeal to a rationality that imparts order and defines context for the details of the faith.

The religions that think theologically—that is, we cannot overstress, that think philosophically about religion—appeal to a common mode of thought, which is that of criticism, and a shared method of inquiry, which is an appeal to a common logic. Theological thought insists upon a single criterion of truth, a mathematics of the divine, so to speak. For both rabbinic Judaism and classical Christianity, a grammar of thought derived from documents valued as authoritative by the faithful suggests a theological system. The common documentary foundation for these systems is a set of writings that both Judaism and Christianity affirm as revealed by God to mankind in an act of self-manifestation: through the Hebrew Scriptures of ancient Israel ("the Torah," "the Old Testament"), if not only through them, mankind knows God as God wishes to be known. The two religions concur on that fundamental point.

Not only so, but because both tell the same story of humanity and God's self-revelation to humanity, both religions organize their thought in large-scale structures that exhibit traits of congruence. Both begin their stories with creation and tell the same story of creation. Both speak of those who know God as "Israel" and affirm the revelation by God to Israel at Sinai. Both see the story of humanity as a tale with a beginning in Eden, a middle here and now, and an end with the last judgment and victory over the grave and entry into eternal life. With so much in common, each organizing much (though not the whole) of its theological system within structures comparable to those of the other, Judaism and Christianity present themselves as ideal candidates for the enterprise of comparison and contrast.

Logically the next question is: given the diversity of Judaisms and Christianities through time and, in particular, in ancient times, of which Judaism and of which Christianity do we speak? In the case of Judaism, on what basis, given the diversity of rabbinic opinion represented in the authoritative writings, do we speak of a cogent theological structure and system at all? In the case of Christianity, on what basis, in light of the diversity of Christian opinion in Greek, Latin, and Syriac, do we claim to compose, for purposes of comparison and contrast, a single theology? To these questions we now turn.

Rabbinic Judaism

For "Judaism" we take up the Judaism of the dual Torah, written and oral, which is conventionally called rabbinic Judaism and which calls itself "the Torah," as in the form of theological utterance composed of "the Torah teaches" plus whatever a rabbinic sage wishes to say that day. From its beginnings in the first six centuries CE to nearly the present day, rabbinic Judaism, represented by Scripture and the oral Torah, defined the normative faith for nearly all practitioners of Judaism (a religious system that privileged the Pentateuch and adopted for its adherents the name Israel). Today when people speak of "Judaism" they still mean the diverse heirs and continuators of rabbinic Judaism. The metaphor derived from comparing theology to language proves especially appropriate in the study of rabbinic Judaism, because the representation of the religious life and experience of that Judaism comes to us in the sole medium of texts, and those texts exhibit remarkably uniform traits of linguistic formalization and expression. So to begin with we take up a Judaism that uses disciplined language to set down in permanent form whatever it wishes to say about knowing God.

All expressions of rabbinic Judaism privilege the Pentateuch and find the meaning of Torah in a set of related texts. These are the Mishnah, a philosophical law code (ca. 200 CE); its amplifications and commentaries: the Tosefta (ca. 300), the Yerushalmi or Talmud of the Land of Israel (ca. 400), and the Bavli or Talmud of Babylonia (ca. 600); and various compilations of exegeses of the Pentateuch and the Five Scrolls, known collectively as Midrash. Along with Scripture, these contain the record of revelation and mediate that record. In these writings we have to do with the oral Torah—the other half of the record, the half unique to Israel. That integral and necessary component of the one whole Torah revealed by God to Moses our Rabbi at Sinai is set forth in vast documents. Their number, more than a score or more in all, scarcely conveys the enormous volume of words that make up that part of the Torah. The oral part of the Torah, like the written part, records that encounter in its own distinctive language, which pervades the entire record. The theology of that part of the Torah becomes accessible when we know how to understand that language for what it is: the this-worldly record of the meeting of the Eternal in time with Israel.

Now it is the simple fact that in the Mishnah, the Talmuds, and the Midrash compilations we find a vast and diverse range of opinion on religious subjects. Yet in these pages we claim to know what "the rabbis" think everywhere, throughout all their distinctive writings. And we further allege that these opinions adumbrate—are animated by—a cogent theological system. Two questions require attention. First, some maintain that Judaism has no theology. By that they apparently mean to claim that Judaism sets forth no dogmatic and systematic theology. It possesses no list of convictions that one must affirm who wishes to claim status as a normative Israelite, that is, a practitioner of Judaism. (We cannot use the term "Jew," which is an ethnic category, but prefer "Israel," meaning "one who knows God.") By that view of matters, rabbinic Judaism is merely law, orthopraxy lacking orthodoxy, deed lacking all deliberation and conviction.

A Comprehensive, Collegial Compendium

But in fact rabbinic Judaism sets forth a rich corpus of theological formulations of religious truth. That corpus begins with monotheism. It continues with the dogma that God revealed the Torah at Sinai, both written and oral. It culminates in the conviction that all Israel has a portion in the world to come—except those who deny the Torah and the world to come. These propositions surely comprise not only religious propositions but a cogent theological structure and system.[5] Everyone knows that holy Israel proclaims God's unity, certainly a principal component of a theological system: "Hear O Israel, the Lord is our God, the one and only God." In due course we shall encounter the statement of the Mishnah, "All Israel [with few exceptions] has a portion in the world to come" (m. Sanhedrin 10:1), which is to say, all Israelites will rise from the dead, stand in judgment, and pass on to eternal life in Eden. So rabbinic Judaism sets forth a mighty abundant corpus of theological convictions indeed! What validates our further insistence that these propositions represent dogma and creed, not merely opinion? Since (rabbinic) Judaism affirms the forms of prayer of a received liturgy that celebrates God as creator of the world, revealer of the Torah, and redeemer and savior of humanity at the end of days, we have no difficulty in outlining the theological dogmas of Judaism. The proclamation of God's unity in the liturgy—"Hear, O Israel"—forms a fundamental theological statement. So much for our speaking of the theology of rabbinic Judaism.

But given the range of diverse, even conflicting opinion in the rabbinic literature cited in these pages, on what basis do we cite certain positions as normative and authoritative theological principles of rabbinic Judaism? On what basis do we portray the beliefs and opinions of the sages through statements we present as representative? "Representative" refers not to broadly held opinion but rather to ubiquitous and

---

5. That is the argument of Jacob Neusner, *The Theology of the Oral Torah: Revealing the Justice of God* (Kingston and Montreal: McGill-Queen's University Press, 1999; Ithaca: Cornell University Press, 1999).

governing modes of rational thought and to the necessary, sufficient, and integral doctrines generated by that rationality. It is within that logic of structure and system that we find a normative theology. By "normative" we mean exactly what Christianity means by creed, that is, the official position of the rabbis, viewed as a collegium and council on the model of the councils that declared catholic and orthodox Christianity. How, then, are we to know what composite[6] represents the whole and was deemed obligatory for all who practiced the religion of "the whole Torah of Moses our Rabbi," i.e., for the religion that the world has long known as Judaism?

Our entire account of the theology of the oral Torah rests on the claim that what we set forth, and the order in which we lay matters out, beginning to end, encompasses all the documents that collectively represent and define that Judaism in its initial statement in the Mishnah, Talmuds, and Midrash. We discern the system that undergirds these various writings by noting logically coherent positions that they share. These positions, whether concerning doctrine or correct modes of thought, determine not only what may be said but also what must not be said. More consequentially, they form a tight fabric, of gossamer weight to be sure, spread over the whole, a thin, translucent tent that holds within everything that belongs and keeps out everything that does not. As with philosophy, so here too with the theology of rabbinic Judaism, consistency with the first-established givens, beginning with the principle of one, sole, omnipotent, just God, opens the way for inclusion; but a statement that would contradict others is excluded.

That inquiry into what represents the logic of the whole web of principal doctrines forms the subtext of our entire account, which claims only that the oral Torah attests to its own integrity by the common criteria of reasoned thought. So by "the logic of the whole" we mean modes of thought that govern throughout, such as analysis through comparison and contrast on the one hand and paradigmatic thinking on the other. By coherence we mean doctrines that fit in place and do not impose stresses or strains on the structure that encompasses them. If, to take an obvious example, the one God who created all things is just, then that generative doctrine cannot accommodate cases of structural injustice. So the doctrine that the wicked (nonetheless) prosper cannot on its own find a place. It must be joined with some other, balancing one. Some solution to anomalies that confront the theologians has to accommodate reality to the system, and the system to reality. And it cannot be a solution that posits two gods or no god or a weak god or an unjust god. This is an obvious instance of systemic coherence.

6. A "composite" is a cogent collection of kindred writings.

The sages themselves, in the character of their writing, also signify what is normative. A fifteen-hundred-year-old tradition of learning serves. Several literary indicators establish the normative view and mark the schismatic one. (1) It is a well-established principle in the legal (hala-khic) documents that a rule that is not attributed to a named authority stands for all authority and thus ordinarily sets the norm. A rule bearing a name is usually schismatic.[7] This convention is stated explicitly in the earliest documents and is taken for granted in the composition of those that reached closure later on. (2) The authors of a cogent composition,[8] all the more so the framers of a composite, set forth their accounts in such a way as to indicate clearly the position they favor. They may announce the intended proposition at the outset and amass evidence to demonstrate it, or they may lead to it at the end by assembling much evidence, most of it affirmative, some not. (3) Within the documents of the oral Torah certain principles are treated as self-evident and generate secondary articulation along lines that said principles dictate. The sages have supplied other signals as well. (4) The selection and arrangement of materials, the juxtapositions of topics beyond the dimensions of composites, and other subtle editorial indications leave little doubt as to the positions deemed authoritative. The documents of the oral Torah set forth coherent statements, making possible the description of the theological system of the writings seen whole. That is because in principle a statement on a given, fundamental topic in a document within the oral Torah that is not contradicted by a statement made by any other document—and none is!—constitutes a reliable indicator of the theology of the oral Torah viewed whole. All the statements here presented as representative of the position of "the rabbis" (i.e., of the oral Torah as a whole) are selected from the sources on the basis of these literary indicators. The rare items of contradictory material here omitted do not meet these criteria and in fact are nearly always formally schismatic.

Our picture of the theology of the oral Torah consequently represents our sages of blessed memory as a collegium. The sages did set forth the orthodox and catholic position of the Torah in law and in lore, the oral in relationship to the written Torah. For the work of setting forth a coherent theological system, they used available instruments of intellect, proposition, evidence, argument, thought, and the writing down of thought. Thus they attained consensus through persuasion, because like the Jewish people in general, the sages had no better options. The people

7. We say this with the proviso that certain names carry within themselves signals as to normative status.
8. A "composition" is a unitary and continuous exposition of a proposition.

had no politics of consequence, so the sages could not work through political institutions. No emperor confirmed their views, no court enforced their judgments. They met, if at all, only irregularly—except on the field of argument. And to have their own say as individuals would have been to lose their integrity by denying the logic of their definitive myth. That, after all, is the meaning of claiming to receive and hand on a tradition, as the sages did when they spoke of the oral tradition of Sinai as a component of revealed Torah.

Their counterparts in the equally complex world of Christianity did two things that sages did not and could not do. From Constantine's time forward, Christian theologians held world councils, sponsored by the Roman Empire, to work out positions embodying orthodox and catholic Christianity. And as individuals, they wrote books. No state sponsored ecumenical meetings of sages, and the sages held none. Nor did the logic of the sages' view that they participated in an oral tradition of a corporate character permit individuals to write books in their own names as did every principal of Christianity beyond the founder himself. Had the sages of the oral Torah met in world councils, as their counterparts in Christian theology did, these are the positions they would have taken and set forth as normative—every one of them. If rabbinic Judaism has no counterpart to the Nicene Creed, we could readily write one out of the table of contents of this book. That claim is what made possible our decision to focus our discussion on the governing logic and to investigate and unpack the principles of coherence and proportion that govern throughout. Each abstract from a source that we set forth speaks for the collegium of the sages, represents the oral Torah viewed whole, and coheres with all others. The documents of rabbinic Judaism do refer to individual opinion, but the role of individuals is only to supply footnotes, clarifications, and alternatives to the mainstream of anonymous consensus. For rabbinic Judaism, the writing of individual, personal documents would begin only in early medieval times.

Readers to whom it may seem strange that we do not describe the theological systems of individual sages in the way that we can describe the distinctive theological systems of Origen or Augustine may find it helpful to imagine what we would know about Christianity if the Christian sources resembled the documentation we have for Judaism in late antiquity:

(1) Not only the New Testament but all the works of the church fathers, from Justin to Augustine, would now be represented as expressions of one communal mind, fully homogenized into a single, harmonious logical structure on various themes. True, they would be shown constantly to disagree with one another. But the range of permissible disagreement would define a vast area of consensus on all basic matters, so that a

superficial contentiousness would convey something quite different: one mind on most things, from beginning to end. The names of the fathers would be attached to some of their utterances. But all would have gone through a second medium of tradents and redactors. These editors of our patristic Talmud, as it were, would have followed their own interests in picking and choosing what to include of Justin, Origen, Tertullian, and Augustine. In the end, the picture of the first six centuries of early Christianity would be the creation of sixth-century editors out of the shards and remnants of people of the first five centuries. Our work then would be to uncover what happened earlier by studying a document portraying a timeless world.

Not only would the document be so framed as implicitly to deny historical development of ideas, but the framers also would gloss over diverse and contradictory sources of thought. I do not mean only that Justin, Irenaeus, and Tertullian would be presented as individual authors in a single, timeless continuum. I mean that all gnostic and catholic sources would be broken up into sense-units and their fragments rearranged in a structure presented as representative of a monolithic Christianity with a monolithic theology. This synthesized ecumenical body of Christian thought would be constructed so as to set out judgments on the principal theological topics of the day, and these judgments would have been accepted as normative from that day to this. So the first thing we must try to imagine is a Christianity which reaches us fully harmonized and whole—a Christianity of Nicea and Chalcedon, but not of Arians, Nestorians, monophysites and the rest. There would be no distinctive Justin or Augustine, no Irenaeus and no gnostics, and surely no Nag Hammadi, but all would be one "in Christ Jesus," so to speak.

(2) Let me emphasize that this would be not merely a matter of early Christian literature's reaching us without the names of the authors of its individual documents. The thing we must try to imagine is that there would be no individual documents at all. Everything would have gone through a process of formation and redaction which obliterated the marks of individuality. Just as the theology would be one, so would the form and style of the documents that preserved it. Indeed, what would be striking about this picture of Christianity would be not that the tractate of Mark lacks the name of Mark, but that all of the tractates of the Gospels would be written in precisely the same style and resort to exactly the same rhetorical and redactional devices. Stylistic unity so pervasive as to eliminate all traces of individual authorship, even of most preserved sayings, would now characterize the writings of the first Christians. The sarcasm of Irenaeus, the majesty of Augustine, the exegetical ingenuity of Origen, the lucid historicism of Aphrahat—all would be homogenized. Everyone would talk in the same way about the same things.

(3) And now to come to a principal task of the study of early Christianity: what would we know about Jesus, and how would we know it, if sayings assigned to Jesus in one book were given to Paul in a second, to John in a third, and to "they said" or "he said to them" in a fourth? Can we imagine trying to discover the historical Jesus on this turf? If even the provenance of a saying could not be established on the basis of all those to whom it is attributed? If often a single *Vorlage* and *Urtext* could not even be postulated? Then what sort of work on the biography and thought of any of the early figures of Christianity would be credible?

If readers can envision such a state of affairs, then they have entered the world of sources and scholarly orthodoxies confronted by us who study the ancient Judaism emergent from the rabbinic literature. A life of Jesus or of Augustine is plausible; a life of Aqiba or Hillel is not. An account of the intellectual biography of Paul and his theology is entirely a propos, the sources answering precisely the questions that are asked. A counterpart picture of Judah the Patriarch, who wrote up the Mishnah, or of Rabbah, Abbayye, or Raba, the greatest geniuses of the Talmud, is not. That accounts for the differences in the presentation of Judaic theology in comparison with that of Christianity.

Classical Christianity

Christian faith understands itself to be grounded in the Holy Spirit, God's communication of the divine self in all its richness. Access to the Holy Spirit is possible because in Jesus Christ God became human. The Incarnation (God's becoming flesh, *caro* in Latin) is what provides the possibility of divine Spirit's becoming accessible to the human spirit. ("Spirit" is often used without the definite article in the New Testament in order to refer to a range of experience in a way that is obscured when we automatically add the article when translating.)

Speaking from the perspective of Christian faith, then, there is a single source of theology: the Holy Spirit that proceeds from the Father and Son. Because God's very nature is love itself, this procession outward to all those he created is unique, the indivisible means of revelation. Human beings are created and blessed with the capacity to know Spirit in this sense. Yet the inspiration of the Holy Spirit has been discovered and articulated by means of distinct kinds of literature in the history of the church. By becoming aware of the diversity of those sources, we may appreciate both the variety and the coherence of Christianity.

The Scriptures of Israel have always been valued within the church, primarily in the Greek translation used in the Mediterranean world. (The Greek rendering is called the "Septuagint," after the seventy-two translators who were said to have produced it; see *The Letter of Aristeas*). Those were the only Scriptures of the church in its earliest, primitive phase, when the New Testament was being composed. In their meetings for prayer and worship, followers of Jesus saw the Scriptures of Israel "fulfilled" by their faith: their conviction was that the same Spirit of God active in the prophets was through Christ available to them in a way that realized its power and constituted Israel, God's chosen people, afresh.

The New Testament was produced in primitive communities of Christians to prepare people for baptism, to order worship, to resolve disputes, to encourage faith, and for like purposes. As a whole, it is a collective document of primitive Christianity. Its purpose is to call out and order true Israel in response to the triumphant news of Jesus' preaching, activity, death, and resurrection. The New Testament provides the means of access to the Spirit spoken of in the Scriptures of Israel. Once the New Testament was formed, it became natural to refer to the Scriptures of Israel as the "Old Testament."

The Old Testament is classic for Christians, because it represents the ways in which God's Spirit might be known. At the same time, the New Testament is normative: it sets out how we actually appropriate the Spirit of God, which is also the Spirit of Christ. That is why the Bible as a whole is accorded a place of absolute privilege in the Christian tradition: it is the literary source from which we know both how the Spirit of God has been known and how we can appropriate it.

"Early Christianity" designates the period between the second and fourth centuries CE during which the church founded theology on the basis of the Scriptures. Although Christians were under extreme—sometimes violent—pressure from the Roman Empire, the early Christian era was a time of unique creativity. From thinkers as different from one another as Bishop Irenaeus in second-century Gaul (now France) and Origen, the speculative, third-century teacher active first in Egypt and then in Palestine, a common Christian philosophy began to emerge. Early Christianity might also be called a "catholic" phase, in the sense that it was a quest for a "general" or "universal" account of the faith, but that designation may lead to confusion with Roman Catholicism after our period and is largely avoided here.

After the Roman Empire itself embraced Christianity in the fourth century, the church was in a position formally to articulate its understanding of the faith by means of common standards. Orthodoxy emerged. During this period correct norms of worship, baptism, creeds, biblical texts, and doctrines were established. From Augustine in the West to Gregory of Nyssa in the East, Christianity for the first and only time in its history approached true ecumenicity.

Texts, Creeds, Philosophies

Jesus and his movement clearly recognized the traditional grouping of the Hebrew canon into the Torah, the Prophets (often divided into Former Prophets [Joshua–2 Kings] and Latter Prophets [Isaiah–Malachi]), and the Writings. That grouping is cited in almost so many words in Luke 24:44. But the Gospels themselves were written in Greek, and the Bible of the church was also Greek in language and Hellenistic in presentation. A great deal of work has been done in recent years on the Greek text of the Septuagint;[9] less attention has been given to the actual structure of the rendering, which amounts to a radical revision of the significance of the Hebrew Bible. The Septuagint truly creates an Old Testament by the time of the first extant manuscript of the whole (Codex Vaticanus, fourth century CE).

As Henry Barclay Swete showed long ago, the ordering of books—the sequence and structure of the canon—follows a pattern in the Septuagint significantly different from that of the Hebrew Bible. In Codex Vaticanus, an order is followed that is as foreign to the Hebrew Bible as it is to the English Bible:

1. Genesis, Exodus, Leviticus, Numbers, Deuteronomy, Joshua, Judges, Ruth, 1–4 Kings, 1–2 Chronicles, 1–2 Ezra;
2. Psalms, Proverbs, Ecclesiastes, Song of Songs, Job, Wisdom of Solomon, Wisdom of Sirach, Esther, Judith, Tobit;
3. Hosea, Amos, Micah, Joel, Obadiah, Jonah, Nahum, Habakkuk, Zephaniah, Haggai, Zechariah, Malachi, Isaiah, Jeremiah, Baruch, Lamentations, Letter of Jeremiah, Ezekiel, Daniel.

This grouping is by no means fixed. Not only does the list of books in the Greek Bible differ from the Hebrew canon (producing the academic category of the "Apocrypha," works of the Septuagint without apparent Hebrew originals) but within the Greek tradition the ordering of books varies from manuscript to manuscript, ancient commentator to ancient commentator. Still, Swete was able to show that Vaticanus attests to a representative order, in which

9. See, for example, Eugene Ulrich, "Origen's Old Testament Text: The Transmission History of the Septuagint to the Third Century CE," in *The Dead Sea Scrolls and the Origins of the Bible* (Leiden: Brill; Grand Rapids: Eerdmans, 1999), 202–23; Julio Trebolle Barrera, *The Jewish Bible and the Christian Bible* (Leiden: Brill; Grand Rapids: Eerdmans, 1998), 301–23; Karen H. Jobes and Moisés Silva, *Invitation to the Septuagint* (Grand Rapids: Baker Academic, 2000); Martin Hengel, *The Septuagint as Christian Scripture: Its Prehistory and the Problem of Its Canon* (Edinburgh: T&T Clark, 2002; repr., Grand Rapids: Baker Academic, 2004).

the first category was "historical," the second "poetical," and the third "prophetic."[10]

Swete argued that this grouping was initially literary, derived from the reception of the Greek Bible in Alexandria, but he also suggested at the close of his discussion that "it may have seemed fitting that the Prophets should immediately precede the Evangelists." This remarkable insight helps us to understand the sequence within the third category, that of Prophecy (which also departs signally from the Hebrew Bible). The Septuagintal order, by commencing with the Minor Prophets, is able to finish off with the greatest literary prophets: Isaiah, Jeremiah (with the additions of Baruch, Lamentations and the Letter), and Ezekiel. Even more strikingly, the canon closes with Daniel, now emphatically and climactically one of the *Prophets* (rather than one of the Writings, as in the Hebrew Bible). Its references to the resurrection (12:2) and to the son of man (7:13; 10:16) make it an ideal transition into the story of Jesus. It is interesting that the canon of the New Testament, which was also solidifying during the fourth century, closes similarly on a strong note of prophecy, with the Revelation of John.

Tertullian in North Africa reflects the strict attachment to the divine Spirit and the imminent expectation of judgment that characterized much of Christianity during the second century. He addressed his *Apology* to those who might be called upon to judge Christians, but in fact it was intended to counter the common prejudice that Christianity encountered. It is as effective an example of rhetoric as one will find, and at the same time it illustrates the legal situation and the popular reaction to the new religion. The *Apology* was written in 197 CE, shortly after Tertullian's conversion to Christianity. The uncompromising stance is characteristic of the climate of the movement in Carthage and may explain why, around 207 CE, Tertullian himself seems to have become a Montanist, attracted by the asceticism which comported with the conviction that each believer was a vessel of the Holy Spirit.

Writers such as Tertullian, who shaped Christian theology out of the raw materials of the Old and New Testaments, the nascent faith in Jesus, and their own attainments in philosophy, are known as the fathers of the church. These patristic theologians were often boldly experimental, as in the case of Tertullian, even to the point of breaking with their own communities and the church at large. Yet they have left a wealth of intellectual reflection on faith that has been mined until this day. Not

10. *An Introduction to the Old Testament in Greek* (Cambridge: Cambridge University Press, 1902; repr., Peabody, Mass.: Hendrickson, 1989), 197–230. See especially 201, 217–19.

even a representative sample of the fathers can be noted here, but a few prominent examples might be cited.

Irenaeus, bishop of Lyons during the second century, countered gnostic understandings of the gospel with what was called by his time a "catholic" faith. Faith as catholic is "through the whole" (*kath' holou*) of the church. It is faith such as you would find it in Alexandria, Antioch, Corinth, Ephesus, Lyons, Rome—wherever. That construction of Christianity was designed to avoid the imposition of any local requirement (such as adherence to one of the esoteric myths of gnosticism) upon Christians as such.

Irenaeus's attempt to join in establishing a generic or catholic Christianity called attention to four aspects of faith that have remained constant in classic definitions of Christianity. First, faith was to be expressed by means of the Scriptures as received from Israel; there was no question of eliminating the Old Testament (which was part of the program of many gnostics). Indeed, one of the reasons for the formation of the canon in Christianity was to refute teachers such as Marcion, who excised from the Bible both the Old Testament and portions of the New Testament that seemed to Jewish to him. Second, faith was grounded in the preaching of the apostles, as instanced in their own writings and (derivatively) in the creeds. Third, communities were to practice their faith by means of the sacraments that were universally recognized at that time, baptism and Eucharist. Fourth, the loyalty of the church to these principles was to be assured by the authority of bishops and priests, understood as successors of the apostles. Taken together, these were the constituents of "the great and glorious body of Christ." They made the church a divine institution: "Where the Spirit of God is, there is the church and all grace, and the Spirit is truth" (Irenaeus, *Against Heresies* 4.33.7). Irenaeus's claims would obviously not have been accepted by followers of Marcion, and there were many variants of Christianity that did not subscribe to his version of a catholic orthodoxy. A "classic" only emerges over time, its status established by the reference to it of later thinkers. In describing Christianity as "classical," we do not claim everyone agreed with each classic, either in the ancient period or today; the designation rather refers to the persistent recourse to these sources by believers over the course of centuries.

Although Irenaeus's conception was designed to be inclusive, it was purposely at odds with emerging gnosticism. The issue was not only the authority of the Old Testament (which was typically contested by gnostics). Gnostics also cherished writings that were not apostolic, sacraments of initiation that were not universal, and leaders who were authorized by private revelation rather than the Spirit moving communally in the church. Irenaeus's concern to establish this fourfold definition of the church is consonant with one of his most vivid observations. Just as there are four quarters of the heavens, four principal winds that circle the world, and four cherubim before the throne of God, he says, so there are four gospels. Indeed, the number four corresponds to the four universal (or catholic) covenants between God and humanity: those of Noah, Abraham, Moses, and Christ (Irenaeus, *Against Heresies* 3.9.8). The Gospels belong to the order of the very basics of life, and—what is equally important in Irenaeus's mind—the basics of life belong to the Gospels. The power of God is not to be abstracted from the terms and conditions of the world in which we live. In insisting upon that, teachers such as Clement of Alexandria and Irenaeus opposed the popular dualism that was a principal appeal of the gnostics. Resisting the widespread fashion of abstracting God from this world, catholic Christians insisted upon the Incarnation as the key to the revelation of God's truth to humanity.

The incarnational emphasis of catholic Christianity is accurately conveyed by its most ancient confession of faith, a second-century composition still in use today under the title "the Apostles' Creed." The form in which it is currently used, however, was considerably developed during a time beyond our period of interest. As a guide to its ancient formulation, the best source is the *Apostolic Tradition* of Hippolytus. Hippolytus sets out the three questions which candidates for baptism answered, "I believe."

> Do you believe in God the Father Almighty?
> Do you believe in Christ Jesus, the son of God,
>> who was born of the Holy Spirit and Mary the virgin
>> and was crucified under Pontius Pilate and was dead
>> and rose again on the third day alive from the dead
>> and ascended into the heavens
>> and sits at the right hand of the Father
>> and will come to judge the living and the dead?
> Do you believe in the Holy Spirit
>> and the holy church and the resurrection of the flesh?[11]

The division of the creed into three sections, corresponding to Father, Son, and Spirit, is evident. That marks the commitment of the early Christian church to the Trinity as a means of conceiving God. Its commitment necessitated a philosophical explanation, which Origen provided

11. See Burton Scott Easton, *The Apostolic Tradition of Hippolytus* (Cambridge: Cambridge University Press, 1934); Philip Carrington, *The Early Christian Church*, vol. 2, *The Second Christian Century* (Cambridge: Cambridge University Press, 1957), 330–31; Francis Xavier Murphy, "Creed," *New Catholic Encyclopedia* (New York: McGraw-Hill,

during the third century. Indeed, the Trinity correlates with the kind of incarnational faith that is expressed in the creed.

The Incarnation refers principally to Jesus as the embodiment of God, as expressed in the prologue of John's Gospel (1:1–18). In the creed, however, that view of the Incarnation is developed further. The longest, middle paragraph shows in its focus on Jesus as God's eternal Son that the ancient practice of Christian catechesis is at the heart of the creed; that paragraph is a fine summary of the Gospels (compare Peter's speech in Acts 10:34–43, where baptism is also at issue). Its level of detail articulates a rigorous alternative to the tendency of gnosticism towards abstraction. But the statement about Jesus does not stand on its own. His status as Son is rooted in the recognition of the Father, understood as the creator of the heavens and the earth. The creed begins with an embrace of the God of Israel as creator and with an equally emphatic (if indirect) rejection of dualism.

The last paragraph of the creed, devoted to the Holy Spirit, also recollects the catechesis of Christians, which climaxed with baptism and reception of the Spirit. That basic understanding was rooted in the catechesis of Peter (again, see Acts 10:34–43, and the sequel in vv. 44–48). But here the common reception of the Spirit is used to assert the communal nature of life in the Spirit. To be baptized is to share the Spirit with the holy church: that is where communion with God, forgiveness, and the promise of the resurrection are to be found.

Finally, the creed closes on a deeply personal and existential note. "The resurrection" refers not to Jesus' resurrection (which has already been mentioned) but to the ultimate destiny of all who believe in him. The creed does not spell out how God raised Jesus and is to raise us from the dead, but it is unequivocal that we are all to be raised as ourselves, as embodied personality. There is no trace here of joining an undifferentiated divine entity, or of some part of us (a soul, an essence) surviving in a disembodied way.

In its assertion of the continuity of the body before and after the resurrection, non-gnostic Christianity came increasingly to stress the complete (that is, material) identity between what had died and what was raised from the dead. Whether the issue was what God raised in

---

1967), 432–38; Joseph Cullen Ayer, *A Source Book for Ancient Church History: From the Apostolic Age to the Close of the Conciliar Period* (New York: Scribner's, 1913), 123–26; Roger E. Olson, *The Story of Christian Theology: Twenty Centuries of Tradition and Reform* (Downers Grove: InterVarsity, 1999), 128–31; Alistair Stewart-Sykes, *Hippolytus: On the Apostolic Tradition: An English Version with Introduction and Commentary* (Crestwood, N.Y.: St. Vladimir's Seminary Press, 2001), 110–27. For the lines here cited, see Stewart-Sykes, pp. 113–14.

the case of Jesus and or would raise in the case of the faithful, material conceptions came to predominate. Resurrection was not only of the spiritual body that Paul refers to in 1 Corinthians 15:44, the identity that figures in the medium of flesh, but of the flesh itself. The Latin version of the creed actually refers to the resurrection of the flesh at its close. Catholic Christianity emerged as orthodox at the moment it became creedal, regularizing faith in terms of certain opinions (*doxai*) which were held to be right (*ortho-*). That development occurred in the context of opposition to gnostic versions of Christianity, and the result was the greater attachment to literal, material theologies of the resurrection from the second century onward.

During the last decade of the second century, Clement of Alexandria offered instruction to Christians in that great city and intellectual center. He was active there until the persecution that broke out in 202 under Septimus Severus. Clement developed a brilliant philosophy of Christian faith, which he produced in conscious opposition to gnostic teachings. His greatest works constitute a trilogy. The first is an introduction to Christianity as a superior philosophical teaching (the *Protreptikos*). The second, the *Paidagōgos* or "Tutor," is an account of how Christ serves as our moral guide in the quest for true knowledge and perfection. Finally, his "Miscellanies," the *Strōmateis* (literally, "Carpet Bags"), is a wide-ranging and complex work. Initially it was intended as a defense of Clement's thesis that Christian revelation surpasses the achievements of human reason, but its structure and expression are obscure. For that reason, the *Paidagōgos* is probably the best introduction to Clement's innovative philosophy of Christianity.

Born in 185, Origen knew the consequences that faith could have in the Roman world: his father died in the persecution of 202. Origen accepted the sort of renunciation demanded of apostles in the Gospels, putting aside his possessions to develop what Eusebius in the fourth century calls the philosophical life demanded by Jesus (*History of the Church* 6.3). His learning resulted in his appointment to the catechetical school in Alexandria, following the great examples of Pantaenus and Clement. Eusebius reports that Origen castrated himself (*History of the Church* 6.8), inspired by Jesus' teaching in Matthew 19:12, but it seems likely that Eusebius was repeating a calumny by Demetrios, bishop of Alexandria, who objected to Origen's ordination by the bishops of Jerusalem and Caesarea.[12] Origen moved from Alexandria to Caesarea in Palestine, to some extent as a result of bitter dispute with Demetrios, his episcopal nemesis. During

---

12. See Jacob Neusner and Bruce Chilton, *The Intellectual Foundations of Christian and Jewish Discourse: The Philosophy of Religious Argument* (London: Routledge, 1997), 75–86.

the Decian persecution (250 CE) Origen was tortured, and he died of ill health in 254.

Origen was the most powerful Christian thinker of his time. His *Hexapla* pioneered the compared study of texts of the Old Testament, while his commentaries and sermons illustrate the development of a conscious method of interpretation. His most characteristic work, *On First Principles*, is the earliest extant comprehensive Christian philosophy. It offers a systematic account of God, the world, free will, and Scripture. His *Against Celsus* is a classic work of apologetics, and his contribution to the theory and practice of prayer in the *Philokalia* (the classic source of meditation edited by Basil the Great and Gregory of Nazianzus during the fourth century) is unparalleled. Throughout, Origen remains a creative and challenging thinker. Condemned by later councils of the church for such teachings as his daring assertion that even fallen angels could theoretically one day repent and be saved (see *Apology* 1.6), Origen is perhaps the most fascinating theologian in the Christian tradition.

Eusebius (260–340), bishop of Caesarea (from 314 CE), was deeply influenced by the martyr Pamphilus, his teacher and model. Eusebius was imprisoned in 309 at the same time Pamphilus was, although Eusebius himself was released. After Constantine embraced Christianity, Eusebius was prominent in the ecumenical church at various councils from Nicea onward as well as a friend of the emperor. His *History of the Church* is the starting point of ecclesiastical history. He expresses better than anyone both the pitiless quality of the persecution under Diocletian and the inexpressible relief that followed. Constantine for him heralds the new day of Christ's revelation to the world.

Gregory of Nyssa inhabited a very different world from that of Clement or even Eusebius. By his time, Christianity was in fashion within the empire. He was the brother of Basil of Caesarea in the Cappadocian region of Asia Minor, and Gregory himself was bishop of Nyssa (between 371 and 394). Together with their friend Gregory, son of the bishop of Nazianzus, they are known as the Cappadocian fathers. Of these champions of the emerging Trinitarian doctrine of their day, Gregory especially represents the interpenetration of the Hellenistic literary tradition with the orientation of Christianity. Deeply influenced by Origen, he also remained married long into his episcopate and took monastic vows only after his wife's death.

Augustine was born in 354 in Tagaste in North Africa, the son of a petty administrator and his Christian wife. A benefactor from Tagaste enabled him to continue his studies in rhetoric in Carthage, where he was deeply influenced by his reading of Cicero, and then accepted the popular philosophy of Manichaeism. Its conception of the struggle between good and evil as two masses opposed to one another appealed to him deeply. Further study in Rome and Milan led to Augustine's conversion to Christianity. Rome brought him into contact with thinkers who showed him that Manichaeism was based upon unproved dogma, while in Milan he heard the sermons of Bishop Ambrose. Ambrose demonstrated to Augustine that the authority of faith did not contradict reason. At the same time, a reading of Neoplatonism enabled Augustine to conceive of God as immaterial, beyond time and space.

Philosophy was the first expression of Augustine's faith. Even while he was preparing for baptism, he wrote treatises, and he continued doing so in Rome afterwards. Then he returned to Tagaste, living and writing with a few friends. A visit to Hippo Regius proved fateful, however. He was made a priest, and later became bishop of the small town. He continued to write extensively, but in a more pointed way against those who attacked the church. He particularly concerned himself with Manichaeism. In addition, he criticized two viewpoints that demanded perfection of Christians. The Donatists attempted to force out of the church those who had cooperated with Roman authorities during the period of persecution, while the Pelagians argued that human effort was sufficient to attain redemption. In those controversies, Augustine's mastery of the concept of grace was brilliantly articulated.

In addition, Augustine wrote on how to instruct new members of the church, and he preached homilies that were the basis of his popular fame. Three profoundly innovative works have influenced the world of letters and Christian doctrine ever since. His *Confessions* (finished in 400) is the epitome of his introspective method: the analysis of his own life enables him to lay out the forces at work in the human soul. The *City of God* (413–425), occasioned by the sack of Rome in 410, sets out the pattern of redemption within the patterns of global history. *On the Trinity*—his great synthetic work begun in 400—is a meditation on the imprint of God's image within us and around us. He died in 430, while Hippo was under siege by the Vandals, whose advent presaged the dissolution of the empire.

The Principal Shared Topics

The body of this book expounds six shared topics or category-formations, all of them taking up the problem of man, his relationship with God, and God's quest for him:

1. *Creation, the nature of man, the loss of Eden.* Appealing to the story of creation as a way of explaining the condition of man, Judaism and Christianity base their mythic monotheism on the narrative of

Genesis 1–3: the story of the creation of the world, human beings, Eden, and how man and woman sinned and so lost paradise. If a Greek philosopher were to read Scripture and translate what he read through philosophical thinking into theological propositions, what system would he put forth? Is the meaning of the narrative to be found in an understanding of the human condition or in a promise of what human beings might become? Rabbinic and patristic theologians addressed that question in characteristic and differing ways.

2. *Christ and Torah.* When asked for the antidote to the sinful human condition, Judaism and Christianity concur that God in his grace provided means of righting the relationship that went wrong at Eden. For each, God provided both a model of regeneration and a medium for renewal. For Judaism, the model is set by the revealed teaching, or Torah, of Sinai. The counterpart model, for Christianity, is the last Adam, who is Jesus Christ. Communion with him—the identification effected by baptism, prayer, ethics, and Eucharist—makes of each believer a child of God according to the model of Jesus' sonship.

3. *Israel and the kingdom of God.* The medium for man's renewal is the formation of a holy community in the model of the Torah or of Christ. For Judaism, that is the sector of humanity that calls itself "Israel"[13] (understood to mean "people that sees God") and seeks to embody the Torah by identifying with and adopting the story, including laws and prophecy, of Scripture. That story, in the context of rabbinic Judaism, has no bearing on an ethnic, territorial, or cultural identity, since one becomes "Israel" by an act of religious conversion, namely, by accepting the Torah as God's revealed will. Then a critical theological component of the Judaic structure will be the situation of God's people among the nations. In the case of Christianity, the key term of reference within the Scriptures is the kingdom of God rather than Israel. Understood as a transformative principle that could remake humanity and creation according to the pattern of God's will and wisdom, the kingdom was presented as the most precious inheritance of Christ.

4. *The Body of Christ and the holiness of Israel.* Rabbinic Judaism finds in Scripture what it means to be Israel in the here and now: "You shall be holy, for I the Lord your God am holy" (Lev. 19:2).

---

13. Not to be confused with the usage of this name for the contemporary state of Israel. Before 1948 when people spoke of "Israel" they meant not a particular location, let alone a political entity, but the holy people of God, the people of whom Scripture speaks and the people that finds its story in Scripture.

The requirements of holiness turn out to entail behavior of an ethical and moral character, culminating in the statement: "You shall not hate your brother in your heart but you shall reason with your neighbor, lest you bear sin because of him. You shall not take vengeance or bear any grudge against the sons of your own people, but you shall love your neighbor as yourself. I am the Lord" (Lev. 19:18).

Using language of "the body of Christ," Paul developed a conception that became classic for Christianity. Baptism for him is the moment of believers' identification with the pattern of Jesus' death and resurrection. What is received in baptism is "the first fruit of the Spirit," such that believers "welcome sonship, the redemption of our bodies" (Rom. 8:23). Identifying with Christ means joining in the victory of life over death and at the same time joining in the living triumph of the Spirit over the letter of the law.

5. *Sin and atonement.* Rabbinic Judaism and classical Christianity concur that man sins by nature. The source of sin is man's will gone wrong, as the story of man and woman in paradise stresses. There God expressed his will in one regard only, and man and woman exercised their freedom of will in that same regard. Sin, therefore, begins with man's will and atonement must correspondingly be an act of will that expresses remorse and brings about reconciliation. How in the two faiths atonement for sin is attained forms the focus of this shared, native category. In Judaism, repentance (*teshuvah*) is attained through resolve not to repeat a sin and sealed by the Day of Atonement, while Christianity relies not on a salvific Torah but on a redemptive Christ.

6. *Resurrection, judgment, and eternal life.* Philosophical monotheism can express its teleology in abstract language. It can speak of God's intervention at the end of days without telling a detailed story of what is going to happen. Mythic monotheism, for its part, delivers the message that God's justice and mercy resolve all conflict through narrative. It reaches its climax in resurrection, judgment, and life eternal. That is because the narrative of creation leaves open questions of what happened to Adam and Eve after the fall from Eden. Once monotheism takes the form of the story of creation and the fall of man, the tale takes over and the conclusion is predetermined. With the resurrection from the grave, the last judgment, and the recovery of Eden in the world to come or paradise, Christianity and Judaism resolve the deepest dilemma of monotheism: the prosperity of the wicked, the suffering of the righteous; in other words, the human condition. Job and Ecclesiastes show the outer limits of theological philosophizing.

They offer no solutions, only responses to that condition. Mythic monotheism, reaching its climax in the correspondence of last things to first things (in Christian terms, the last Adam to the first; in Judaic terms, the answer of Israel to Adam), resolves the dilemma of monotheism and affirms God's justice in all things.

2

Creation, the Nature of Man, and the Fall

Judaism and Christianity begin with the start of creation, not with a doctrine of the one and only God; theirs is a mythic, not a philosophical monotheism. By "philosophical monotheism" we mean a monotheism grounded in proofs based on proposition, evidence, argument, and reasoning. That would come in due course, but that is not how matters originated. By "mythic monotheism" we mean monotheist theologies that convey their teachings through reflection upon Scripture's myth, that is, its account of truth in the form of a tale. The Torah (written and oral) and the Bible (Old Testament and New) share a common preference for truth embodied in narrative. Rabbinic Judaism and classical Christianity begin their respective systems not with propositions and proofs but with stories of creation and the knowledge of God revealed therein.

The two monotheisms of one Scripture concur on three points. (1) Theology commences in story, transforming story into proposition and forming the consequent body of propositions into a coherent, proportionate, rational statement. Rabbinic Judaism takes the further step of translating the propositions into the norms of the social order by restating theology in the form of laws of correct conduct. Christianity concerns itself with the transformation of human nature which began with Jesus and will be completed at the end of time. (2) This way of proceeding is possible because Scripture portrays in narrative form the truths that theology means to articulate in abstract language. The theology animates the story and is embodied therein. And rabbinic Judaism finds in the written Torah—particularly in Exodus, Leviticus, Numbers, and Deuteronomy—the imperative to form out of Israel a kingdom of priests and a holy people, and to do so through law. (3) In portraying what man knows about God and how man knows it, theology begins in the beginning. On this there is no disagreement between Judaic and Christian theologians, because Scripture declares that man is made by God "in our image, after our likeness" (Gen. 1:26). Differences take over when the two groups specify who embodies that image and that likeness on earth.

Monotheist theologies of Christianity and Judaism commence at Genesis 1 with the story of the creation of the world. In that story Eden is the setting, man and woman are the climax, and the conflict between God's word and man's and woman's will is the starting point of human history. Specifically, the theologies of rabbinic Judaism and classical Christianity take as their critical problem man's relationship with God. They find in Scripture, specifically in Genesis, the story of who and what man is from God's perspective. Neither defines God as a philosophical abstraction, nor do the early theologians undertake systematic proofs of God's existence. For both, Scripture is the starting point. But for neither does a mere rehearsing of the scriptural story of Eden suffice.

The story that precipitates the theological adventure of rabbinic Judaism and classical Christianity focuses upon the character of man: Adam and Eve and their consequent relationship with God. God created the world in orderly perfection, but in making man "in our image, after our likeness," God imparted to man, alone in all creation, the freedom to make choices. The story of mankind unfolds in the conflict between God's word and man's will. It takes on depth and meaning in the tragic consequences of that conflict and in God's yearning for a response to the love that he poured out in making the world and man in it: "And God saw everything that he had made and behold, it was very good" (Gen. 1:31).

The Theology of Rabbinic Judaism

The Torah—the written part as mediated by the oral—tells a simple story, the story of how God created the world he pronounced good, but in the aftermath of man's exercise of his free will to reject God's will, how God gave up on mankind and wiped out all but one family, Noah's. The story goes on to narrate how again God met disappointment until he found in Abraham the one on whom to build, and how God sustains creation through the just moral order realized in the people to whom he has made himself known, Abraham's heirs, holy Israel.

The theology narrates the unfolding tale of humanity from the creation of the world to the resurrection of the dead to eternal life with God. It is a tale that sustains complex articulation and extension without losing coherence. That simple story tells about a world governed by the moral order imposed by God's ultimate reason and justice. God's means for man's regeneration is set forth in the Torah of Sinai, in oral and written traditions. Through the Torah God intended to realize in Israel—defined as those who accept the Torah and know God therein—that perfection of creation that was not accomplished in the beginning. The generative doctrine of God's perfect justice in his creation and governance of the world imparts integrity to the details and proportion to the whole. That story portraying the requirements of justification encompasses the entire tale of humanity in general and of Israel in particular. The tale provides a dense record of the reasonable rules that account for what happens in public and at home, to the people in general and in particular instances.

The rabbinic sages in the chain of tradition from Sinai, who flourished in the early centuries of the Common Era, compare the story of Israel's possession and loss of the Land with the story of Creation and Adam's and Eve's possession and loss of Eden. The key is their quest for patterns, and in Scripture they find a huge pattern. From their perspective, the entire narrative of Scripture from Genesis through Kings shows how Israel recapitulates the story of Adam and Eve, but it is a pattern with a difference: Adam and Eve lost paradise, never to return, but Israel after its exile returned to the Land and, with the Torah for guidance, would endure there.

In this reading, the books of Genesis through Kings tell a simple story. First, the prologue (Gen. 1–11) sets forth the human condition, telling how Adam and Eve were given paradise but sinned and brought pain, suffering, and death to the world, and then how God tried again, with Noah, this time finding in Abraham and Sarah the beginnings of a humanity worthy to be designated "in our image, after our likeness." Then, from Genesis 12 through the end of the book of Kings, the story shows how just as Adam was given Eden but lost it through sin in the form of rebellion against God's will, so also Israel was given the Land but lost it. But here comes the difference between Adam, without the Torah, and Israel, with the Torah: while Israel, like Adam, sinned and lost the Land, Israel also breaks out of the pattern. Guided by the Torah,

Israel could recover and now hold the Land by loyalty to God's will expressed in the Torah.

The rabbinic sages thus took Scripture to form not a one-time narrative but a model and a pattern, in the theory that the deeds of the founding generations (in Genesis, Abraham and Sarah, Isaac and Rebecca, Jacob and Leah and Rachel) define a paradigm for their descendants. So they went in quest of the patterns implicit in the narratives.

Adam and Israel: The Parallel Stories

Now to the centerpiece of their reading of Scripture. In the case at hand, they found intelligible markers in parallel details of two stories: Adam's and Israel's. Everything follows from that discovery. The text before us derives from Genesis Rabbah, the reading of the book of Genesis by the rabbinic sages in the fifth century CE. Seeking patterns in abundant data, like natural historians in a tropical forest, the rabbinic sages constantly cite verses of Scripture to provide the facts at hand. But they construct with those verses a pattern that permits the comparison they have in mind. Notice how various books of Scripture—the Torah and the Prophets and the Writings—contribute to the exposition. Scripture is now turned into a vast corpus of facts, and the task of the faithful sage is to discern out of those facts the patterns and regularities that signal the workings of laws, just as in natural history the philosopher turns the facts of nature into natural laws. Now to the text, comparing Israel to "a man," that is, Adam:

> 2. A. R. Abbahu in the name of R. Yose bar Haninah: "It is written, 'But they [Israel] are like a man [Adam], they have transgressed the covenant' [Hos. 6:7].
> B. "'They are like a man,' specifically, like the first man. [We shall now compare the story of the first man in Eden with the story of Israel in its land.]"

Now the sage identifies God's action in regard to Adam with a counterpart action in regard to Israel, in each case matching verse for verse, beginning with Eden and Adam. Adam is brought to Eden as Israel is brought to the Land, with comparable outcomes:

> C. "'In the case of the first man, I brought him into the garden of Eden, I commanded him, he violated my commandment, I judged him to be sent away and driven out, but I mourned for him, saying "How . . ."' [which begins the book of Lamentations, hence stands for a lament, but which, as we just saw, also is written with the consonants that also yield, 'Where are you'].

D. "'I brought him into the garden of Eden,' as it is written, 'And the Lord God took the man and put him into the garden of Eden' [Gen. 2:15].

E. "'I commanded him,' as it is written, 'And the Lord God commanded . . .' [Gen. 2:16].

F. "'And he violated my commandment,' as it is written, 'Did you eat from the tree concerning which I commanded you' [Gen. 3:11].

G. "'I judged him to be sent away,' as it is written, 'And the Lord God sent him from the garden of Eden' [Gen. 3:23].

H. "'And I judged him to be driven out.' 'And he drove out the man' [Gen. 3:24].

I. "'But I mourned for him, saying, "How . . ."' 'And he said to him, "Where are you"' [Gen. 3:9], and the word for 'where are you' is written, 'How. . . .'"

Now comes the systematic comparison of Adam and Eden with Israel and the Land of Israel:

J. "'So too in the case of his descendants, [God continues to speak,] I brought them [Israel] into the Land of Israel, I commanded them, they violated my commandment, I judged them to be sent out and driven away but I mourned for them, saying, "How. . . ."'

K. "'I brought them into the Land of Israel.' 'And I brought you into the land of Carmel' [Jer. 2:7].

L. "'I commanded them.' 'And you, command the children of Israel' [Exod. 27:20]. 'Command the children of Israel' [Lev. 24:2].

M. "'They violated my commandment.' 'And all Israel have violated your Torah' [Dan. 9:11].

N. "'I judged them to be sent out.' 'Send them away, out of my sight and let them go forth' [Jer. 15:1].

O. "'. . . and driven away.' 'From my house I shall drive them' [Hos. 9:15].

P. "'But I mourned for them, saying, "How. . . ."' 'How has the city sat solitary, that was full of people' [Lam. 1:1]."

Genesis Rabbah XIX:IX.1–2

We end with Lamentations, the writing of mourning produced after the destruction of the Temple in Jerusalem in 586 BCE by the Babylonians. Here we end where we began, Israel in exile from the Land, like Adam in exile from Eden. But the Torah is clear that there is a difference, which we shall address in its proper place: Israel can repent.

These persons, Israel and Adam, form not individual, particular, one-time characters, but exemplary categories. Israel is Adam's counterpart, the other model for man, the one lacking the Torah, the other possessing and possessed by it. Adam's failure defined Israel's task, marked the occasion for the formation of Israel. Israel came into existence in the aftermath of the failure of Creation with the fall of man and his ultimate near-extinction; in the restoration that followed the flood, God identified Abraham to found in the Land, the new Eden, a supernatural social entity to realize his will in creating the world. Called variously a family, a community, a nation, a people, Israel above all embodies God's abode in humanity, his resting place on earth. I hardly need repeat that this definition of "Israel" cannot be confused with any secular meanings attributed to the same word, e.g., nation or ethnic entity, counterpart to other nations or ethnic groups.

These are the critical points of the theology of rabbinic Judaism in the setting of creation and the fall of man: (1) God formed creation in accord with a plan which the Torah reveals. It is a world that is perfectly rational and perfectly just. Israel with the Torah knows that plan, the nations with idolatry do not. World order can be shown by the facts of nature and society set forth in that plan to conform to a pattern of reason based upon justice. Those who possess the Torah constitute Israel. They know God, and those who do not—called the gentiles—reject him in favor of idols. What happens to each of the two sectors of humanity responds to their relationship with God. But how to account, then, for the condition of those who know God, namely, Israel? Israel in the present age is subordinate to the nations, because like Adam Israel has sinned, and like Adam Israel has lost its Eden. But God has designated the gentiles as the medium for penalizing Israel's rebellion, meaning through Israel's subordination and exile to provoke Israel to repent. When Israel fully realizes the Torah's teaching, then Israel will recover its Eden, the Land. Private life, like the public order, conforms to the principle that God rules justly in a creation of perfection and stasis.

(2) The perfection of creation, realized in the rule of exact justice, is signified by the timelessness of the world of human affairs and its conformity to a few enduring paradigms that transcend change. No present, past, or future marks time, but only the recapitulation of those patterns (theology of history). Perfection is further embodied in the unchanging relationships of the social commonwealth, which assure that scarce resources, once allocated, remain in stasis (theology of political economy). A further indication of perfection lies in the complementarity of the components of creation and in the correspondence between God and man in God's image (theological anthropology).

(3) Israel's condition, public and personal, flaws creation. What disrupts perfection is the sole power capable of standing on its own against God's power, and that is man's will. What man controls and God cannot

coerce is man's capacity to form intention and therefore to choose either arrogantly to defy, or humbly to love, God. Because man defies God, the sin that results from man's rebellion flaws creation and disrupts world order. The paradigm of the rebellion of Adam in Eden governs; the act of arrogant rebellion leading to exile from Eden thus accounts for the condition of humanity. But, as in the original transaction of alienation and consequent exile, God retains the power to encourage repentance through punishing man's arrogance. In mercy, moreover, God exercises the power to respond to repentance with forgiveness, that is, a change of attitude evoking a counterpart change. Since, commanding his own will, man also has the power to initiate the process of reconciliation with God, it is possible for man through repentance, an act of humility, to restore the perfection of the order that through arrogance he has marred.

(4) God ultimately will restore the perfection that embodied his plan for creation. In the work of restoration, death, which comes about by reason of sin, will die; the dead will be raised and judged for their deeds in this life; and most of them, having been justified, will go on to eternal life in the world to come. The paradigm of man restored to Eden is realized in Israel's return to the Land of Israel. In that world or age to come, however, that sector of humanity that through the Torah knows God will encompass all humanity. Idolaters will perish, and humanity that comprises Israel at the end will know the one true God and spend eternity in his light.

How do these principles emerge from the narrative of the written Torah? The rabbinic sages read the facts and traditions of Scripture as philosophers read nature. They thought philosophically about Scripture. The logic that they uncovered imparted rationality and coherence to the theological convictions they set forth in devising a system to account for the unity of being. All reality conforms to the few simple rules of reason that God embodied in his works of creation. The rabbinic sages sought in Scripture the evidence of God's rules for creation, treating its episodes as cases and these cases as units of a series. So Scripture's facts are shown to be ordered and to yield regularities. That accounts for the critical position of the creation story in their account of God and the world. In their view, the revealed Scriptures, read together as a single coherent statement, tell why things are now as they are. And they show the logic of that reason, revealing its integrity in the working of justice throughout. As the sages portray the written part of the Torah and set forth the oral part, the Torah lays heavy emphasis upon the perfection of the timeless, flawless creation that God forms and governs in accord with wholly rational and accessible rules. If everything fits together and works coherently, it is because, as philosophers maintain in their realm of reflection, a single, unitary logic (*logos*) prevails—the monotheistic logic centered on the one just, reasonable, and benevolent God.

Generalizing from Scriptural Data

Scripture's facts are organized and sorted out in such a way as to present a generalization. Generalizations are to be formulated through that same process of collecting kindred facts and identifying the implications that all of them bear in common. But Scripture may also be asked to provide illustrative cases for principles that are formulated autonomously, as the result of analytical reasoning distinct from the sorting out of scriptural precedents. Then Scripture is asked only to define in concrete terms what has been said abstractly. Successive propositions organize and rationalize a vast body of data, all of the facts pointing to conclusions that are proposed as generalizations. The proof then lies once more in the regularity and order of the data that are collected. The balance and coherence of the opposed laws yield the desired generalizations. Nothing about this method will have appeared alien to elementary students of natural history or of simple logic in the schools of certain ancient philosophical traditions.

So the sages set forth the rational version of the myths of Scripture: creation and its flaws, Eden and the loss of Eden. But their logic, involving as it did the insistence on a perfect and unchanging world, sought out what complements and completes an account, modes of thought that will occupy us later on.[1] Thus, they also taught how Eden is to be recovered. Adam and his counterpart, Israel, in the cosmic drama enacted daily in the humble details of Israel's ordinary life, embodied the simple story of the world: unflawed creation, spoiled by man's act of will, restored by Israel's act of repentance. The rationality of an orderly and balanced world set forth in the oral Torah comes to full realization in the matching of Eden and the Land of Israel, Adam and Israel, paradise and paradise lost, with one difference. Adam had no Torah, Israel does. Adam could not regain Eden, but Israel can and will regain the Land. The sages' teleology (theory of the end and purposes of things) imposed itself on eschatology (theory of the last things), thus forming a theology of restoration.

How, out of the materials of nature and Scripture, do the rabbinic sages demonstrate their view of creation? A single statement in detail of that view in general suffices to call attention to the regularities and order, the correspondences, that the sages found linked nature and man in a perfect match. Stated very simply, to the sages man and nature correspond. God created the same matching traits in nature and in man:

1. See also pp. 94, 197 below.

A. R. Yose the Galilean says, "Whatever the Holy One, blessed be he, created on earth, he created also in man. To what may the matter be compared? To someone who took a piece of wood and wanted to make many forms on it but had no room to make them, so he was distressed. But someone who draws forms on the earth can go on drawing and can spread them out as far as he likes.

B. "But the Holy One, blessed be he, may his great name be blessed for ever and ever, in his wisdom and understanding created the whole of the world, created the heaven and the earth, above and below, and created in man whatever he created in his world.

C. "In the world he created forests, and in man he created forests: the hairs on his head.

D. "In the world he created wild beasts and in man he created wild beasts: lice.

E. "In the world he created channels and in man he created channels: his ears.

F. "In the world he created wind and in man he created wind: his breath.

G. "In the world he created the sun and in man he created the sun: his forehead.

H. "Stagnant waters in the world, stagnant waters in man: his nose [namely, rheum].

I. "Salt water in the world, salt water in man: his urine.

J. "Streams in the world, streams in man: man's tears.

K. "Walls in the world, walls in man: his lips.

L. "Doors in the world, doors in man: his teeth.

M. "Firmaments in the world, firmaments in man: his tongue.

N. "Fresh water in the world, fresh water in man: his spit.

O. "Stars in the world, stars in the man: his cheeks.

P. "Towers in the world, towers in man: his neck.

Q. "Masts in the world, masts in man: his arms.

R. "Pins in the world, pins in man: his fingers.

S. "A king in the world, a king in man: his head.

T. "Grape clusters in the world, grape clusters in man: his breasts.

U. "Counselors in the world, counselors in man: his kidneys.

V. "Millstones in the world, millstones in man: his intestines [which grind up food].

W. "Mashing mills in the world, and mashing mills in man: the spleen.

X. "Pits in the world, a pit in man: the belly button.

Y. "Flowing streams in the world and a flowing stream in man: his blood.

Z. "Trees in the world and trees in man: his bones.

AA. "Hills in the world and hills in man: his buttocks.

BB. "Pestle and mortar in the world and pestle and mortar in man: the joints.

CC. "Horses in the world and horses in man: the legs.

DD. "The angel of death in the world and the angel of death in man: his heels.

EE. "Mountains and valleys in the world and mountains and valleys in man: when he is standing, he is like a mountain, when he is lying down, he is like a valley.

FF. "Thus you have learned that whatever the Holy One, blessed be he, created on earth, he created also in man."

Avot de Rabbi Nathan XXXI:III.1

Shorn of theological and mythic language, the statement says no less than natural philosophy does in its insistence upon the teleology of nature, its hierarchical order. As philosophers follow a procedure of comparison and contrast, resting on the systematic sifting of the data of nature, so too do sages. But here, nature and Scripture (without differentiation as to source or effect of derivation from nature rather than from Scripture) yield correspondences that are deemed concrete and exact. We begin with a proposition clarified by a parable and then proceed systematically through the parts of nature and their counterparts in the body of man.

The sages accordingly find in the Torah's story of creation the account of the balanced and orderly world that God has made. That then serves as counterpart to the philosophers' reasoned picture of man's domain and its laws, nature's realm and its regularities. Corresponding to the book of nature, which philosophers consult to read this tangible world's laws of physics or biology or astronomy, is the Torah. There, and not in nature—though concurring with natural philosophers that teleology and intentionality yield a rational and ordered universe—the sages find the record of God's purpose in creating the world:

A. "In the beginning God created" [Gen. 1:1]:

B. The word ["in the beginning"] means "work-plan."

C. [In the cited verse] the Torah speaks, "I was the work-plan of the Holy One, blessed be he."

D. In the accepted practice of the world, when a mortal king builds a palace, he does not build it out of his own head, but he follows a work-plan.

E. And [the one who supplies] the work-plan does not build out of his own head, but he has designs and diagrams, so as to know how to situate the rooms and the doorways.

F. Thus the Holy One, blessed be he, consulted the Torah when he created the world.

G. So the Torah stated, "By means of 'the beginning' [that is to say, the Torah] did God create . . ." [Gen. 1:1].

H. And the word for "beginning" refers only to the Torah, as Scripture
   says, "The Lord made me as the beginning of his way" [Prov. 8:22].

Genesis Rabbah I:I.2

In the Torah God wrote out the record of his plans and acts. Read rightly, the laws of the Torah yield law for the wise who can discern regularity and perceive purpose. The facts of nature take second place to the facts of the Torah. The Torah gives the encompassing account of the realm of perfection promised in Eden and actualized in Torah's social counterpart: Israel both as kingdom of priests and as individual.

The Theology of Classical Christianity

Christianity typically and persistently interprets the knowledge of God in terms of our knowledge of persons. St. Paul, for example, shows how one's personal knowledge of God is the basis of understanding that the creation of the world is divine. In other words, knowledge of God is not predicated on the intellectual assumption that God made all things; rather, God is known as creator because he is known personally.

When Paul describes his own conversion, he does not refer to external phenomena, although the story as given by St. Luke in Acts 9 and 22 does involve supernatural occurrences. Paul himself, however, simply speaks of the moment when "it pleased God—who had separated me from my mother's womb and called me through his grace—to reveal his Son in me" (Gal. 1:15, written around 53 CE). That simple statement is a vivid, existential description and at the same time a normative account of how Christians know God personally. God creates us, calls us, and provides the image of his own humanity—his Son—within us. That, rather than an understanding of propositions, is the basis of our knowledge of God. Knowing God as the one (and the only one) who does these things is our special knowledge of God.

Knowledge of God within Christianity is not first of all a matter of what we can say about God but a function of personal familiarity with God and trust in God. St. Paul's statement needs some explanation in order for us to see the kind of personal familiarity with God he had in mind. Fortunately, he himself provides very clear indications of how he sees us as created, called, and shaped within ourselves by God, and by following his explanations we can understand how Christianity conceives of how we know about God. For St. Paul and the other theologians mentioned here, God is conceived of personally, and therefore (given conventions in Greek and Latin) in terms of what "he" does with "his" creation, and how that creation approaches "him." We will simply follow that usage.

St. Paul on the Creator, the Spirit, the Son

St. Paul wrote very extensively to a Christian community in Rome around 57 CE (four years after he wrote to the Galatians in Asia Minor). The resulting letter to the Romans is the fullest explanation of Paul's theology. In an opening section, Paul concerns himself with the issue of how God may be conceived of as judging people when they do not know him. His response is that God's power and divinity are primordially evident to people from the world around them, a divinely created order:

> What is known of God is evident to them, because he has manifested it to them. His invisible qualities, his eternal power and divinity, have been demonstrated perceptibly from the creation of the world by the things that have been made. (Rom. 1:19–20)

To Paul the particular qualities of God, because they are behind the world rather than in it, are invisible. God's being God means that he is transcendent in his divinity, beyond the terms of reference of time and space. But his power is also evident, demonstrated by our perception of things made in the world around us.

The world is not just an accident of our environment, but that which is created by God. Paul's conviction is consonant with the story of the creation in Genesis 1 and with much else in the Old Testament. Sometimes the joyful expression that we live in a divine creation approaches romanticism. In 1712, Joseph Addison in England wrote a paraphrase of Psalm 19 which was subsequently set to music written by Franz Josef Haydn. The hymn is still used in many churches:

> The spacious firmament on high,
> With all the blue ethereal sky,
> And spangled heavens, a shining frame,
> Their great Original proclaim.
> The unwearied sun from day to day
> Does his Creator's power display;
> And publishes to every land
> The work of an almighty hand.

Addison's paraphrase is typical of the English Enlightenment in its stress upon the regular pattern of creation in its relation to the recognition of God. In fact, the final stanza of Addison's paraphrase makes it clear beyond a doubt that, for him, the existence of God is an inference of reason:

What though in solemn silence all
Move round the dark terrestrial ball?
What though no real voice nor sound
Amid their radiant orbs be found?
In reason's ear they all rejoice,
And utter forth a glorious voice;
Forever singing as they shine,
"The hand that made us is divine."

Writing in a period in which the angels in heaven were being steadily replaced by laws of nature, Addison paraphrased the psalm along the lines of the Pauline insight: the natural world attests the invisible power and transcendence of God. In this case, as in others to which we will call attention during our discussion of Christianity, the force of the classical ideas becomes especially evident when we consider their influence long after the age of classical Christianity came to an end.

Of course, Paul did not limit his claim to the inferences of reason. He concluded that what could be known of God was "evident," a matter more of immediate perception than of reasoned argument. But Addison clearly pursued Paul's insight in a new key, adding an almost romantic sense of delight in nature (a sense which Haydn's music reinforces).

When Paul refers to God's separating him from his mother's womb (Gal. 1:15), there is nothing abstract or theoretical about the imagery of creation. The emphasis rather falls on the immediate and personal link between God and Paul's own being. The imagery is not original with Paul: he is picking up the language of the Old Testament, for example in the book of Psalms. Psalm 22:9 and Psalm 71:6 offer praise to God for taking the speaker from the womb and keeping him safe from childhood. The image is also used in the prophetic literature, when the prophet is said to have been taken from the womb for the purpose of giving his prophecy (Isa. 49:1; Jer. 1:5). In all these cases, as in Paul's usage, the imagery expresses the experience not only of an ordered creation but also of God's care within that creation. The prophetic usage enhances the emphasis on one's personal sense of purpose by applying the image to a particular mission one is to accomplish. Paul shares that emphasis as well.

The prophetic dimension of Paul's reference to God comes out again in his description of God's "calling" him. The motif that God "calls" is so widespread in the biblical tradition that its significance might be overlooked. The basic meaning of the motif is expressed in the story of the prophet Samuel's call (1 Sam. 3:1–14). The boy Samuel is staying with the priest Eli, attending the ark and its sacrificial worship. It was a time when "the word of the LORD" and vision were rare. But when

Samuel slept at night near the ark, the LORD called to him so clearly that Samuel thought Eli was calling him. Three times he went to Eli to ask what he wanted, then Eli finally instructed him to answer, "Speak, LORD, for thy servant hears." The result is that God begins to tell Samuel what he is about to do. Samuel commences his prophetic ministry, which leads to the anointing of David as king of Israel.

Calling, then, is understood to establish a link between God and the person called, so that God's word may be delivered. Who is called? It might be a prophet, or all Israel, or Jesus himself. Matthew 2:15 cites one of the prophets to present the infant Jesus as called from Egypt for his vocation in Israel: "Out of Egypt I called my Son" (Hos. 11:1). Hosea applies these words to the people Israel, liberated at the time of the exodus. That wording is then interpreted afresh in Matthew to refer to Jesus. That is possible because much of the language of the Old Testament, including reference to God's calling and God's separating a person from the womb, is deliberately developed in the New Testament. The usage of the Old Testament is the point of departure for new applications and unusual developments designed to convey a sense of intimacy with God.

God initiates the biblical call, but the call must be answered to produce the intended communication. Indeed, the fact of God's call can be the basis upon which people take it upon themselves to call upon God. "Answer me when I call, O God of my righteousness" (Ps. 4:1) is an appeal predicated on the response of the psalmist and the psalmist's community to God's prior call.

The reciprocity of call and response is particularly developed by Paul in his teaching in regard to the Spirit of God. 1 Corinthians 2 shows how, in a letter written a year or two before Romans, Paul sees the Spirit at work. If one asks how we can know what God has prepared for us, the answer is that Spirit alone is able to communicate divine purposes. Paul develops his position by quoting (in 1 Cor. 2:9) a passage from Isaiah 64:4 that speaks of things beyond human understanding that God has readied for those who love him, and then goes on to say:

> God has revealed them to us through the Spirit; for the Spirit searches all things, even the depths of God. For who among men knows the things of man except the spirit of man which is in him? So also no one has known the things of God except the Spirit of God. (1 Cor. 2:10–11)

As Paul sees human relations, one person can only know what another thinks and feels on the basis of their shared "spirit." "Spirit" is the name for what links one person with another, and by means of that link we can also know what God thinks and feels. The Spirit at issue in knowing

God, Paul goes on to say, is not "the spirit of the world," but "the Spirit which is of God" (1 Cor. 2:12). The human spirit, which is the medium of ordinary, human exchange, becomes as the result of God's effective calling the vehicle of divine revelation.

Paul's remark in 1 Corinthians 2 is part of a complete anthropology that is spelled out further in 1 Corinthians 15, his classic explanation of what resurrection involves. When Paul thinks of a person, he conceives of a body as composed of flesh. Flesh in his definition is physical substance that varies from one created thing to another (for example, people, animals, birds, and fish; 1 Cor. 15:39). But in addition to being physical bodies, people are also what Paul calls "psychic bodies," by which he means bodies with souls (1 Cor. 15:44). (Unfortunately, the phrase is wrongly translated in many modern versions, but its dependence on the noun for "soul" [*psychē*] shows what the real sense is.) In other words, people as bodies are not just lumps of flesh but are self-aware. That self-awareness is precisely what makes them "psychic bodies."

In addition to being physical body and psychic body, Paul says we are or can become "spiritual body" (1 Cor. 15:44). That is, we can relate thoughts and feelings to one another and to God, as 1 Corinthians 2 has already shown us. Jesus is therefore the last Adam, a "life-giving spirit" (1 Cor. 15:45), just as the first Adam was a "living being" or "soul" (the two words are the same in Greek, *psychē* again). Jesus is the basis on which we can realize our identities as God's children, the brothers and sisters of Christ, and know the power of the resurrection. In presenting Jesus in this way, Paul defines a distinctive Christology as well as a characteristic spirituality. At the same time, this theological perspective makes the primordial myth of creation existential: the drama of the first human being is realized in the transformation of final humanity.

The initial terms of Paul's knowledge of God, then, are his awareness of God's power and care and his access to the Spirit of God. But that is by no means the whole of Paul's knowledge of God. Its distinctive feature is that God was pleased "to reveal his Son in me" (Gal. 1:15–16): that is how Paul knows in the first place that he has been separated from the womb and called by God. The revelation of God's Son in the midst of one's being is the distinctive basis of Christian knowledge of God. In fact, Paul conceives of the moment of receiving God's Spirit in a highly specific manner, linked inextricably to Jesus:

Because you are sons, God sent the Spirit of his Son into our heart, crying, Abba—Father. (Gal. 4:6)

Baptism is the moment at which, by accepting the revelation of the Son, one can accept that Spirit which is truly divine. Only what has come from God can acknowledge and respond to God: that is the revelation of God's Son within.

Paul brings us, then, to the most characteristic aspect of the Christian understanding of the knowledge of God and of its disclosure as producing a new creation—its emphasis upon Jesus, the Son of God, as the central mediator of that knowledge. One's own acknowledgment of and response to God remain vital, but they are understood to be possible only because God has already been at work within, shaping a spiritual eye to see him at work and a spiritual ear to hear his call. As Paul conceives of Jesus, he is first of all the Son of God revealed within us. Of course, Paul is aware of the primitive teaching concerning Jesus' deeds and teaching, including a graphic account of his crucifixion (see Gal. 3:1). But his interest in Jesus is not historical. Rather, his attention is taken up by how the revelation of the Son of God might shape our minds and hearts to know God.

The most famous expression of this theme occurs in the letter to the Philippians. Whether written by Paul himself or (as I believe more likely) composed after his death by his follower Timothy (ca. 90 CE), it represents a mature Pauline theology, much of it on the basis of what Paul personally had thought. It was composed when Christians in the Greco-Roman world were largely of the servant class, so that its appeal to the form of Jesus as a servant is especially poignant:

> Let this thought prevail among you, which was also in Jesus Christ: Who, being in God's form, did not consider the presumption of being equal to God, but emptied himself, taking a servant's form; existing in men's likeness, and found as a man in shape, he humbled himself, becoming obedient unto death, death on a cross. (Phil. 2:5–8)

The point of Paul and Timothy together (see Phil. 1:1) is that it is possible, on the basis of the revelation of the Son of God within one, to think as Jesus did, although in one's own circumstances. Here is an example of the imperative to imitate Christ within the New Testament. Its object is not a slavish mimicry of the historical person but an embrace of that humble disposition of Christ which makes the knowledge of God possible, proceeding as it does from God's own loving nature.

Knowledge of God, then, involves the capacity to acknowledge God as the source of one's being, the ability to respond to God's call and to hear him, and an acceptance within oneself of Christ's own loving disposition, his humility unto death. How, then, do we know God? By discovering and reshaping who we truly are in the image of God's Son, joining God in the act of creation, which began primordially and can be completed only eschatologically.

Once we appreciate how we know God within the creation, it is easy to see why in Christianity God is principally known as Father, Son, and Spirit. Those are God's aspects as he creates us, provides the image of his humanity within us, and calls us. That God is to be known as the Trinity may seem to be a confusing statement, because it can be mistaken for an assertion that there are three gods. Christianity avoids any such claim and insists that it is speaking of the one God. At the same time, the Trinity is held to express how God relates both to himself and to humanity. In terms of the confusions that are possible today—and in terms of its historical development—the teaching of the Trinity is best approached by beginning with the Son in relation to the Father. The place of the Holy Spirit is more easily determined once the fundamental question of Christology has been dealt with.

The passage from Philippians just cited closes its praise of Jesus' example with a conclusion setting out that praise in the clearest possible terms:

> So that at the name of Jesus every knee should bow, in heaven and earth and in the depths, and every tongue acknowledge that Jesus Christ is Lord, to the glory of God, the Father. (Phil. 2:10–11)

There is no mistaking the imagery of every knee bowing and every tongue acknowledging Jesus as Lord: God himself says in Isaiah 45:23, "To me every knee shall bow, every tongue shall swear." Paul and Timothy are applying that prophecy to Jesus, thus putting him in the position of God.

St. Augustine on the Trinity

In the interpretation of the classic theologian of the Trinity, St. Augustine, the passage from Philippians revealed a fundamental truth about God. His treatise *On the Trinity,* some twenty years in the making (from 400 CE), represents the intellectual climax of his career. The central problem that he wrestled with for years before and after his conversion was that of the nature of God. For Augustine, the divine nature or essence was precisely what the Trinity concerned.

In Philippians 2:6–7, Christ is praised because he "did not consider the presumption of being equal to God, but emptied himself, taking a servant's form." That can only be said, according to Augustine, because the Son existed prior to becoming flesh and freely chose the form of servanthood. He did not consider assuming equality with God, but he might have done so. After all, he was "in God's form" when he decided instead to become a servant, the only mortal form he ever took (*On the*

Trinity I.11, 13; II.11). The Son was an eternal aspect of God's being before becoming known as the man Jesus Christ. By becoming human and taking on the form of a servant, he permitted those who would be servants of others after him to discover the way of God on earth.

The implications for understanding Christ are evident, and Augustine does not hesitate to spell them out:

> Even then, when the Lord was born of a virgin . . . it was not the Word of God in his own substance, by which he is equal and co-eternal to the Father . . . but assuredly a creature . . . which could appear to bodily and mortal senses. (*On the Trinity* III.11)

Here Augustine provides the key to a Christian evaluation of Jesus. He is a mortal person, a "creature" within natural conditions and historical time, and can be understood as such. But just this person also embodies God's "Word," the divine plan for all time. That "Word" was revealed to the prophets of Israel according to their own perception of it, but in the case of Jesus that "Word"—God's own loving design for humanity—actually became flesh. For that reason, all that has been accurately said in the Old Testament has been fulfilled in the New Testament. In his association of Christ with the prophetic Word of God, Augustine reflects a tradition of thought that reaches back to the opening of the Gospel according to John (see John 1:1–18). But he is more acute than most Christian thinkers in his assessment of the distinction between the created person called Jesus and the eternal Son who is the Father's equal.

God, then, creates as Father and redeems as Son. Likewise, God as Holy Spirit communicates a uniquely divine essence; Spirit is God's gift of himself (*On the Trinity* V.11–16). Augustine acknowledges that no established vocabulary can convey the meaning of the Trinity. He is familiar with the reference to "essence" and "nature" among some Greek theologians, to whom we will refer in a moment. He admits that, to refer to what unifies the Trinity, "essence" (*ousia*, in Greek) serves better than the common Latin term "substance" (*substantia*, *On the Trinity* V.2–4; see also VII.4–5). His worry about "substance" is that its meaning might be confused with material composition. But whether seen as singular essence or unique substance, Father, Son, and Spirit are to be understood as the exalted Trinity, in which each is truly God, but there are not three gods (*On the Trinity* V.8). That is so because they are all aspects of a single and unique essence, the substance of divinity alone.

Augustine's Greek predecessors in the exposition of the Trinity are known as the Cappadocian fathers (Basil of Caesarea, Gregory of

Nazianzus, Gregory of Nyssa). The Cappadocian fathers borrowed from the vocabulary of Greek philosophy in order to explain the relationship between Father, Son, and Spirit. The statement of faith called the Nicene Creed had already established the Son as being "of one substance" (*ousia* in Greek, *substantia* in Latin) with the Father, but how could the differences within the Trinity be expressed? The Cappadocians spoke of one substance (Greek *ousia*) in three "individuals" (Greek *hypostaseis*). This terminology was problematic for Augustine because the Latin *substantia*, generally used to represent Greek *ousia*, was etymologically equivalent to the Greek *hypostasis*. For that reason he accepted the Latin practice of speaking of three "persons" (Latin *personae*) and used the word "essence" (Latin *essentia*) as an alternative for *substantia*. But he warned his readers that the words used have no authority in themselves; we only employ them "in order that we might not be obliged to remain silent" (*On the Trinity* V.9). Despite such warnings, however, different uses of language to explore the Trinity have caused a deep rift between what came to be called the Orthodox Church in the East and what came to be called the Catholic Church in the West.

Knowledge of the Trinity must obviously be beyond words, because words emerge from the terms and relations of this world, not directly from God. When Augustine turned to explore the true nature of God, he found that the best possible medium would be to analyze love. After all, God is love (1 John 4:7–10) and God commands love (Mark 12:28–34 and parallels); it must be that love is the gift of God within us, so we must understand love in order to know God. In general terms, we can even say that the Trinity is reflected in the relationship between the lover, the beloved, and love itself (*On the Trinity* VIII.7–IX.2).

Augustine's emphasis on the interior gift of love led him to turn away from exterior relations among people (which the Cappadocian Fathers had in any case explored) and to seek the truth of love within the human mind. There, his favorite analogy to the Trinity was that a mind is possessed of memory, understanding, and will, and these are not "three minds, but one mind":

> For I remember that I have memory, understanding, and will; and I understand that I understand, will, and remember; and I will that I will, remember, and understand. (*On the Trinity* X.11–12)

Augustine's analogy of a single human mind has led to the accusation that he minimized the differences within the Trinity. On the other hand, the Cappadocians' analogy of three people living in a village had led to the accusation that their picture of the Trinity was practically of three gods. In the climate of controversy during the fourth and fifth centuries, it is doubtful that any analogy of the Trinity, no matter how refined, could have avoided causing offense in some quarter or another.

But the fundamental insight which animates the work of the Cappadocians and Augustine alike is that the one God is known to us in three aspects, and that God is related to himself in those same aspects. The Trinity is not just a way of knowing God, but an account of how God is. His creativity, his redemption, his communication of himself are all essential and distinct aspects of his being God that human beings can also partake of and mirror within their lives. The nature of God is the interior logic of the economy of salvation, which is conveyed to us by God's Spirit.

If we wish to convert the Cappadocian and Augustinian analogies into a fresh perspective, we might return to our reflection on how we come to know another human being. Among all the people I can name, I might come to know and to love a person as I become familiar with him. A person, as distinct from the multitude of people whom I might know (but do not), has particular intentions and purposes that become evident as I get to know him. These intentions are associated with a particular personality and character. And both the intentions and the personality become familiar to me because the person communicates, shares himself. A useful analogy of the Trinity, then, is how we know another person as a person; the image of God in creation (Gen. 1:27) is the best image of God in theological reflection, provided it is considered in the perspective of love.

Just as love is the principle within our experience that enables us to know God, so it is the basis of our coming into a direct and redeeming relationship with God. The passage in 1 John that says that God is love is worth citing at some length to show to what extent loving is held to be a principle of comprehensive transformation:

> Beloved, we ought to love one another, because love is from God, and everyone who loves has been begotten from God and knows God. He who does not love does not know God, because God is love. By this has the love of God been made evident among us, that God sent his only begotten Son into the world, that we might live through him. (1 John 4:7–9)

God's creation of the world in love, the purpose and power of the Father, corresponds to a fully human character, the personality of the Son. For that reason, the imperative to love as God loves us is also a call to follow the example of the Son.

Imitation of Christ

The connection between loving as God loves and following the example of the Son is explicitly made in 1 John:

> In this we know love, that he laid down his life for us, and we ought to lay down our lives for the brethren. (1 John 3:16)

The call to realize the symmetry between Christ and the believer, which is usually known as "the imitation of Christ" (*imitatio Christi*), is a perennial theme of Christian ethics, and its most characteristic theme. The reason for that emphasis is that Jesus provides the model and the reality of God in human form. Imitating him is at one and the same time the imitation of God.

Once the *imitatio Christi* is understood in this fashion, two otherwise puzzling and persistent features of Christian theology become explicable. First, curiosity about Jesus in his own context—in the modern period, "the historical Jesus"—is by no means a purely speculative concern. The moving force of that curiosity is a desire to understand that life which, by imitation, transforms our lives into the likeness of God. Second, because imitating Jesus is imitating God, it is perfectly natural for Christians to wonder in what precise ways Jesus' divinity was evident during his lifetime. Those two issues—Jesus in his actual life and Jesus in relation to the Father and the Spirit—are profoundly Trinitarian and have been prominent in every major epoch of Christian thought and life. Expressions of the two concerns are enormously varied; the concerns in themselves are consistent.

The crux of Christian life, however, is not speculative. Whatever one might think of God, the purpose of life, as Gregory of Nyssa put the matter (in *What Is Meant by the Profession "Christian"?*), was to imitate God through Christ and to be transformed into an eternal child of God on that basis. For all that it is intellectually stimulating, the Trinity's proper function is to arouse the sort of active love which is at its source. That is possible principally because, in addition to being created by God and provided with the Son's love as an example, love is communicated to us by means of the Holy Spirit.

The ways in which the Holy Spirit is experienced are, to say the least, varied within Christian tradition. Within the modern period, the Quaker discipline of waiting upon what are usually called "movings" of the Spirit provides many examples. Perhaps the most accessible is that of John Woolman (1720–1772), who left a detailed diary of his personal understanding of what was happening to him. He did not begin his diary until he was thirty-six years old, and speaks in retrospect of a gradually growing seriousness of reflection and an intentional quietness in his life. The result was he learned to speak "under a strong exercise of spirit":

> My understanding became more strengthened to distinguish the language of the pure Spirit which inwardly moves upon the heart . . . until I felt that rise which prepares the creature to stand like a trumpet through which the Lord speaks to his flock.[2]

Within the social history of the United States, Woolman's influence extended far beyond his personal practice and the Quaker meetings he began to address. He refused to draw up bills of sale for slaves, as required by his employer in Philadelphia. In addition to resisting slavery, he opposed paying taxes for war and accepting payment for quartering troops. He advocated fair wages and working hours, affordable education, and a "reformation" of society on the basis of nonviolent confrontation. When he considered making one of his many tours to oppose the practice of slavery, Woolman had a vision:

> . . . as I opened my eyes I saw a light in my chamber at the apparent distance of five feet, about nine inches diameter, of a clear, easy brightness and near the center the most radiant. As I lay still without any surprise looking upon it, words were spoken to my inward ear which filled my whole inward man. They were not the effect of thought nor any conclusion in relation to the appearance, but as the language of the Holy One spoken in my mind.[3]

Such experiences, which punctuate Woolman's diary, drove him to extraordinary lengths. Despite a recent bout with pleurisy, he traveled to England in 1772. (He also traveled in steerage to share the conditions of young seamen.) He wished to speak out for the poor in the North and to influence the London Yearly Meeting of Quakers against the slave trade. After extensive travels in England following that successful meeting, Woolman died in York of smallpox.

Woolman's diary makes it plain that experience of the Holy Spirit may not be understood as a single, aberrant event. The visions which punctuate his diary occur within a regular practice of reading the Scriptures (and much else). His reflection on God as creator led him to see justice toward all creatures as an imperative. His experience of "the love of God through Jesus Christ to redeem me" awakened compassion within him. Woolman's reflective practice and rational consideration, as well as his

2. Phillips P. Moulton, ed., *The Journal and Major Essays of John Woolman* (New York: Oxford University Press, 1971), 31.
3. Ibid., 58.

political judgments, were involved within a meditative focus on God as Creator, Redeemer, and Sanctifier.

That has been the typical pattern of Christians' experience of God, which is characteristically Trinitarian (whatever a given Christian might say about the doctrine of the Trinity). As such, it is understood to derive from God himself, communicating himself as Spirit to our spirits. What is discovered when we encounter God, then, is not a definition of what divinity is or a limitation of God's creative power to the primordial past. Rather, God's essence is such that it awakens a realization of who we are, and on that basis we can become familiar with God. The One who made us human also loves us and reveals himself to us. It is God's very nature to be making and loving and revealing. That is why we are who we are called to be—his children in the imitation of Christ. And that is why it is that only in becoming what we are in our truest selves (the selves that God has given), we come to know God and join his endless creativity.

Comparing Theologies

Judaism on Christianity

Sharing the narrative in its main outline—creation, fall, restoration at the end of days—Judaism and Christianity part company at the important turnings in the story. Who carries forward the legacy of Adam and forms the new Adam, Israel or Christ? The case for Judaism begins in Professor Chilton's statement that Christianity interprets the knowledge of God in terms of our knowledge of persons: God is known personally. Judaism finds in the Torah knowledge of what God wants of humanity, but does not claim to know more than that. Indeed, Moses in the cleft of the rock, Elijah hearing the thin voice of silence, the prophets in their struggles with God's insistence—these all attest to the humility of Judaism. Israel knows what God wants Israel to know—no less, no more. What accounts for the difference and explains the fundamental incompatibility of the two continuators of Scripture is the figure of Christ. Christianity can claim to know God personally because of its affirmation of God in Christ. Judaism alleges no counterpart knowledge.

Yet Judaism finds the Christian claim wanting. For what Judaism affirms in the Torah is knowledge of the way the world works, the divine design of the cosmos: *Thus the Holy One, blessed be he, consulted the Torah when he created the world.* Judaism thus encompasses within the Torah all sciences, all knowledge of the natural world and of the working of the social order. Whatever the mind of humanity discovers about creation contributes to that Torah that formed the design of creation and thus affords access to the mind of God.

What Judaism knows about God in the Torah forms an adumbration of the working of the mind of God. That is because the premise of all Judaic theological discourse is that the Torah was written by God and dictated by God to Moses at Sinai—word for word, in God's grammar and syntax. In their analysis of the deepest intellectual structures of the Torah, the sages of Judaism therefore supposed that they were entering into the mind of God, showing how God's mind worked when God formed the Torah, written and oral alike. And that leads into the mysteries of creation, a quest nourished by mathematics and the natural sciences. So the heavens declare the glory of God, and the Torah guides us to the encounter with God in the world.

Thus in discerning in the Torah how God's mind worked, the sages claimed a place in that very process of thought that had given birth to the Torah. Compared with that claim of knowledge of God, the counterpart claim of Christianity may be judged necessary but insufficient.

Christianity on Judaism

The power of a paradigm for a world that is perfectly rational and perfectly just attracts the admiration of anyone concerned with justice and reason, Christians included. That promise of the Torah has quickened the eschatological imagination of believers from the time of Jesus to our own. But in Christ the *eschaton*, the "end" of which eschatology speaks, has begun already to reach its accomplishment. Christ is the climax of the story, apart from which the sense of the beginning and the middle cannot be fathomed.

The paradigm of Genesis strikes Christianity as having been improvised to deal with the reality of human sin, so that its enduring timelessness seems questionable. "Adam" is only the beginning of the story, not the beginning and the end. God's creation of this "living being" was a glorious breakthrough, and yet Adam constitutes only a prelude to the transformation that makes all those raised from the dead, beginning with Jesus, "life-giving spirit." And because this shift in the whole constitution of humanity copes directly and immediately with human beings in all their variety, it looks as if the Scriptures of the Torah express God's aim rather than spell out a detailed plan.

Proposition, proportion, and regularity are all qualities of the ideal world the Torah of the sages delineates, but Christianity does not view the human constitution as ideal. The issue here—separating the two religions irrevocably—turns not on what people *do* ("the human condition") but on what they are constitutionally. Judaism of course acknowledges the condition of sin, but Christianity insists that human reason is so clouded that not even its perception of an ideal *eschaton* is reliable. People require a change not merely in their behavior but in their very being, and the act of believing in God through Christ puts them on the path of this transformation because they receive the Spirit of the divine Son.

Just as the gulf between Christian and Judaic anthropologies is profound, so the relationship between God and nature differs sharply between the two systems. For St. Paul and Joseph Addison in the passages discussed above, the order of nature attests a divine power that is beyond the natural order itself, insusceptible of complete understanding by human beings. Humanity lives suspended between the hope of a fulfilled *eschaton* and the obscurity of what has produced the world in which we live. The Torah sets out to explain how we know God in this world, but the indirection involved is so great that a more immediate insight into God is plainly required before people can have any knowledge at all. That is precisely what the Spirit accomplishes. In that accomplishment, God appears to be as dynamic as human beings are, as we look at him in a dim mirror until that time when we can see God face to face (1 Cor. 13:12).

3

Christ and Torah

What then is to be done about man, the climax and catastrophe of creation? God has pronounced creation "very good" (Gen. 1:31) and declared man—Adam and Eve—"in our image, after our likeness" (Gen. 1:26). The truth here expressed in mythic garb is that what makes man like God is that man possesses free will. He is asked to name the components of creation. But in exercising his freedom, man sins. Telling the same story, Judaic and Christian theologians faced the task of identifying God's next step in the ongoing story of man. Both concurred that man's free will accounted for—defined, really—the human condition. Then how to regenerate man, so as to make doing God's will as natural as, for Adam and Eve, obedience had proved unnatural? Judaism responded by pointing to the Torah, and Christianity to Christ. Here is how the two theological worlds addressed the same question but presented superficially unrelated answers. Our task is to see how different answers to the same question in fact intersect.

For the theology of rabbinic Judaism, God's second chance at creation took place at Sinai. Summoning to Sinai that portion of humanity that enters a covenanted relationship with him to do his will, God gives the Torah, the antidote to sin, its laws intended to "purify the heart of man," which is what God most craves. For rabbinic Judaism, therefore, the Torah is the answer to the question of the fall of man from grace, and Israel (those who know God through the Torah) represents God's second chance at perfecting creation. Keeping the laws of the Torah, Israel undertakes a new beginning.

To expound this chapter in the theology of rabbinic Judaism, we turn to its principal medium of thought and expression, which is discourse about law, that is to say, theology in the medium of norms of conduct. This is the fully realized, acted out, and embodied theology that forms the principal medium of rabbinic Judaism. It takes two forms. First comes amplification, exegesis, and extension of Scripture's account in writings that produce discourse such as we saw in chapter 2. This mode of theological expression is called collectively *aggadah*, lore. Second comes the definition of theology through law regarding concrete deeds of commission and omission. This is called *halakhah*. While the aggadah contains diverse views, the halakhah sets forth normative rules. It governs how people are to behave, and its rules of conduct, properly observed, realize in the life of the entire community of faithful Israel the theological convictions implicit in the halakhah itself. In this chapter, then, we shall follow the halakhic part of the Torah's address to Eden. In preferring the halakhic to the aggadic medium while making use of both, rabbinic Judaism carries forward the manner of Moses in Scripture, who conveys God's will in practical instructions on the actualities of the holy society, Israel.

On the Christian side, the centrality of Israel's Scriptures is axiomatic for St. Paul because, he said, from the Israelites came "the sonship, the glory, the covenants, the giving of the law, the worship, and the promises" (Rom. 9:4). If you want to know what these things are, you need the Scriptures of Israel. Paul also understands that all these gifts are only fully realized in the final gift of Israel: the coming of the "Christ according to the flesh" (Rom. 9:5). You cannot perceive *that* Christ fulfills unless you appreciate *what* he fulfills, and that tale is told only in Israel's Scriptures. But the central term of Israel's promise and its realization is not Torah but sonship. Sonship is what the whole story of God with his people is about, first on Paul's list of Israel's gifts to all believers (with law-giving a distant fourth; Rom. 9:5). Sonship belongs to us because it belongs to Jesus, and vice versa. "I am sure," said Paul, "that neither death nor life nor angels nor principalities nor things present nor things to come nor powers nor height nor depth nor anything else in all creation will be able to separate us from the love of God that is in Jesus Christ our Lord" (Rom. 8:38–39).

How did it come about that the very content of Scripture was understood in such radically different ways? In this chapter, we will consider first why Paul could make his assertion about sonship as a statement that Christians generally could accept. That clarification will underline the conceptual innovation involved in the development of rabbinic Judaism.

The Theology of Classical Christianity

From the time of the New Testament, Christianity has taught that describable practices afford the believer access to the sonship that belongs to them through Jesus. In this sense, theology is in the first instance practical, enacted through growth into the image of Christ. Baptism signals the moment of receiving the Spirit of God consciously within oneself; prayer is the practice of the filial consciousness that results from this Spirit. Ethics is determined by a programmatic dedication to conduct that mirrors Christ's relation to the world. Finally, Eucharist—a sacrament understood in many ways over time—finds its pivotal importance as a summation of what baptism, prayer, and ethics should be.

Baptism

The Synoptic Gospels are designed to show what divine sonship is and how people may become God's children through Jesus. In aggregate, they initially highlight baptism, a single moment of communion which is both public and private.[1] They address that moment by relating the baptism of Jesus at the hands of John the Baptist (Matt. 3:13–17; Mark 1:9–11; Luke 3:21–22). Here Jesus is addressed unequivocally by God as "my Son," and from that point the Spirit that descends upon him governs his actions. The emphasis upon the latter motif is such that Jesus, after the baptism, is portrayed as being brought by the Spirit into the wilderness for his temptation (Matt. 4:1; Mark 1:12; Luke 4:1). His baptism commences the public ministry and the spiritual dynamism of Jesus.

In a passage commonly regarded as a reflection of a truly evangelical (i.e., gospel-conveying) oral tradition, Peter in the book of Acts preaches in the house of the Roman centurion Cornelius and begins the gospel of Jesus with reference to the baptism preached by John (Acts 10:37–38). The result of his preaching is that the Holy Spirit falls upon those present (v. 44), and Peter proceeds to baptize them with water (vv. 46c–48). Peter is here portrayed as authorizing the baptism of gentiles, despite the astonishment of his companions, who are "of the circumcision" (v. 45). The Synoptic Gospels tell the story of Jesus' baptism for people who

1. See Bruce Chilton, *Jesus' Baptism and Jesus' Healing: His Personal Practice of Spirituality* (Harrisburg: Trinity Press International, 1998).

themselves could be baptized because the movement's membership was no longer exclusively Jewish. The content of baptism had been changed: it was now baptism "in the name of Jesus Christ" (v. 48, a formulation found frequently in Acts).

The notion of baptism into Jesus' name represents a transformation of John's program of ritual and ethical purification. It is impossible, on the face of the texts of the Synoptic Gospels, to determine what "happened" to Jesus, as distinct from what happened in the practice of predominantly gentile Christians. That indeterminacy between what occurred in the past and what is appropriated in the present is enshrined within the texts themselves. At the crucial moment, when it concerns the experience of being baptized, the Synoptic Gospels present interesting (and distinctive) qualifications:

> Having been baptized, immediately Jesus arose from the water; and lo, the heavens were opened, and he saw God's Spirit descending as a dove, coming upon him. (Matt. 3:16)

> And he was baptized in the Jordan by John. And immediately, arising from the water, he saw the heavens split, and the Spirit as a dove descending upon him. (Mark 1:9c–10)

> And Jesus having been baptized, while he was praying, heaven was opened, and the Holy Spirit descended in bodily form as a dove upon him. (Luke 3:21b–22)

Although the Synoptic Gospels are comparable here, there is no question of a verbatim identity among them.

Nonetheless, each presents the baptism as a function of Jesus' own experience as well as of what was said and done. In Matthew, the statement is made that the heavens were opened, but then the descent of the Spirit is described as what Jesus—and, apparently, Jesus alone—saw. Mark's wording presents both the heavenly tear and the descent of the dove of the Spirit as matters of what only Jesus could have attested. Luke's language might seem to refer to objective events, but what is related is cast as a matter of what transpired while Jesus was praying after his baptism.

What is the reason for such frustrating indeterminacy? Why not merely state what happened and say what it means? Scholars of the New Testament commonly appeal to what are taken to be the looser standards of ancient historiography, but such explanations are superficial. The catechumen who was prepared for full admission into the society of Christians in the different cities in the Mediterranean world where the Gospels were composed was to be baptized into Jesus Christ's name, and therefore to receive the Spirit of God. The narrative of Jesus' baptism was naturally presented as a paradigm of what the catechumen was to experience. The voice which addresses Jesus as the divine Son in whom God is well pleased (Matt. 3:17; Mark 1:11; Luke 3:22b) is saying what Jesus, God, and the church know, but what Jesus' contemporaries are said not to have grasped. The Gospels deliberately speak out of time in order to convey their timely knowledge to the catechumen. The indeterminacy between what might be said of Jesus and what may be said by the follower at baptism is, then, no quirk of the Synoptic Gospels nor a matter of literary presentation alone. It is not an unfortunate confusion but a systemic feature of Christianity: the narrative identification in baptism between the believer and Jesus Christ.

We may note similar claims of this identification in New Testament documents other than the Synoptics. The Gospel according to John (written in Ephesus ca. 100 CE) does not refer to Jesus' baptism, although it presupposes that Jesus belonged to the group around John the Baptist. John the Baptist is chiefly important within the Fourth Gospel as a witness (cf. 1:6–8), and he is the vehicle of claims made in the Synoptics by means of Jesus' baptism. He is portrayed as attesting that Jesus is "the lamb of God" on the basis of John's own vision of the Spirit descending as a dove and resting upon Jesus (John 1:29–32). The Baptist goes on to explain that "He who sent me to baptize with water said to me, 'Upon whomever you should see the Spirit descend and rest upon him, he is the one baptizing with Holy Spirit'" (v. 33). For that reason, John says he knows that Jesus is the Son of God (v. 34), which is precisely the message of the divine voice in the Synoptics. John the Baptist's testimony here has totally swallowed up any specific reference to the fact that Jesus was baptized; significance has overwhelmed narrative within the Johannine idiom. Yet there is a common theme in the Johannine discourse and the Synoptic story: baptism in Jesus' name will alone give access to Holy Spirit.

Paul presumes even more daringly upon the previous catechesis of his readers, as when he says, around 55 CE, to those in Corinth who styled themselves sophisticated Christians:

> I do not want you ignorant, brethren, that our fathers were all under the cloud and all passed through the sea, and all were baptized into Moses in the cloud and in the sea, and all ate the same spiritual food and all drank the same spiritual drink—for they drank from a spiritual rock that followed, which rock was Christ. (1 Cor. 10:1–4)

The confident assumption here is that you know the reference to "our fathers" will introduce a typology of the exodus.

Within the typology, the Israelites' dwelling under the protection of the divine cloud in the wilderness (Exod. 13:21–22; 14:19–20, 24–25) and their passing through the sea (14:21–22) corresponds to baptism by Spirit and water in the name of Jesus. The thought of baptism then triggers a reference to the Eucharist. The miraculous provision of food and drink in the wilderness (Exod. 16–17) relates to the underlying reality of the rock from which the water came, which is Christ. Unless we know that baptism and Eucharist are standard practices among Corinthian Christians and that they have appropriated the Scriptures of Israel as their own we are at a loss to explain what Paul is talking about. Once we know what we need to know, it becomes clear that, for Paul, baptism is a matter of receiving the Spirit while being immersed in water in Jesus' name. As a consequence, each Christian is God's son, much as Israel was at the time of the exodus (Exod. 4:21–23).

The use of Scripture as an instrument of analogy, in which texts of Israel in the past are applied to the church of the present, is no Pauline idiosyncrasy. First Peter, written for the churches in the northern portion of Asia Minor around 90 CE (that is, well after the apostle's death ca. 64 CE), inherits the common habit of applying scriptural figures to the present. In order to exhort its readers to patient suffering, the letter invokes the example of Jesus:

> For Christ also suffered for sins once for all, the righteous on behalf of the unrighteous, so that he might bring you to God. Put to death in flesh, he was made alive in Spirit, in which also he went to preach to the spirits in prison, who were formerly disobedient, when God's patience waited in the days of Noah while the ark was prepared in which a few lives—that is, eight—were saved through water. The antitype of that, baptism, now saves you, not a removal of dirt from flesh but an appeal of clear conscience to God, through the resurrection of Jesus Christ, who having gone to heaven is at the right hand of God where angels and authorities and powers are subjected to him. (1 Pet. 3:18–22)

The flourish of the statement in the Greek text of 1 Peter is all the greater in that it stands as a single sentence in the original. Its elements, however, are fairly easily identified. It is Jesus' resurrection now that makes baptism efficacious; the roots of the practice in issues of ritual purity are no longer of concern.

Because Jesus was righteous and was raised from the dead, he becomes the spiritual basis of the commendation of clear consciences to God. Within that grounding logic, the statement in regard to Noah is a corollary. Made alive in Spirit, Jesus was able to address the dead who had no opportunity to receive him when they were living. Those who were disobedient in Noah's day are examples of that group; the ark in the water is taken as a type of baptism, the foreshadowing of the more effective reality, which is known as the antitype. (In classical terms, a "type" [*typos*] is the impression something might make, while the "antitype" [*antitypos*] is the thing itself.) The salvation of eight lives—Noah with his three sons and the wives of all four—is asserted because the number is symbolic. It is evocative of the eighth day of one's life, when circumcision is to occur within Judaic practice (following Gen. 17:12). Baptism is the reality (the antitype) of the salvation for which the ark is a type and of the incorporation within God's people for which circumcision is a type.

Baptism is located less within the "life" of Jesus than as a place where endowment with Spirit and identification as God's son are realized. That narrative representation by the Synoptic Gospels is confirmed by the discursive representation of Jesus as the source of Holy Spirit in John's Gospel. The Johannine emphasis upon the Baptist's testimony to Jesus as the one who baptizes in Spirit as God's Son is achieved without specific reference to the fact that Jesus was literally baptized. In their differing ways, 1 Corinthians and 1 Peter utterly submerge the initial ritual sense of baptism within an understanding that baptism into Jesus' name is fundamentally a quickening by the Spirit of Christ, which is related to the Hebrew Scriptures as antitype (fulfillment) to type (promise).

Prayer

In his letter to the Galatians, Paul articulates the commonly agreed sense of baptism and goes on to demonstrate that a close connection between baptism and prayer was presupposed:[2]

> When the fullness of time came, God sent forth his Son, born of a woman, born under law, in order that he might redeem those under law, in order that we might obtain sonship. And because you are sons, God sent forth the Spirit of his Son into our hearts crying, Abba, Father! (Gal. 4:4–6)

Contrary to what is sometimes claimed, the application to God of the Aramaic term "Abba," a direct form of address, would be at home within sources of Judaism prior to the New Testament.

In Paul's understanding it is possible (even for a Greek-speaking gentile) to refer to God as "Abba" because in baptism the Spirit of God's own Son possesses one's heart. A similar conviction, expressed more fulsomely,

2. For discussion with reference to recent secondary literature, see Bruce Chilton, *Jesus' Prayer and Jesus' Eucharist: His Personal Practice of Spirituality* (Valley Forge: Trinity Press International, 1997).

appears in Paul's letter to the Romans (8:1–17), which was written some four years after the letter to the Galatians. Accepting the Spirit of God's Son puts one in a fresh relationship to God, and one addresses him in a new way. "Abba" is the Aramaic word that has best survived multiple translations during the history of the church, because it has been accepted as the paradigm of how one stands in relation to God through Christ.

To address God as Father initially in baptism implies that a continuing and intimate relationship has been established. In fact, in the same chapter of Romans in which Paul refers to Christians' address of God as "Abba," he also avers:

> Similarly, the Spirit also comes to the aid of our weakness; for we do not know just how we should pray, but the Spirit itself intercedes in wordless sighs. (Rom. 8:26)

That is, a liturgical understanding of prayer is expressly set aside in favor of an intimate, spontaneous, and even nonverbal conception of prayer.

Paul's claim meshes with the fact that that there are many imperatives to pray within the New Testament (at every level), and several warnings about the abuse to which formal prayer may lead, but only one actual text of prayer. The single exception is what is commonly called the Lord's Prayer, which is better considered a template or outline of prayer than a liturgical form. The prayer is presented only by Matthew and by Luke, not by Mark. The omission in Mark does not appear deliberate; there are some two hundred verses in Matthew and Luke (largely examples of Jesus' teaching) which are not found in Mark. They appear to reflect a source which no longer exists and may never have existed as a whole in writing. Originally a compendium of sayings such as the disciples of a rabbi would treasure (a mishnah), the so-called Q collection of sayings was shaped by the fervent expectation of final judgment within the churches in Syria, where it was transmitted. Fundamentally, the Lord's Prayer is a guide to the sorts of intimacy that prayer in the Spirit of Jesus might lead to, a model teachers might commend to catechumens who had already been instructed in the purpose of prayer.

Of the two versions of the Lord's Prayer in the New Testament (Matt. 6:9–15; Luke 11:2–4), Luke's is widely considered the earlier in form, and it does seem plain that Matthew presents what is, in effect, a commentary woven together with the prayer:

Matthew	Luke
Our Father,	Father,
who is in the heavens,	

Matthew	Luke
your name will be sanctified,	your name will be sanctified,
your kingdom will come,	your kingdom will come.
your will happen	
as in heaven, even on earth.	
Our bread that is coming,	Our bread that is coming,
give us today,	be giving us each day.
and forgive us our debts,	and release us our sins,
as we also have forgiven our debtors,	because we also ourselves
	release everyone who is indebted to us,
And do not bring us to the test,	And do not bring us to the test.
but deliver us from the evil one.	

Certain elements appear to be expansions on a common model. The reference to God's "will" in Matthew, for example, provides a categorical commentary on the meaning of God's "kingdom."

The distinctiveness of the Lord's Prayer in Matthew as compared to Luke should make it plain beyond a doubt that one gospel cannot be explained simply on the basis of scribal copying from another. The Gospel of Matthew gives us the received view of the prayer in its community, just as Luke provides us with the received view in its. Both of them might have kept the silence of Mark, where the matter is not taken to be a part of initial catechesis. Had they followed suit, the version of the prayer in *Didache* 8, which is comparable to Matthew's, would have been our only literary source of the Lord's Prayer from documents of primitive Christianity. There, the Lord's Prayer is to be said thrice daily, as is the Amidah in Judaism. An increasingly liturgical portrayal of the prayer, from Luke through Matthew and further in the *Didache*, is obvious.

The relative sparseness of Luke has won it virtually unanimous recognition among scholars as the nearest to the form of an outline which Jesus would have recommended. This verdict seems warranted in view of the tendency we have seen towards an increasingly liturgical presentation, a filling out of the model, but caution is in order. Scholars have persisted in confusing two categories, one literary and the other historical. When they reach what they believe is the earliest form of a passage, they frequently equate that with a dictum of Jesus. What falsifies that equation is that none of the Gospels (as it stands) can reasonably be called historical. A given gospel might be catechetical, as in the case of the Synoptics (and even then, the catechesis involved is construed distinctively in each), or theologically discursive (as in John). There is no stemma of the relationship among them, so that the "most primitive" is identifiable from the outset, and even if there were, our experience of the texts at hand would make us suspicious of any claim that what was most primitive happened also to be the most historical. All of the texts are programmatic for the communities that produced them; none of them is historical in its governing intention, even to the extent that, say, Josephus's work is.

Yet the Gospels refer back to Jesus as their source: the literarily historical Jesus is a fact of which any reading of the Gospels must take account, even if the question of the historical Jesus remains problematic. That is to say, we cannot understand the documents at all unless we can identify what they believe they are referring to (whether or not we accept that they are relating historical facts at each point). That reference constitutes the literarily historical Jesus for a particular document, and the community which produced it. The disentanglement of the literarily historical Jesus from the historical figure we would call Jesus requires an investigation behind the texts at hand,[3] but for the present purpose that is beside the point. If our concern is with the religious system which the texts served and which produced those texts, the typically modern fixation with writing Jesus' biography must simply be put to one side. The fundamental issue for the critical study of religion is not what Jesus said as the Lord's Prayer, but what generated the texts before us.

In terms of a generative exegesis (that is, an exegesis engaged first of all with the religious system and how texts were produced within it), Luke's version of the Lord's Prayer, as compared to Matthew's and the *Didache*'s, appears the most likely of the three to have produced the other two. But having identified lapses of logic in historicist exegesis, we must avoid cognate errors in generative exegesis. The fact that Luke's version is the simplest does not necessarily mean that it actually generated the other two: there is no evidence of direct contact among the versions. All we can say is that the form of a model is better conveyed by Luke than by Matthew or the *Didache*. The possibility of secondary formations within Luke remains.

The generative model of the Lord's Prayer consists of calling God Father, confessing that his name should be sanctified and that his kingdom should come, and then asking for daily bread, forgiveness, and not to be brought to the test. Because a model is at issue, rather than a liturgy, attempts to fix a precise form of words simply exceed the bounds of any achievable certainty. Luke 11:2b–4 appears to function as a paradigm in its brevity, and its terse petitions for elemental needs—bread, pardon, integrity—appear nearly anticlimactic in comparison with the sorts of appeals which were possible within the early Judaism of the period. The

---

3. For a narrative inference on the basis of a literarily historical reading of the sources, see Bruce Chilton, *Rabbi Jesus: An Intimate Biography* (New York: Doubleday, 2000).

Lukan context (11:1–2a, 5–13) presents the prayer in a didactic manner, as something to be learned in contrast to other formulations. The
Matthean context is the more liturgical, invoking as it does the issues
of almsgiving (6:2–4), inappropriate and appropriate places of prayer
(vv. 5–6), putting prayer into words (vv. 7–8), and fasting (vv. 16–17).

The generative model permits us to specify the elements within the
recommended outline of prayer under two major headings:

1. an address of God (a) as Father, (b) with sanctification of God's
   name, and (c) vigorous assent to the coming of God's kingdom;
2. a petition for (a) bread, (b) forgiveness, and (c) constancy.

The two major headings are clearly distinguished in grammatical terms.
The address to God as Father is followed by imperatives in the third
person ("your name be sanctified," "your kingdom come"), while the
plea for bread is second-person imperative ("give"), as are the appeals
for forgiveness ("forgive") and for constancy ("do not bring").

Observable symmetry links the elements of the two major divisions of
the outline. In 1a, God is called Father, an address which calls to mind
his merciful provision for Israel, as in the Psalms:

Father of orphans and judge of widows is God in his holy dwelling.
(Ps. 68:5)

That Father is asked for the bread of the day in 2a. The invocation of the
sanctity of God in 1b, commonly instanced in the Hebrew Scriptures
(as in the same verse from Psalm 68), is then related to the petition
for forgiveness in 2b. The link between sanctity and forgiveness is also
straightforward, in that the forgiveness of sins is what may prepare one
for fellowship with the holy God. Just that connection is repeated many
times in the book of Leviticus from 4:20 onwards, when reference is
made to forgiveness in order to describe people's fitness to engage in
sacrifice again after an offering has been made for sin. The fundamental
conception is that God's appeasement by means of sacrifice leads to a
forgiveness which makes continuing participation in worship and in
the community possible again. Finally, the prayer for God's kingdom
in 1c corresponds to the appeal for constancy in 2c. The kingdom is a
conception of systemic importance, to be investigated in chapter four,
but for the moment we may observe that by the time of Jesus and his
followers, its sense within their Judaism was that God as king was extending himself to all peoples, and that they might either embrace or
reject him. A typical expression of hope in God's royal judgment of the
world is found in Psalm 96:

Say among the gentiles that the LORD reigns,
that the world is established so as not to move:
he will judge the peoples with equity. (Ps. 96:10)

God's extension into the world is to include judgment, so that loyalty to his righteousness, the resistance of any test leading to disloyalty which is the final plea of the prayer, becomes imperative.

Assessed by its individual elements, the Lord's Prayer may be characterized as a fairly typical instance of the Judaic piety of its period. To call God "Father" was—as such—nothing radical, and the association of his fatherly care with his actual provision for prayerful Israel is attested, as in Psalm 68:5. The same passage shows that the connection of God's holiness to his fatherhood was seen as natural, and the importance of sanctifying God's name within the earliest of rabbinic texts of prayer—such as the Kaddish, which means "Sanctified [be God's name]"—is well known. That his holiness is consistent with people being forgiven and accepted by him is also unexceptionable. Finally, the idea that God's being king amounts to a "kingdom" which was about to be revealed is amply precedented within the Aramaic paraphrases of the Hebrew Bible known as the *targumim*, and they insist upon the loyal response of God's people to that revelation.

The frequently repeated remark, therefore, to the effect that the Lord's Prayer is essentially a prayer of early Judaism, is perfectly understandable, and—from an atomistic point of view—justifiable. Indeed, the observation is consistent with the number of Aramaisms either present or implicit within the prayer. Prominent among them are the reference to God as "Father" (*Abba* in Aramaic, attested in early Judaism within nonliturgical prayers), the usage of the "kingdom" as a convention for divine self-disclosure, the assumption that the term "debt"—*hovya'* in Aramaic, used routinely of sin within the *targumim*—means "sin," and the understanding that *nisyona* ("the test") is the ultimate test which might prove us disloyal.

The deceptive simplicity of the generative model could cause one to overlook its significance. From the point of view of content and general structure, as we have noticed, claims of material originality—which are sometimes still made on behalf of the Lord's Prayer—seem to be wide of the mark. But it is apparent that the prayer must in some way be distinctive. After all, the tradition of prayer within the New Testament is not enthusiastic about formal texts, which is why the Lord's Prayer stands out in the first place. Matthew portrays Jesus as lampooning formal prayer (whether Judaic or gentile) in the passage immediately preceding the Lord's Prayer (6:5–8), and Luke conveys the prayer in didactic terms, as the equivalent of John the Baptist's teaching (11:1–2a).

The treatment of the Lord's Prayer in the two gospels indicates that it was seen as having distinctive character that made it a valuable model of prayer for the church.

The initial point of the model is that God is to be approached as Father, his named sanctified, and his kingdom welcomed. The act of prayer along those lines, with great variety over time and from place to place and tradition to tradition, has been a hallmark of Christianity. The claim of intimacy with God, of his personal involvement with the one who prays as a divine child, is intrinsic within the first step of praying. And it is in one sense an odd thing, but in another sense profoundly revealing, that Christians otherwise in dispute, even violently opposed to one another, can and do nonetheless pray together in the words their savior taught them. Whatever the realities and the forces of institutional, theological, ethnic, social, economic, linguistic, and other divisions, the mutual, filial consciousness of Christians when they say "Our Father" makes them family in a moment of time which is unconditioned by time. Unquestionably, those divisions remain. The scandal of Christians at violent odds with one another is not lost on Christians themselves. But because their unity is a unity in prayer, and often in prayer alone, the scandalous discrepancy is between earth and heaven, not just between theory and practice. What divides Christians from one another is not that they are Christians but that they are human beings; their prayer, however, permits them to see humanity as one in the invocation of a single Father, intimately accessible to all.

The sanctity of God is not diminished by the approach to him as Father. The intimacy between parent and child is not the intimacy of lovers or of friends on equal terms. Parents will usually know more, overlook more, care more, fret more, provide more, than anyone else. It is precisely their greater love, however, which will predictably distance them from their children, and even at times alienate their children from them. God as Father is altogether different from us and from what we know, as transcendent and unknowable as his love knows no boundaries. What is holy is what stands apart from us and our usual relationships, a center of privilege but also of danger, unlike all that we are familiar with, even as it permits us to exist. To address God as one's Father, and yet to sanctify his name, acknowledges the ambivalence which might permeate our attitude toward God. He approaches us freely and without restraint, and yet is unapproachable, as holy as we are ordinary. The welcoming of his kingdom, of his comprehensive rule within the terms of reference of our world, wills away our ambivalence. His intimate holiness is to invade the ordinary, so that any ambivalence is overcome by God's own force. The kingdom is dynamically ingressive and is welcomed in the act of prayer, however others might react to it.

The three elements which open the prayer, then, characterize a relationship and an attitude toward God which the one who prays makes his own or her own. The distinctiveness of the prayer is nothing other than that consciousness of God and of one's relationship to him that the prayer implies. Whoever prays after this model recapitulates that consciousness. Such an awareness of God and of oneself is what Christians kindle when they pray the Lord's Prayer. And at the same time, the prayer is nothing other than the Lord's; whatever the merits of such a consciousness, it is only ours because it was Christ's first. That is why the filial consciousness of praying in this manner is as strong as it is: one is God's child and Jesus' sister or brother in the same instant.

The conscious relationship to God conveyed and reinforced in the first three elements of the prayer, in which God is approached, is then extended into the last three elements, in which God is besought as a holy Father and King. The apparent modesty of the requests is linked to the purpose of the prayer. One asks for bread; its reception every day is to be taken as of God's fatherly provision. One requests forgiveness; one's need for it as a requirement of divine sanctity is therefore granted. The petition to be guarded from temptation presumes the dread of any apostasy from the hope of God's kingdom. Precisely because the three elements for which one pleads are ordinary, they mark the purpose of the prayer as the acquisition of the filial consciousness of Jesus, enacted as one eats, enjoys forgiveness, and remains loyal to God.

Much as baptism represents the narrative identification with Christ, so the Lord's Prayer (understood as the model of the sort of prayer in which one will engage) represents the appropriation of that consciousness of God which is initiated and made possible by Christ.

Ethics

Jesus' consciousness of God as Father as conveyed and promulgated in the Lord's Prayer is the basis of the portrait of him in the last moments before his arrest. The agreement of the Synoptic Gospels in presenting some version of Jesus' prayer to be spared the cup of his suffering attests its importance for ancient Christian catechesis. The highly schematic quality of the scene in Gethsemane suggests its usage as a model of Christian reflection in the midst of crisis.[4]

In Mark's version (14:32–42), we see Jesus and his disciples coming to the parcel of land called Gethsemane after his prediction of his

---

4. Regarding ethics, see Bruce Chilton, *Pure Kingdom: Jesus' Vision of God* (Studying the Historical Jesus 1; Grand Rapids: Eerdmans; London: SPCK, 1996).

betrayal (14:18–21), his final meal with the disciples (14:22–25), and his prediction of their denial of him (14:26–31). Within the scene itself, Jesus commands his disciples to sit while he prays alone, but he takes Peter, James, and John with him some way further (14:32–33a). In deep distress, he asks them to remain and stay alert (vv. 33b–34). Only then does he start to pray; proceeding a little further, he falls to the earth, and asks that the "hour" which has come upon him may pass (v. 35). The words of his prayer are also given:

> Abba, Father: everything is possible for you.
> Take this cup away from me.
> Yet not what I will, but what you will. (Mark 14:36)

The reminiscence of the Lord's Prayer seems deliberate, because next, finding Peter and his companions sleeping, Jesus tells them to stay alert and pray, "so that you do not come to a test" (14:37–38). The scene is then repeated a second (14:39–40) and a third time (14:41a), when Jesus announces that the hour has come; the son of man is now betrayed (14:41b–42).

The passage is an example of the catechetical method followed in the Gospels. The text appears to be an incident concerning Jesus at prayer, but some care is taken to exclude the very witnesses which the scene would require to be historically credible in all its detail. At the crucial moment, Jesus is alone, but for the presence of three sleeping disciples in his vicinity. Who was there to hear how he prayed? But the matter of his prayer turns out, in any case, to be predictable on the basis of the Lord's Prayer, whose paradigmatic importance is therefore confirmed. The substance of the prayer is more a presupposition than the point of the passage: the scene in Gethsemane is more important for its setting than for Jesus' words and deeds there.

Those disciples who seem to be distanced from the action are in fact deeply implicated within it. After all, they are the group from which the betrayer comes; they are the ones who share a meal with Jesus as he tells them of his fate; their denial of Jesus (with Peter at their head) is openly predicted. And now, in Gethsemane, they cannot even watch and pray. Such prayerful attention is precisely the way of Jesus, his steeling for the hour that comes upon him, and the disciples are as yet no match for that "hour."

As in the case of the Lord's Prayer, what Jesus does is paradigmatic, but here the paradigm has more to do with the crisis he faces than with what he says in the midst of it. The sleep of the disciples and the repetition of the notice of their inattention as contrasted with Jesus' agonized struggle are deliberately schematic, because the burden of the passage is how (and how not) to face the hour of trial without disloyalty (the "test" of which Jesus speaks in 14:38, as in the Lord's Prayer).

In that the principal concern of the scene is how followers of Jesus are to face crisis, the portrayal of Jesus' own behavior (as well as his disciples') is deliberately unheroic. The catechesis is designed to identify catechumens with Jesus, and their fears are transferred to him within the narrative. He asks for what indeed seems impossible. The logic of his own action to that moment, a calculated visit to Jerusalem and a forceful—even violent—controversy with the authorities of the Temple, could only have led to that "hour" which indeed must come upon him. The single plausible alternative to arrest is flight, which is just the alternative the disciples will avail themselves of later in the narrative (see Mark 14:43–52). Yet Jesus asks for what any catechumen might desire: freedom from persecution, no matter how inevitable such persecution might be. He is shown praying after the model that the catechumen has learned and being as deeply conflicted as any recent convert might be.

Within the world of the Gospels, persecution is a likely result of baptism. Public identification with Jesus might bring with it a fate comparable to his. That reality casts its shadow on a principle motif of the New Testament, that of believers' call to the imitation of Christ. The importance of 1 Peter as reflecting of the place of baptism within the church has already been observed. It is consistent with that emphasis that the Epistle addresses a plain word of advice to domestic servants who might suffer as a result of their faith (2:21): "for you were called to this, because Christ also suffered for you, leaving you an example in order that you might follow in his footsteps." The example of Christ comes at the close of a fairly well-developed sequence of imperatives of a general nature (2:11–17) and is obviously a fitting conclusion, but the ease of the transition is predicated upon the mention of domestic servants or slaves and their predicament from v. 18.

If one is baptized into Christ and practices the consciousness of Christ in prayer, how is one to be and behave in a world that has largely rejected Christ? The advice of 1 Peter to domestic slaves is to remain obedient to masters, good and bad, "for this is grace, if—on account of a consciousness of God—someone bears pain, suffering unjustly" (2:19). The position of oppression, provided it is combined with the will to do good (v. 20), enables one to walk in Jesus' footsteps. For that reason, a social status comparable with Jesus' vulnerability at the end of his life was commended. That commendation simultaneously affirmed the position of the early Christians themselves, who were encouraged to see their position within underclasses as an indication of divine approval.

The framing of the Gospels, the Epistles, and the other writings of the New Testament for those who were about to be or had been baptized resulted in appropriations of Jesus within environments quite unlike his own. The rabbi, as we have seen, became a slave in the Epistles. And not only in the Epistles. Within the Gospel according to John, the last meal of Jesus with his disciples in chapter 13 is a symposium, complete with a discourse which continues for several chapters thereafter and dominates the Johannine account of this meal. The introduction (13:1–12b) has Jesus perform the menial task of washing his disciples' feet in order to exemplify the sort of mutual service he demands from his followers. The Johannine point is driven home without symbolic embellishment:

> He said to them, Do you know what I have done for you? You call me teacher and lord, and you say well; I am. If, then, I—lord and teacher—washed your feet, you also ought to wash one another's feet. For I have given you an example, so that just as I have done to you, so you also might do. Truly, truly I say to you, a servant is not greater than his lord, nor an apostle greater than the one who sent him. If you know these things, you are blessed if you do them. (John 13:12c–17)

John's placement of the scene as the formal equivalent of the "last supper" in the Synoptics suggests the importance of the behavior that Jesus models. Serving others is the active equivalent of Jesus' ministry, the performance of his purpose.

The relative privilege of poverty within early Christianity is reflected in a pivotal catechetical section of the Synoptics (Matt. 19:16–30; Mark 10:17–31; Luke 18:18–30), beginning with the story of a would-be disciple with property. The enthusiastic catechumen is told, much to his dismay, to sell all and give to the poor in order to gain treasure in heaven (Matt. 19:16–22; Mark 10:17–22; Luke 18:18–23). The normative value of the cautionary story is reinforced by Jesus' statement about rich people and the kingdom of God: a camel would have an easier time wriggling through the eye of a needle than the rich would have getting into the kingdom. Only God's capacity to overcome what is humanly impossible gives them any hope (Matt. 19:23–26; Mark 10:23–27; Luke 18:24–27). Peter, speaking for the body of Jesus' peripatetic followers, calls attention to their voluntary poverty. In response Jesus promises rewards (Matt. 19:27–30; Mark 10:28–31; Luke 18:28–30).

The message of the passage may appear mixed, but it is pointed. Those who are poor simply because of their underclass status enjoy relative proximity to the kingdom, while the rich may enter only by means of the exceptional grace of God. But Peter and his companions, by means of their voluntary poverty for the sake of the movement, are assured of life everlasting. The pericope reflects the stringent practice

of Christianity in the circle of Peter; from that circle, the story of Ana-
nias and Sapphira in Acts also derives. That couple claimed to have
sold their property for the benefit of the apostles but in fact retained
some of the profit, and they died separately under Peter's interrogation
(Acts 5:1–11). Within the Petrine group, there seems little question but
that voluntary poverty was a principal means of following Jesus, that
is, of enacting his ethos. The only evident alternative was the obvious
alternative to eternal life.

Even the Petrine transformation of Jesus from a rabbi with the resources of fishermen and artisans at his disposal into a peripatetic
mendicant allowed that the rich might wriggle in through the needle's
eye. The voluntary acceptance of poverty on the basis of an analogy with
Jesus' ministry, however highly it was recommended, was not taken by
itself to be a fulfillment of the imperative to follow Jesus. Simply accepting poverty did not make one like Jesus and worthy of eternal life.
The Petrine circle and other communities of the New Testament knew
that the needle's eye was open for those with property because voluntary
poverty was in the service of a more basic means of enacting the ethos
of the Christ. Other means than voluntary poverty might realize that
program. The purest form of the Petrine statement of the larger principle appears in Matthew and Mark (Matt. 22:34–40; Mark 12:28–34).
In them both, Jesus is asked by someone outside his group (a Pharisee
in Matthew, a scribe in Mark) what is the great (so Matthew) or first (so
Mark) commandment. He replies by citing two commandments, to love
God (drawing from Deut. 6:4–5), and to love one's neighbor (drawing
from Lev. 19:18). Jesus concludes in Matthew that all the Law and the
Prophets hang from those two commandments, and in Mark that no
other commandment is greater than these.

Matthew and Mark construe the sense of the teaching distinctively.
In Matthew, the organic connection among the commandments assures that they all hang together (with the teaching of the prophets)
on the principle of love towards God and neighbor (22:40). Mark, on
the other hand, has the scribe who initiated the scene conclude that to
love is more than all burnt offerings and sacrifices (12:32–3). The construal of Matthew is in the direction of claiming that Jesus represents
the fulfillment of the Law and the Prophets, a thematic concern of the
Gospel generally. Mark takes the tack that Jesus' principle establishes
a noncultic means of approval by God. Both find their center of gravity,
however, in the conviction that the commandment to love God and love
one's neighbor is the action that unites one with Jesus in an approach
to God. The emblem of that approach is fulfillment of the Law and
the Prophets in Matthew (22:40), nearness to the kingdom of God in
Mark (12:34). The differences between those construals are not to be

minimized: they represent the substantive independence of the Gospels as catechetical instruments. But equally striking is the systemic agreement between Matthew and Mark that love is the means of access to God after the pattern of Jesus.

It is a commonplace of critical study to observe that Hillel—in a dictum comparable to Jesus'—is said to have taught that the Torah is a commentary on the injunction not to do what is hateful to one's neighbor (*b. Shabbat* 31a). The centrality of the commandment to love one's neighbor is also asserted by Aqiba, the famous second-century rabbi (*Sifra*, Lev. 19:18). Differences of emphasis are detectable and important, but the fact remains that Jesus simply does not appear to have been exceptional in locating love at the center of the divine commandments. Any rabbi, a teacher in a city or a local village, might have come up with some such principle, although the expressions of the principle attributed to Jesus are especially apt. The principle itself is little more than proverbial: love, after all, is not easily dismissed as a bad idea, or beside the point.

Precisely because Jesus' teaching has precedents in the early Judaism of his day, it becomes clear that the Petrine tradition presented in aggregate by Matthew and Mark is offering a transformation of that teaching. Jesus' citation of the two biblical passages that demand and define love is for that transformation no longer simply a matter of locating a coherent principle within the Torah, which is what the question of the Pharisee or scribe hinges on. Rather, the twin commandment of love is now held to be a transcendent principle that fulfills (so Matthew) or supersedes (so Mark) the Torah. Christ himself, by citing and enacting that principle, is held to offer the ethical key to communion with God.

The Lukan version of the teaching concerning love makes it especially apparent that the significance of Jesus' message lies at least as much in who is speaking as in what he says. There (Luke 10:25–28), an unidentified lawyer asks what to do in order to inherit eternal life; formally, the fact that the rich man in 18:18 asks the same questions is striking. Clearly the Lukan community at Antioch (the likely place of origin of this gospel) appreciates the relation between the latter question, which leads Jesus to commend poverty, and the question that leads Jesus to demand love. Indeed, by reversing the order of the passages as compared to Matthew and Mark, Luke presents poverty as the subordinate virtue: the lawyer's question is the precedent of the rich man's question in Luke, while the discussion of love only appears after the praise of poverty in Matthew and Mark.

Yet it is not Jesus in Luke who cites the twin principle of love, but the lawyer (10:27). At first, Jesus merely confirms what the lawyer already knows (10:28); Jesus' peculiar contribution comes in the response to the lawyer's further question, Who is my neighbor (10:29)? The question and the response appear in uniquely Lukan material, the presentation of Jesus' teaching concerning love which was characteristic of the church in Antioch (10:29–37). The Lukan transformation of the principle, in distinction from the Petrine transformation, explicitly makes Jesus' application of the commandment, not its formulation, his systemic innovation.

The innovation is effected in the parable of the Good Samaritan (Luke 10:29–37). Whether Jesus himself told the parable is beside the present point. What concerns us is (1) that the parable invests the commandment to love with a new meaning, and (2) that this new meaning is the systemic center of Lukan ethics, as distinct from Matthean and Markan ethics. Formally, the parable is designed to answer the question, Who is my neighbor? And that formal issue is also addressed at the close of the parable, when Jesus tells his questioner to go and do what the Samaritan did, that is, show himself a neighbor to one in obvious need (10:36–37). But the formal issue here is distinct from the systemic issue.

The systemic challenge is not the goodness of the Samaritan, but the fact that he is a Samaritan. The victim of the mugging is in no position to complain, but especially as a recent pilgrim to Jerusalem he might well otherwise have objected to contact with a Samaritan, since sacrifice on Mount Gerizim was seen as antagonistic to and impure in respect of sacrifice on Mount Zion. A priest and a Levite have already passed by, motivated by concerns for their special status; after all, the victim is described as half dead (10:30), and he presumably would have been taken for dead—and therefore unclean—by any person who did not, out of pity, look more closely than would an ordinary passerby (see 10:33). In the parable, then, a victim who seems impure is aided by a Samaritan who actually is impure, and that action nonetheless fulfills the commandment to love one's neighbor as oneself.

The parable of the Good Samaritan, then, is a story which formally conveys how to be a neighbor, and which is shaped systemically to insist that one viewed as "impure" may be a neighbor to one who is "pure." The commandment to love is such that, in its application, it creates a new sphere of purity transcending any other notion of clean and unclean. The purity issue was crucial to the church in Antioch. In Galatians 2:11–13, Paul describes factional fighting among three groups, classed according to their leaders. On one extreme, Paul himself taught that gentiles and Jews might freely eat with one another; on the other, James insisted upon the separation of those who were circumcised. Peter and Barnabas were caught somewhere in between. Much later, around 90 CE, Luke represents how the issue was resolved within Antiochene Christianity: the question of the boundaries established by purity was settled in terms of ethical engagement rather than dietary practice. It is no accident, then, that Luke conveys this unique parable and its peculiar perspective on the distinctiveness of Jesus' teaching regarding love.

Much as Jesus provides the model of a consciousness of God in prayer, so his performance of an ethos of love under duress provides a paradigm of loving service. The link with catechumens' social situation is so strong that their lives are mirrored in his as much as his is in theirs, even when one might expect the texts to be straightforwardly historical. In the case of both Jesus and believers, the ethos which goes by the name of love is transformed by distinctive conditions, so that love might be—for example—the integral principle of the Torah (Matthew), or a principle beyond cultic Judaism (Mark), or the single term of reference which determines the purity of one person for another (Luke).

Eucharist

An awareness of how Jesus' apparently proverbial teaching concerning love was transformed in a signally different way in Luke as compared to Matthew and Mark provides the point of departure for our consideration of the next medium of communion with God in Christianity. Eucharist has been the object of even more dramatic transformations. In one understanding or another, it is claimed as a hallmark of identity—along with baptism, prayer, and ethics—by nearly every group of Christians, and yet how Eucharist is understood has been a greater and more frequent cause of division than any other single issue. Division, of course, has proven to be a regular feature of Christendom, but the regularity with which Eucharist has been cited as a matter of contention between groups over the centuries is striking. A principal cause of the contention can now be identified: the New Testament already presents multiple mutually conflicting transformations of the meaning of Eucharist. A systematic assessment of Christianity is impossible without an appreciation of those sacramental transformations.

Six types of Eucharist in early Christian tradition may be distinguished within the text of the New Testament. Each type, with attendant words and gestures, is the meaning of the Eucharist for particular circles of Christians. These types were generated within distinct circles of the movement during its formative stages. The first two were produced by Jesus, the first during the larger part of his ministry, the second after his abortive attempt to occupy the Temple and influence sacrificial worship there. The third type is that of Peter and his network in Judah, Galilee, and beyond, while the fourth bears the imprint of James's group, the prestigious church headquartered in Jerusalem. The fifth type represents an attempt to rationalize the variant views of Eucharist that had emerged by the mid-fifties. The Pauline group attempted a radical appropriation of the type of Peter and a rejection of the type of James, while in the group that shaped the Synoptic Gospels a symbolic reconciliation of elements included in previous types was practiced. Just at that stage, "This is my body" and "This is my blood" came to mean that bread and wine become for the believer a direct communion with Christ in his martyr's death. The Gospel according to John, an example of the sixth type, demonstrates the extent to which the understanding of the Eucharist as a consumption of Christ's body and blood dominated the movement by the end of the century. In a longer study, I have isolated each type according to a generative exegesis designed to analyze the meanings that produced particular texts, but here we may follow through the types in their chronological order in a summary way:[5]

1. *The purity of the kingdom.* Jesus' frequent meals with his disciples throughout his ministry represent the practice of purity in anticipation of the kingdom. Each meal is a pledge that the kingdom is to come. As Jesus says in a famous dictum: I shall not again drink of the fruit of the vine until I drink it new in the kingdom of God (Matt. 26:29; Mark 14:25; Luke 22:18). The intention of the saying within its originating context was to assure Jesus' followers that every meal taken in his fellowship was a warrant of the festal kingdom which was shortly to come.

2. *The surrogate of sacrifice.* After Jesus' occupation of the Temple, and his failure to change arrangements in the cult, he presented his "blood" and "body"—his meals in anticipation of the kingdom—as a replacement of conventional sacrifice. The sense of the gesture is straightforward: pure wine and bread, shared in a community created by mutual forgiveness, is a better sacrifice than the priesthood of the Temple is willing to permit. The gesture is confrontational but does not involve the formal blasphemy that a later interpretation of the saying would require. Jesus did not in history refer to himself as "blood" and "body"; he referred to his meals with followers under those terms in order to designate them as a surrogate of sacrifice within the Temple.

3. *The covenantal sacrifice.* Jesus' practice at the end of his life ran the risk—if simply repeated by his followers—of being taken as a challenge to the regular practice of sacrificial offering. That was how the authorities in the Temple had understood Jesus' own meals after his failed raid on the outer court. The Petrine circle

5. See Bruce Chilton, *A Feast of Meanings: Eucharistic Theologies from Jesus through Johannine Circles* (Supplements to Novum Testamentum 72; Leiden: Brill, 1994).

saw Jesus' meals after the manner of Moses' sacrifice with his followers in Exodus 24, where the Mosaic covenant had been inaugurated. That transformation enabled those around Peter to proceed with regular worship in the Temple while insisting upon the normative value of what Jesus had done.

4. *The Passover.* Passover became the paradigmatic association within the circle of James (which focused on maintaining the covenantal identity of Israel; Acts 15:13–21). However emphatic the association, it is also artificial: the Gospels admit that the authorities wished (with good reason) to execute Jesus prior to the feast. The paschal connection of the meal was a most effective means of incorporating Jesus' movement fully within cultic worship, which was the program of James. In a stroke, the meal was more tightly linked to the liturgical year than it ever had been before, and Jerusalem—the hub of Jacobean influence—was accorded irreducible importance as the single place where Passover/Eucharist could fully be observed with its full meaning.

5. *The heroic sacrifice for sin: Pauline and Synoptic symposia.* Hellenistic Christians most naturally associated the dominical meal with a philosophical symposium, the sober version of gatherings that for other purposes could be uproarious. Paul stresses the importance of order and moderation at meals in the Lord's name (see 1 Cor. 11:17–34). In resistance to Jacobean hegemony, he also insists that the primitive tradition (1 Cor. 11:23) made no tight connection with the Passover but simply with the night in which Jesus was betrayed. Paul so emphasizes the connection with Jesus' death (1 Cor. 11:26) that the older, Petrine understanding of the meal in terms of covenantal sacrifice is lost on non-Jewish readers. The understanding that Jesus offered himself in connection with the meal as a martyr's sacrifice for sin was current in the emerging consensus of Hellenistic Christianity and is assumed by Paul elsewhere (Gal. 1:4; Rom. 3:21–26). The association with Jesus' death becomes so fundamental in his thought that he believes that anyone who does not discern the Lord's body and blood in the proceedings is condemned (1 Cor. 11:27–30).

The Synoptic Gospels reflect the conception of Jesus as a heroic sacrifice for sin (*hata'at,* see Lev. 4) that characterized the Hellenistic catechesis invoked by Paul. The blood of the covenant is "poured out" in the Synoptic tradition in the manner of the blood of the sacrifice for sin, in the interest of the communities for which the Gospels were written (Matt. 26:28; Mark 14:24; Luke 22:20). That same basic thought is spelled out differently in each gospel.

6. *Miraculous food*. The Johannine Gospel identifies the story of the feeding of the five thousand with Passover (6:1–15, v. 4) and then develops fully a quasi-magical exposition of the eucharistic bread as manna, the miraculous bread of Exodus 16 (John 6:26–71). Conceptually, John marks a daring advance beyond the Hellenistic catechesis represented in the Synoptics. Jesus no longer merely offers solidarity in martyrdom by means of his symbolic body and blood: Jesus now claims that he is what is consumed, the true bread of heaven (John 6:35). The fact that the new identification is developed within the complex of the feeding rather than within a narrative of the "last supper" may indicate self-conscious creativity.

By now it should be clear that Christianity as a movement was fated to define itself along differing lines in eucharistic terms. The ministry of Jesus itself set in motion a process of transformation in which an initial practice of purity by means of forgiveness at meals was transformed into a surrogate of sacrifice after Jesus' occupation of the outer court of the Temple. Peter's circle changed that type into a new sort of covenantal sacrifice, not a permanent replacement but a foundational act permitting Jesus' followers in the Petrine circle to go on worshiping in the Temple while they accepted Jesus' view of purity. If the Petrine transformation of the meal may be regarded as a domestication of dominical types, what happened at the next stage was even more emphatically so. James's circle linked the Eucharist tightly to the Temple in the manner of Passover.

The fifth type of Eucharist, however, became normative in the history of the church. The Synoptic reading proved to have the resilience to reconcile the stark alternatives represented by the Petrine and Jacobean circles. The Synoptic reference to the "body" and "blood" within a biographical context permitted the association with Jesus himself at the point of martyrdom. Solidarity with him could be regarded as being as literal as eating bread and drinking wine. Although the Synoptic tradition did not impose that understanding, it was open to such a reading. A notion which would have been unthinkable at earlier stages, eating a person's flesh and drinking his blood, became the ordinary paradigm of Christian worship at the stage represented by John's Gospel.

To say we consume Jesus' "flesh" and his "blood"—as is plainly asserted by the time of John—is to say that the very means of our communion with Christ are alternative to any reasonable construction of purity within Judaism. It is no longer Jesus' practice but his very self which is the substance of Eucharist. Precisely when Eucharist discloses

its systemic force, the divergence of Christianity from Judaism is accomplished. Communion in Christ's body and blood is separation from
classic constructions of purity within Judaism, even as it is held to be
communion with God, the culmination and focus of baptism, prayer,
and ethics.

The Theology of Rabbinic Judaism

For Adam and Eve the fall brooked no looking back; sin marked
the end of Eden. Ten generations later, God gave up hope, finding
only Noah righteous in his generation. Ten generations after that, God
identified Abraham, of all mankind, as faithful and obedient: him did
he call, with him he made a covenant, and to his heirs (both heirs
after the flesh and heirs by reason of an act of will, all of them called
Israel), God made himself known by fully spelling out his will at Sinai
in the Torah (or Teaching). For the new moral entity called Israel, sin
is not indelible because the Torah provides a twofold antidote. (1) The
Torah's commandments educate the heart of man, so that by nature
he will want to do what God wants. Through keeping the laws of the
Torah, Israel would learn to keep God's will and express love for God:
"You shall love the Lord your God with all your heart, with all your
soul, and with all your might" (Deut. 6:5). (2) For failures and sins, defined as rebellion against God, the Torah makes available the means of
washing sins away: sacrifices that atone for inadvertent sin, confession
and the Day of Atonement, reconciliation with the wronged party, and
associated acts of repentance, as we shall see in a later chapter. These
constitute public transactions involving God and Israel and therefore
represent only communal—not familial, let alone personal—categories.
The Torah through its law therefore accomplishes the task of forming
the new moral entity, Israel, within the very framework of providing
for the atonement of sin.

This reference to the setting forth of God's will (for both behavior
and belief) in the form of law brings us to an unfamiliar medium of
theological discourse. We find routine the formulation of theology in
propositional form. But in the form of acts of omission or commission
that *imply* diverse but harmonious propositions, we confront theology
in an unaccustomed medium: deliberate action or restraint from action
as an expression of coherent theological convictions. In specifically
commanding in the Torah that one should or should not do a given deed
or feel a given emotion or form a given attitude, God gives mankind a
second chance. So we have to ask, how, in detail, does the law of the
Torah form a medium of theological instruction?

Rebellion in Eden and in Israel

Let us start with how the halakhah responds to the story of what happened in Eden: man's rebellion through an act of disobedience at the moment of creation's perfection and Adam's and Eve's consequent exile from Eden. The halakhah does simply not set out to recapitulate Eden by restoring the conditions of paradise. It also takes account of the tragedy of Eden and accordingly institutes a new moral entity equipped with a transaction not available to Adam and Eve. In Eden God had made no provision for atonement for sin, but in the unfolding of man's story God grasped the full measure of man's character, drew the necessary conclusion, and acted on it.

The halakhah embodies in norms of behavior deep reflection on the meaning of human nature. Endowed with autonomous will, man has the power to rebel against God's will, and it follows that rebellion lurks as an ever-present possibility. Therefore the halakhah finds urgent the question how man, subject to God's rule, is to atone for the sin that because of his rebellious nature man is likely to commit. To answer that question the Torah formulates rules that govern man both under God's dominion and in rebellion against God's will. These represent the two aspects of the one story that commences with Eden, leads to the formation of Israel through Abraham, Isaac, and Jacob (God's antidotes to Adam), and climaxes at Sinai. But Israel also is human, so that story accommodates both Adam's fall and Israel's worship of the golden calf, both Adam and Eve's exile from Eden and Israel's ultimate exile from the Land. How, then, does God propose to repair the world he has made to take account of man's character and Israel's own proclivity? It is through the halakhah, which formulates norms of everyday conduct.

These fall into two sets, the one on atonement for sin, the other on the regulations of life in God's kingdom. We follow the halakhah that pertains to the shift from the condition of Eden to the long-term consequences of what happened there: sin but also atonement, and Israel's resolve to live by God's will as revealed to Moses at Sinai in the commandments of Torah. The first of the two critical passages of the halakhah—sin but also atonement—reveals the effort not only to restore Eden but also to recapitulate, with a different result, what took place there. The halakhah registers that sin is not permanent; man can atone and attain reconciliation with God. The second then sets forth how life is to be lived in God's kingdom, subject to God's dominion. The Torah both accommodates Israel's character and educates its conscience.

In both passages, Israel, like Adam but for the Torah, takes over the tasks of Adam. Since the whole story of Eden is set in motion when man uses his freedom of will to act in rebellion against God's will, the halakhah must in setting out to restore Eden focus on precisely that innate human trait. The regeneration of man will mean the nurturing of Israel's capacity not only to atone but to accept, submit, obey—in perfect freedom. Furthermore, the sages note that Adam and Eve, creatures of the sixth day, did not remain in Eden long enough even to enjoy the seventh, which was meant to be its crowning moment. Israel therefore makes up on the Sabbath for the original failure of man. Just as the original act of rebellion took place within a brief spell before the Sabbath of creation, so Israel's rebellion erupted in the fashioning of the golden calf in the very shadow of Sinai, in fact while Moses was yet on the mount.

So what is to be done, if, as the Torah insists time and again, Israel itself embodies the innate flaws of man as it does? Deliberately or otherwise, Israel is going to sin: that fact defines the human condition. The task of the halakhah, then, is to provide for the natural condition of Israelite man, to afford media for reconciliation: atonement for sin and regeneration, grace not accorded to the original man. If, as the Torah underscores, "the wickedness of man was great in the earth and every imagination of the thoughts of his heart was only evil continually, so that the Lord was sorry that he had made man on the earth" (Gen. 6:5–6), the Torah also tells the tale of God's search for a successor to the original, ultimately incorrigible man. That succession runs via Noah through Abraham to Israel at Sinai. Israel too would write a record of rebellion and sin. But responding to Noah's offering of every clean animal and bird as burnt offerings on the altar, God determined "in his heart never again to curse the ground because of man, for the imagination of man's heart is evil from his youth, nor ever again to destroy every living creature" (Gen. 8:21). That is the context in which atonement finds its place: in response to the offering presented in good faith, God resolves to bear with man and not to destroy him. Just as the story of Noah proves integral to the tale commencing with man, so the provision of media of atonement proves essential to the logic defined by man's disobedience.

But we cannot leave matters at just that point. Clearly God could not rest there but would have to provide exercises of transcendence as opportunities for man to change his nature. Therefore God gives Israel not only the means to atone for sins but also numerous opportunities to engage with God as God had always wanted, that is, to carry out God's instructions, or commandments, thus showing itself regenerate. This latter view is succinctly expressed as follows:

> A. R. Hananiah b. Aqashia says, "The Holy One, blessed be he, wanted to give Israel occasion to attain merit.

> B. "Therefore he gave them abundant Torah and numerous com-
> mandments,
> C. "as it is said, 'it pleased the Lord for his righteousness' sake to
> magnify the Torah and give honor to it'" [Isa. 42:21].
>
> *m. Makkot* 3:16

The entire narrative of Scripture would then tell the tale of Israel's exile
and return to the Land, parallel to man's loss of Eden but with a different outcome. Abundant Torah and numerous commandments would
form the remedy to man's innate capacity to rebel and sin.

The tale of the Torah accordingly falls into two parts, the one comple-
menting the other. First, Israel is given the Torah and commandments,
so afforded the occasion to show itself obedient to God's will. Then Israel
overcomes Adam's heritage. But, second, Israel also sins, whether willingly or inadvertently. So, unlike Adam, Israel is allowed the opportunity
to atone. The halakhah devotes a principal chapter of its statement to
the medium of atonement and reconciliation, which is the Temple offering, especially its blood-rite. To the halakhic nurture of a long-term,
stable relationship between God and Israel despite Israel's sinfulness
we devote the present chapter. Then comes the halakhah governing the
life of Israel under the Torah.

The recapitulation whereby Israel and the Land of Israel (defined as
the sector of humanity and the segment of the humanity's territory that
are fully permeated by God's will in the Torah—an understanding far
removed from the mundane realities of contemporary politics and wars)
reverse the rebellion of Adam is spelled out in *Genesis Rabbah* XIX.[6]
Adam lived in Eden but rebelled against God and was driven out. Israel
lived in the Land of Israel and for a brief moment, upon entry, Israel
recapitulated Eden. But as the Torah (Scripture) says in the authorized
history from Genesis through Kings, Israel rebelled against God and
was driven out. But what distinguishes Israel from Adam is that Israel
possessed the Torah, which held the power to transform the heart of
man and so turn man from rebellion to loving submission. And when
the Israelite man, regenerate in the Torah, fully conformed to the Torah,
then Israel would recover its Eden, the Land of Israel.

Israel represents the new Adam, God's way of correcting the errors of
the initial creation. The Land of Israel stands for the new Eden. Just as
Adam entered a perfect world but lost it, so Israel was given a perfect
world—in repose at the moment of Israel's entry—but sinning against
God, lost it. The difference, however, is that Israel has what Adam did

---

6. This passage is quoted above, pp. 44–45.

not have, which is the Torah, a point that does not enter here except by indirection. The Torah leaves no ambiguity about who man is and what God wants of him. What God craves is man's willing submission to God's will, made known in the Torah, beginning with the drama, for which the halakhah legislates, of the proclamation of God's dominion and God's unity: "Hear, Israel, the Lord our God is unique. And you shall love the Lord your God with all your heart, with all your soul, and with all your might" (Deut. 6:4–5).

Restoration

The restoration of Israel to the Land then forms a chapter in the story of the redemption of all of mankind. The last things are to be known from the first. In the just plan of creation man was meant to live in Eden, and Israel in the Land of Israel, in time without end. The restoration to the Land will bring about that long and tragically postponed perfection of the world order, sealing the demonstration of the justice of God's plan for creation. Risen from the dead, having atoned through death, man will be judged in accord with his deeds. Israel for its part, when it repents and conforms its will to God's, recovers its Eden. When the consequences of rebellion and sin having been overcome and the struggle of man's will with God's word resolved, God's original plan will be realized at last. The simple, global logic of the system, with its focus on the world order of justice established by God but disrupted by man, leads inexorably to this eschatology of restoration, the restoration of balance, order, proportion—eternity. Holy Israel, the people defined theologically and not politically, then assembles at prayer and expresses the hope that, in the end of days, God will call all humanity to his worship, as, even now, he has called holy Israel. Then everyone will acknowledge the sovereignty of the one and only God and accept his dominion.

Realizing the law of the Torah, Israel would regain paradise. For, having been granted what man had missed, which is the Torah, and being guided by the Torah, holy Israel would restore Eden. This it would do in the Land that God had given it for Eden but that had been lost to sin. The Torah, setting forth the halakhah, the rules for the social order of restored Eden, would make of Israel—even sinful Israel, just as capable of rebellion against God's will as Adam was—a worthy occupant of the Eden that the Land was meant to be, had been for a brief moment, and would once again become.

By "Eden" the halakhah understands Scripture to mean that place, whole and at rest, that God sanctified; "Eden" stands for creation in perfect repose. That is, in the halakhah as set forth in the Mishnah, Tosefta,

Yerushalmi, and Bavli, Eden stands for not a particular place but nature in a defined condition, at a particular moment: creation in Sabbath repose, sanctified. Then a place in repose at the climax of creation, at sunset at the start of the seventh day, whole and at rest, embodies, realizes Eden. The halakhah means to systematize the condition of Eden, to define Eden in its normative traits, and also to localize Eden within Israel. How does the halakhah localize that place? Eden is the place to the perfection of which God responded in the act of sanctification at the advent of the seventh day. Where is that place? Here, as elsewhere, the halakhah accommodates itself to both the landed and the utopian condition of the people Israel. So, on the one hand, that place is or ought to be the Land of Israel. The halakhah of the oral Torah finds in Scripture ample basis for identifying with the Land of Israel that place perfected on the Sabbath. It is the Land that, in the written Torah's explicit account of matters, claims the right to repose on the seventh day and in the seventh year of the septennial cycle. But on the other hand, as we shall see, it is the location of Israel wherever that may be at the advent of sunset on the eve of the seventh day of the week of creation. We begin with landed Israel—that is, the Land of Israel—at the moment when Eden was made real: when Israel entered into the Land at the moment of perfection. When that moment is recovered, Eden is restored. This is therefore the correct starting point for a theology of the halakhah that claims the whole holds together as a systematically restorationist theology.

That is the explicit position of the halakhah of *Shevi'it*. This halakhah, which deals with the Sabbatical or seventh year, elaborates the written Torah's commandment:

> When you enter the land that I am giving you, the land shall observe a Sabbath of the Lord. Six years you may sow your field and six years you may prune your vineyard and gather in the yield. But in the seventh year the land shall have a Sabbath of complete rest, a Sabbath of the Lord; you shall not sow your field or prune your vineyard. You shall not reap the aftergrowth of your harvest or gather the grapes of your untrimmed vines; it shall be a year of complete rest for the land. But you may eat whatever the land during its Sabbath will produce—you, your male and female slaves, the hired hand and bound laborers who live with you, and your cattle and the beasts in your land may eat all its yield. (Lev. 25:1–8)

The sages thus find in Scripture the explicit correlation of the advent of the Sabbath and the condition of the Land, meaning, "the land that I am giving you," which is the Land of Israel. After six years of creation, the Land is owed a Sabbath, as much as is man. A second, correlative commandment is treated as well:

> Every seventh year you shall practice remission of debts. This shall be the nature of the remission: every creditor shall remit the due that he claims from his neighbor; he shall not dun his neighbor or kinsman, for the remission proclaimed is of the Lord. You may dun the foreigner, but you must remit whatever is due you from your kinsmen. (Deut. 15:1–3)

The Torah represents God as the sole master of creation, the Sabbath as testimony to God's pleasure with the perfection, and therefore sanctification, of creation. The halakhah of *Shevi'it* sets forth the law that in relationship to the Land of Israel embodies that conviction. The law set forth in the Mishnah, Tosefta, and Talmud of the Land of Israel systematically works through Scripture's rules, treating (1) the prohibition of farming the land during the seventh year; (2) the use of the produce in the seventh year solely for eating, that is to say, its purpose and function by its very nature; and (3) the remission of debts. During the Sabbatical year, Israel relinquishes its ownership of the Land of Israel. So the Sabbath involves giving up ownership, a point to which we shall return later in this chapter. At that time Israelites in farming may do nothing that in secular years effects the assertion of ownership over the land.[7] Just as one may not utilize land one does not own, in the Sabbatical year the farmer gives up ownership of the land that he does own.

What links the Sabbatical year to Eden's restoration? The reason is clear: the Sabbatical year recovers that perfect time of Eden when the world was at rest, all things in place. Before the rebellion, man did not have to labor on the land; he picked and ate his meals freely. And, in the nature of things, everything belonged to everybody; private ownership in response to individual labor did not exist, because man did not have to work anyway. These then represent the halakhah's provisions for the seventh year. Reverting to that perfect time, the Torah maintains that the land will provide adequate food for everyone, including the flocks and herds, even—or especially—if people do not work the land. But that is on condition that all claim of ownership lapses; the food is left in the fields, to be picked by anyone who wishes, but it may not be hoarded by the landowner in particular. Alan J. Avery-Peck states this matter as follows:

> Scripture thus understands the Sabbatical year to represent a return to a perfected order of reality, in which all share equally in the bounty of a holy land that yields its food without human labor. The Sabbatical year provides a model through which, once every seven years, Israelites living in the here-and-now may enjoy the perfected order in which God

---

7. Alan J. Avery-Peck, trans., *Shebiit* (Chicago Studies in the History of Judaism: The Talmud of the Land of Israel: A Preliminary Translation 5; Chicago: University of Chicago Press, 1991), 2.

always intended the world to exist and toward which, in the Israelite world view, history indeed is moving. . . . The release of debts accomplishes for Israelites' economic relationships just what the agricultural Sabbatical accomplishes for the relationship between the people and the land. Eradicating debt allows the Israelite economy to return to the state of equilibrium that existed at the time of creation, when all shared equally in the bounty of the Land.[8]

The Priestly Code expresses that same concept when it arranges for the return of inherited property at the Jubilee year to the family that originally owned it:

You shall count off seven weeks of years, so that the period of seven weeks of years gives you a total of forty-nine years. . . . You shall proclaim release throughout the land for all its inhabitants. It shall be a Jubilee for you; each of you shall return to his holding and each of you shall return to his family. (Lev. 25:8–10)

The Jubilee year is observed as is the Sabbatical year, meaning that for two successive years the land is not to be worked. The halakhah we shall examine in due course will establish that when land is sold, it is for the span of time remaining to the next Jubilee year. That then marks the reordering of landholding to its original pattern, when Israel inherited the land to begin with and began to enjoy its produce.

Just as the Sabbath commemorates the completion of creation, the perfection of world order, so does the Sabbatical year. So too, the Jubilee year brings about the restoration of real property to the original division. In both instances, Israelites so act as to indicate they are not absolute owners of the Land, which belongs to God and which is divided in the manner that God arranged in perpetuity. Avery-Peck states the matter in the following way:

On the Sabbath of creation, during the Sabbatical year, and in the Jubilee year, diverse aspects of Israelite life are to return to the way that they were at the time of creation. Israelites thus acknowledge that, in the beginning, God created a perfect world, and they assure that the world of the here-and-now does not overly shift from its perfect character. By providing opportunities for Israelites to model their contemporary existence upon a perfected order of things, these commemorations further prepare the people for messianic times, when, under God's rule, the world will permanently revert to the ideal character of the time of creation.[9]

8. Ibid., 3.
9. Ibid., 4.

Here we find the halakhic counterpart to the restorationist theology that the oral Torah sets forth in the aggadah. Israel matches Adam, the Land of Israel, Eden, and, we now see, the Sabbatical year commemorates the perfection of creation and replicates it. (Later in this chapter we shall see that the same conception of relinquishing ownership of one's real property operates to facilitate everyday activities on the Sabbath.)

Prohibition and Self-Restraint

That brings us to a natural companion of the halakhah of *Shevi'it*, which is that of *Orlah*, the halakhah devoted to the prohibition of the use of a tree's fruit for the first three years after its planting and the restriction of its use in the fourth year. The halakhah of *Orlah* elaborates the Torah's commandment:

> When you come to the land and plant any kind of tree for food, you shall treat it as forbidden. For three years it shall be forbidden, it shall not be eaten. In the fourth year all its fruit shall be set aside for jubilation before the Lord, and only in the fifth year may you use its fruit, that its yield to you may be increased: I am the Lord your God. (Lev. 19:23–25)

The produce of the fourth year after planting is brought to Jerusalem ("for jubilation before the Lord") and eaten there. But the main point of the halakhah centers upon the prohibition of the fruit for the first three years.

In the halakhah, the role of man in precipitating the effect of the prohibition takes priority. Man has a role in bringing the prohibition into effect, but man cannot by his intentionality change the facts of the case. How does the Israelite farmer's intentionality govern? It is man's assessment of the use of the tree that classifies the tree as a fruit tree or as a tree of some other category, e.g., one meant for lumber. If man deems the tree planted for fruit, then the prohibition applies. But man cannot declare as a fruit tree, thereby subjecting the produce to the prohibition, a tree that does not bear fruit at all. Man's actions reveal his original intentionality for the tree, e.g., how the tree is planted.

Here is an explicit statement, in connection with the exegesis of the halakhah, that intentionality dictates whether or not a tree that can bear fruit actually is covered by the prohibition. Trees not used for fruit are not affected by the prohibition, so the farmer may use the lumber even in the first three years from planting; and parts of trees not intended for fruit are not subject to it either, so they may be pruned off and used for fuel. But intention cannot classify what nature has already designated for one or another category. In the following, Simeon b. Gamaliel refines the law by insisting that man's intention conform to the facts of nature. That is to say, if one planted a tree for lumber or firewood but it is not appropriate for such a use, then his intentionality is null.

> A. ". . . trees for food":
> B. this excludes the case of planting trees for fence posts or lumber or firewood.
> C. R. Yose says, "Even if he said, 'The side of the tree facing inward is to be used for food and the side outward is to be used as a fence, the side of the tree inward is liable to the laws of *orlah*, and the side of the tree facing outward is exempt" [*m. Orlah* 1:1A–D].
> D. Said Rabban Simeon b. Gamaliel, "Under what circumstances? When he planted it as a fence for lumber or for firewood, a use appropriate for those trees. But when he planted it as a fence, for lumber, or for firewood in a case not appropriate for that species, the tree is liable to the laws of *orlah*" [*t. Orlah* 1:1C–H].
> E. How do we know the law given just now?
> F. Scripture says, "all kinds of trees."

The matter of appropriateness will recur many times, since the intense interest of the halakhah in the correct classification of things comes to expression in an interesting notion. A thing has its inherent, intrinsic purpose, and when it serves that purpose, it is properly used; when not, it is improperly used. How does that make a difference? What is edible is food, and produce that may serve for food or for fuel, if it is of a sacred status, cannot be used for anything but food. So intentionality meets its limits in the purpose that a thing is supposed to serve; that is to say, intentionality is limited by teleology. That explains why, also, if the farmer planted the tree for firewood and changed his mind, then the change of his intentionality effects a change in the status of the tree:

> G. If he planted it for firewood and then gave thought to use the tree for food, how do we know that it is liable?
> H. Scripture says, "And you will plant every kind of fruit tree."
> I. From what point do they count the years of the tree for purposes of determining liability to *orlah*?
> J. From the time that it is planted [*t. Orlah* 1:1I–L].

Sifra CCII:I.1

The connection of the tree to the land dictates liability; a fruit tree planted in an unperforated pot is exempt from the law. The law extends not only to the whole fruit but also to defective produce and parts of the fruit. Interestingly, the initial planting marks the starting point for reckoning the three years, not the farmer's subsequent decision to use it for fruit rather than lumber. In that case, the actuality takes over and sets aside the intentionality. The farmer's initial intent may classify the tree as other than a fruit tree, but the potentiality as a fruit tree persists, so when the farmer has second thoughts, the initial status of the tree, not the intervening one, is what counts. This very profound way of seeing the matter is rich in potential consequences that are not explored here.

The power of the metaphor of Eden emerges, we shall now see, in specificities of the law. These turn out to define with some precision a message on the relationship of Israel to the Land of Israel and to God. In Sifra's reading of matters, our attention is drawn to a number of quite specific traits of the law of *orlah*, and these make explicit matters of religious conviction that we might otherwise miss. The first is that the prohibition of *orlah*-fruit applies solely within the Land of Israel and not to the neighboring territories occupied by Israelites, which means that, once again, it is the union of Israel with the Land of Israel that invokes the prohibition:

> A. "When you come [into the land and plant all kinds of trees for food, then you shall count their fruit as forbidden; three years it shall be forbidden to you, it must not be eaten. And in the fourth year all their fruit shall be holy, an offering of praise to the Lord. But in the fifth year you may eat of their fruit, that they may yield more richly for you: I am the Lord your God" (Lev. 19:23–25).]
>
> B. Might one suppose that the law applied once they came to Transjordan?
>
> C. Scripture says, ". . . into the land,"
>
> D. the particular Land [of Israel].

> *Sifra* CCII:I.1

What that means is that some trait deemed to inhere in the Land of Israel and no other territory must define the law, and a particular message ought to inhere in this law.

This same point registers once more: only trees that Israelites plant in the Land are subject to the prohibition, not those that gentiles planted before the Israelites inherited the land:

> A. "When you come into the land and plant":
>
> B. excluding those that gentiles have planted prior to the Israelites' coming into the land.
>
> C. Or should I then exclude those that gentiles planted even after the Israelites came into the land?
>
> D. Scripture says, "all kinds of trees."

> *Sifra* CCII:I.2.

A further point of special interest requires that the Israelite plant the tree as an act of deliberation; if the tree merely grows up on its own, it is not subject to the prohibition. So Israelite action joined to Israelite intention is required:

A. "... and plant ...":
B. excluding one that grows up on its own.
C. "... and plant ...":
D. excluding one that grows out of a grafting or sinking a root.

Sifra CCII:I.4.

The several points on which *Sifra*'s reading of the halakhah and the verses of Scripture that declare the halakhah alert us to a very specific religious principle embedded in the halakhah of *orlah*.

(1) As with *Shevi'it,* the law takes effect only from the point at which Israel enters the Land. That is to say, the point of Israel's entry into the Land marks the beginning of the Land's consequential fecundity. In simpler language, the fact that trees produce fruit matters only from Israel's entry onward. To see what is at stake, we recall that the entry of Israel into the Land marks the restoration of Eden. Only after that point does God take cognizance of the fruit produced by the Land. The halakhah has no better way of saying that the entry of Israel into the Land compares with the moment at which the creation of Eden took place. In this way, moreover, the law of *Shevi'it* finds its counterpart. Just as *Shevi'it* concerns telling time in that it marks off seven years to the Sabbath of creation, so also the halakhah of *orlah* also means telling time in that it marks the time of the creation of produce from the moment of Israel's entry into the Land. Israel's entry into the Land marks a new beginning, comparable to the very creation of the world, just as the Land at the end matches Eden at the outset.

(2) Israelite intentionality is required to subject a tree to the *orlah* rule. If an Israelite does not plant the tree with the plan of producing fruit, then the tree is not subject to the rule. If the tree grows up on its own, not by the act and precipitating intentionality of the Israelite, the *orlah* rule does not apply. If an Israelite does not plant the tree to produce fruit, the *orlah* rule does not apply. And given the character of creation, which marks the norm, the tree must be planted in the ordinary way; if grafted or sunk as a root, the law does not apply.

(3) The entire issue of the halakhah comes down to Israelite restraint in using the produce of the orchards. What is the counterpart to Israelite observance of the restraint of three years? And why should Israelite intentionality play so critical a role, since, *Sifra* itself notes, the *orlah* rule applies to trees planted even by gentiles? The answer becomes obvious

when we ask another question: Can we think of any other commandments concerning fruit trees in the Land that—the sages say time and again—is Eden? Of course we can: "Of every tree of the garden you are free to eat; but as for the tree of knowledge of good and evil, you must not eat of it" (Gen. 2:16). But the halakhah of *orlah* imposes upon Israel a more demanding commandment. Of *no* tree in the new Eden may Israel eat for three years. That demands considerable restraint. Israel must exceed the humble requirement of obedience in regard to a fruit tree that God assigned to Adam; the Land imposes obligations far exceeding those carried by Eden. And the issue devolves upon Israel's will or attitude, much as Eden turned tragic by reason of man's rebellious will.

That is because Israel's own intentionality—not God's—imposes upon every fruit-bearing tree—and not only the one of Eden—the prohibition of three years. That is the point of the stress on the effects of Israel's desire for the fruit. So once Israel wants the fruit, it must show that it can restrain its desire and wait for three years. By Israel's act of will, Israel has imposed upon itself the requirement of restraint. Taking the entry point as our guide, we may say that, from the entry into the Land and for the next three years, trees that Israelites value for their fruit and plant with the produce in mind must be left untouched. And, for all time thereafter, when Israelites plant fruit trees, they must recapitulate that same exercise of self-restraint; that is, they must act as though, for the case at hand, they have just come into the Land.

To find the context in which these rules make their statement, we must ask that details, not only the main point, carry the message. So we ask, why three years in particular? A glance at the narrative of Creation provides the obvious answer. Fruit trees were created on the third day of creation. When Israel by intention and action designates a tree as fruit-bearing, Israel recapitulates the order of creation and so must wait for three years, as creation waited for three days. Then the planting of every tree imposes upon Israel the occasion to meet once more the temptation that the first Adam could not overcome. Israel now recapitulates the temptation of Adam then, but Israel, the new Adam, possesses, and is possessed by, the Torah. By its own action and intention in planting fruit trees, Israel finds itself in a veritable orchard of trees like the tree of knowledge of good and evil. The difference between Adam and Israel (that while Adam, who was permitted to eat all fruit but one, ate the forbidden fruit, Israel refrains for a specified span of time from fruit from all trees) marks what has taken place through the people Israel in the Land of Israel, namely, the regeneration of humanity. The connection of the halakhah with the Land bears that very special message, and I can imagine no other way of making that statement through law than in the explicit concern the sages register for the fruit trees of the

Land of Israel. No wonder, then, that within the Priestly Code *orlah* law finds its position in the rules of sanctification.

So when Israel enters the Land, in exactly the right detail Israel recapitulates the drama of Adam in Eden, but with this formidable difference. The outcome ought not to be the same. By its own act of will Israel addresses the temptation of Adam and overcomes the same temptation, not once but every day through time beyond measure. Adam could not wait out the week, but Israel waits for three years—corresponding to the days God waited in creating fruit trees. Adam picked and ate. But here too there is a detail not to be missed. Even after three years, Israel may not eat the fruit wherever it chooses. Rather, in the fourth year from planting, Israel will still show restraint, bringing the fruit only "for jubilation before the Lord" in Jerusalem. That signals that the once-forbidden fruit is now eaten in public, not in secret, before the Lord, as a moment of celebration. That detail too recalls the Fall and makes its comment upon the horror of the fall. That is, when Adam ate the fruit, he shamefully hid from God for having eaten the fruit. But when Israel eats the fruit, it does so proudly, joyfully, and above all publicly, before the Lord. The contrast is not to be missed, so too the message. Faithful Israel refrains when it is supposed to, and so it has every reason to cease refraining and to eat "before the Lord." It has nothing to hide, and everything to show.

And there is more. In the fifth year Israel may eat on its own, the time of any restraint from enjoying the gifts of the Land having ended. That sequence provides fruit for the second Sabbath of creation, and so through time. How so? Placing Adam's sin on the first day after the first Sabbath, thus Sunday, then calculating the three forbidden years as Monday, Tuesday, and Wednesday of the second week of creation, reckoning on the jubilation of Thursday, we come to the Friday, eve of the second Sabbath of creation. So now, a year representing a day of the Sabbatical week, just as Leviticus says so many times in connection with the Sabbatical year, the three prohibited years allow Israel to show its true character, fully regenerate, wholly and humbly accepting God's commandment, the one Adam broke. And the rest follows.

Here, then, is the message of the *Orlah* halakhah, the statement that only through the details of the laws of *orlah* as laid out in both parts of the Torah, written and oral, the halakhah could hope to make. By its own act of restraint, the new Adam, Israel, in detailed action displays its repentance in respect to the very sin that the old Adam committed, the sin of disobedience and rebellion. Facing the same opportunity to sin, Israel again and again over time refrains from the very sin that cost Adam Eden. So by its manner of cultivation of the Land and its orchards, Israel manifests what in the very condition of humanity has changed by the giving of the Torah: the advent of humanity's second chance, through Israel. Only in the Land that succeeds Eden can Israel, succeeding Adam, carry out the acts of regeneration that the Torah makes possible. And that is what is to be done about man.

Comparing Theologies

Christianity on Judaism

The Torah alone can deal with humanity's brokenness—provided the Torah is truly Scripture's own meaning.

Some Christian teachers have assumed that the Torah is the key to the Bible of Israel and have therefore rejected it. During the second century a teacher in Rome named Marcion insisted that the New Testament should stand alone as Scripture. He liked only Paul's letters and one gospel (Luke), and wanted them expurgated of anything connected with Judaism, including the "Old Testament." Marcion has been called the first textual critic in the church, and his theology has had pale imitators ever since, but the church then and now has authoritatively rejected the idea that the Old Testament can be dispensed with. As we have seen, the letters of Paul, which Marcion made the basis of his views, undermined his position. Christians believe with Paul that the Holy Spirit has always spoken in the Scriptures of Israel.[10] When believers read them with accurate sympathy, that same Spirit—identical to the Spirit of Christ—becomes active in them. A teacher of the second century, Justin Martyr, spells this out:

> Long ago . . . there lived men more ancient than all the so-called philosophers, men righteous and beloved of God, who spoke by the divine Spirit and foretold things to come, that even now are taking place. These men were called prophets. They alone both saw the truth and proclaimed it to men, without awe or fear of anyone, moved by no desire for glory, but speaking only those things which they saw and heard when filled with the Holy Spirit. Their writings are still with us, and whoever will may read them and, if he believes them, gain much knowledge of the beginning and end of things, and all else a philosopher ought to know. For they did not employ logic to prove their statements, seeing they were witnesses to the truth. . . . They glorified the creator of all things, as God and Father, and proclaimed the Christ sent by him as his Son. . . . But pray that, before all else, the gates of light may be opened to you. For not everyone can see

10. On Paul and Israel's Scriptures, see p. 68 above.

or understand these things, but only the one to whom God and his Christ have granted wisdom. (*Dialogue with Trypho* 7)[11]

For Justin and for Christianity after him, the Scriptures of Israel are fundamentally prophecies and only incidentally books of law. Of course commandments are included in them; reference is also made to differing political authorities and to widely varying arrangements for worship. But the Scriptures' idiom throughout is that they articulate that Holy Spirit which is humanity's only real hope. Laws and commandments come, go, and change: prophecy timelessly attests and awakens the Spirit.

Judaism on Christianity

Christianity reads the Israelite Scriptures as an instrument of analogy, in which texts of Israel in the past are applied to the church of the present. Thus Professor Chilton states above: "As a consequence, each Christian is God's son, much as Israel was at the time of the exodus (Exod. 4:21–23)." That is the only point at which the two religious traditions intersect when we compare Torah to Christ: Christians are like Israelites, finding in the Torah a counterpart to their encounter with Christ. On the surface Judaism finds a ready response: you deprive the Torah of its concrete and specific meaning; you empty it of its claim to guide the formation of a kingdom of priests and a holy people, God's people. But, on behalf of Christianity, it must be said that the purpose of the Torah and the purpose of Christ in the context of the human condition do not radically differ. Both represent solutions to the crisis of the fall from grace. Through Torah God educates the heart of humanity to love, which cannot be coerced. The Torah purifies the heart of humanity, the commandments are media of regeneration and sanctification. And so, Christians claim, is the task of the last Adam, Christ.

If the tasks assigned to Torah and Christ, respectively, prove comparable, then the question presents itself: which medium of regeneration more effectively engages with the human condition? The answer depends upon how we assess that condition. What constitutes the flaw in humanity to which Torah or Christ (but not both) represents the remedy? The rabbinic sages find the origins of sin in the attitude of arrogance, the beginnings of virtue in that of humility. Arrogance leads to rebellion against God, humility, to submission to him. Israel, therefore, is in command of its own fate. Redemption depends upon righteousness, just

11. See Andrew Greeley, Jacob Neusner, Bruce Chilton, and William Scott Green, *Forging a Common Future: Catholic, Judaic, and Protestant Relations for a New Millennium* (Cleveland: Pilgrim, 1977), 51–52.

as the present age comes about by reason of arrogance. The impulse to do evil can be overcome, specifically through Torah study, which is its opposite and complement:

> 1. A. "At that time Abimelech and Phicol the commander of his army said to Abraham, 'God is with you in all that you do'" [Gen. 21:22].
>   I. R. Joshua b. Levi said, "The cited verse refers to the impulse to do evil.
>   J. "Under ordinary circumstances if someone grows up with a fellow for two or three years, he develops a close tie to him. But the impulse to do evil grows with someone from youth to old age, and, if one can, someone strikes down the impulse to do evil even when he is seventy or eighty.
>   K. "So did David say, 'All my bones shall say, "Lord, who is like unto you, who delivers the poor from him who is too strong for him, yes, the poor and the needy from him who spoils him"' [Ps. 35:10]."
>
> *Genesis Rabbah* LIV:I.1

Now the antidote is made explicit:

> L. Said R. Aha, "And is there a greater thief than this one? And Solomon said, 'If your enemy be hungry, give him bread to eat' [Prov. 25:21]. The meaning is, the bread of the Torah [which will help a person resist the enemy that is the impulse to do evil], as it is said, 'Come, eat of my bread' [Prov. 9:5].
> M. "'If he is thirsty give him water to drink' [Prov. 25:21], that is, the water of the Torah, as it is said, 'Ho, everyone who is thirsty, come for water' [Isa. 55:1]."
> N. R. Berekhiah said, "The verse says, '. . . *also* his enemies' [Prov. 16:7], with the word 'also' encompassing the insects of the house, vermin, flies and the like."

Sometimes Torah study is treated in concrete terms, with an explanation of precisely how the Torah serves as antidote to sin, and sometimes, as here, in symbolic terms. The result is the same: a coherent system that explains many things in a few simple ways. We find ourselves facing a metaphor for the human condition comparable to Christ: Torah as the regenerative force. The rabbinic sages leave no doubt that Torah study changes disciples, producing humble persons prepared to love the Lord our God with all our heart, soul, and might.

4

Israel and the Kingdom of God

⊷✳︎⊶

Scripture's story of mankind accounts for the human condition: some know God, many do not. While the theologies of both rabbinic Judaism and classical Christianity aspire to persuade all mankind that God is one, unique, and made known in a medium of his own choosing, each theological structure has to answer a critical question. That is, how are we to account for the current condition of mankind, the manifest failure of the many to affirm what to the few is self-evident? Both found necessary a theological interpretation of the condition of mankind. For Christianity, what was required was a theology of history, an account within the system of the faith of what happened from Eden through Calvary and Easter. For rabbinic Judaism, with its capacity to discern the paradigms of human existence, what was needed was a theological anthropology, that is, a systematic religious theory, based on the Torah, to describe and explain the actualities of the whole human condition—those like Adam via Noah, those like Abraham via Isaac and Jacob, that is, the nations and Israel, idolaters and those who know God. To be "Israel" then is to affirm the one and only God and to accept his dominion: to live in God's kingdom. That is the meaning of proclaiming, "Hear, O Israel." Simply put: both circles of theologians had to explain why the knowledge of God has yet to reach the entirety of mankind. And each had to construct that explanation within its theory of itself.

For Judaism, that meant an account of Israel and the nations, that is, those who know God and those who do not. For Christianity, that required theology to produce an extension of Scripture's story of man, to include a principle of transformation that held out the prospect that all God's promises, however long delayed, could and would be kept. "The kingdom of God," a conception inherited from Israel's Scriptures to describe the final, divine hegemony, became for Christianity the pivotal phrase in describing how God transforms human experience past, present, and future.

The Theology of Rabbinic Judaism

The generative question is readily identified: What is "Israel"? And who are "the nations" or "the gentiles"? The criterion of the successful theological system now presents itself. The same theology that defines "Israel" has to explain everybody else, "the gentiles," or "the nations." Thus "Israel" is defined both negatively and positively. Israel means "those who know God by reason of God's self-revelation at Sinai." But, then, Israel also means "not gentile." One prominent antonym in the Torah for "Israel," unsurprisingly, is "gentile," and definitions of both come easily: gentiles worship idols, while Israel worships the one unique God. It is that simple.

God rules as sovereign over all mankind, but the two sectors thereof compete and one, the gentiles, presently dominates the other, Israel. Power relationships between the two respond to three rules. (1) As the prevailing theory of world order maintains in its definition of justice, each action provokes an equal and commensurate reaction. (2) God responds to the attitude as much as to the action of the human actor, especially prizing humility over arrogance. (3) God's special relationship to those who know him through the Torah may require him to use the gentiles to penalize Israel for disobedience, to encourage their return to a proper attitude and consequent action. In combination, these rules respond to the critical issue of Israel's life: why do the gentiles, who do not acknowledge the one God, prosper while Israel, which does, languishes?

The Election of Israel

The answer responds to these givens. Because Israel accepted the Torah, God loves Israel. The Torah therefore defines Israel's life and governs Israelites' welfare. In genus Israel does not differ from the gentiles, deriving from the same ancestry in Noah. In species, matters are otherwise. Distinguished by the Torah, Israel is alone in its category (sui generis), proved by the fact that what is a virtue to Israel is a vice to the nations; what is life-giving to Israel is poison to the gentiles. Israel's condition of weakness comes about by reason of its own sin, which God justly and reasonably punishes through, among others, political means. Still, if Israel sins, God forgives that sin, having punished the nation on account of it. Such a process has yet to come to an end, but it will and in time is going to culminate in Israel's complete regeneration and consequently the restoration of Eden, now in Israel's framework. Meanwhile, Israel's assurance of God's love lies in the many expressions of special concern, in his provision of numerous commandments for Israel to carry out for its own sanctification.

How in the sages' theology did Israel and the nations relate? To answer that question, as to deal with all others of a profound character, the rabbinic sages, like philosophers, turned to the simple logic of classification: comparison and contrast in a process of hierarchical classification. Israel in no way constituted what we should label a secular category, that is, a people or nation like any or all others—even an empire like Rome. We are used to thinking of "Israel" as a political category, referring to the state of Israel, and of "the Jews" as an ethnic group, not a corporate religious community, But for the rabbinic sages, the categories "nation" and "ethnic group" did not serve; they regarded "Israel" as unique, sui generis, a social entity with no counterpart in the rest of humanity, because by "Israel" they meant "the group of those who know God."

A more secular language would yield a simpler statement: their understanding of "Israel" as a category would rather correspond to Christianity's "church" (in its various formulations) or Islam's *dar el Islam* (abode of Islam). For by "Israel" the sages understood the enchanted Israel of which the Scriptures speak, that is, the supernatural social entity called into being by God. And even though the Scriptures appear to tell the story of a nation or people like any other, that is not how the sages read them. Since in their view one became (part of) Israel by coming under the wings of the Presence of God and accepting the dominion of God in the Torah, genealogy gave way to theology. To elect, sanctified Israel, the nations in no way compared except in one: they too found definition in their relationship to God. By the nations, which is to say, everyone else, the sages understood idolaters, those who come under negative definitions: they do not know and worship the one and only true God; they worship no-gods.

What about Israel's sin? That question brings us to the center of the structure built upon the election of Israel and carries within itself the answer to the anomaly of Israel's condition among the nations. God's response to Israel's sin produces the probative mark of divine love for Israel, God's capacity to bear with, even to forgive Israel. Israel tested God ten times, and God forgave them ten times:

> A. It has been taught on Tannaite authority: Said R. Judah, "Ten trials did our ancestors impose upon the Holy One, blessed be he: two at the shore of the sea, two in the water, two in regard to the manna, two in regard to the quail, one in regard to the [golden] calf, one in the wilderness of Paran."
>
> *b. Arakhin* 3:5 II.3/15a–b

The systematic collection of facts and analysis and reconstruction of them into probative propositions now commences. Here are the data that when seen all together prove the point:

> B. "Two at the sea": one in going down, and one in coming up.
> C. In going down, as it is written, "Because there were no graves in Egypt [you have taken us away to die in the wilderness]" [Exod. 14:11].
> D. "In coming up": That accords with what R. Huna said.
> E. For R. Huna said, "At that time the Israelites were among those of little faith."
> M. "Two in the water": at Marah and at Refidim.
> N. At Marah, as it is written, "And they came to Marah and could not drink the water" [Exod. 15:23]. And it is written, "And the people complained against Moses" [Exod. 17:3].
> O. At Refidim, as it is written, "They encamped at Refidim, and there was no water to drink" [Exod. 17:1]. And it is written, "And the people struggled with Moses" [Exod. 17:2].
> P. "Two in regard to the manna": as it is written, [15B] "Do not go out," but they went out, "Do not leave any over," [Exod. 16:19] but they left some over. [The first is not a direct quotation of a verse but summarizes the narrative.]
> Q. "Two in regard to the quail": in regard to the first [quail] and in regard to the second quail.
> R. In regard to the first: "When we sat by the fleshpots" [Exod. 16:3].
> S. In regard to the second: "And the mixed multitude that was among them" [Num. 11:4].
> T. "One in regard to the [golden] calf": as the story is told.
> U. "One in the wilderness of Paran": as the story is told.

Scripture yields ample evidence of God's unlimited capacity to forgive Israel, so that the relationship between God and Israel is ordered by the principles of love and forbearance, shown by God through all time.

Defining Israel Politically: The Kingdom of Heaven

But that (Sinai) was then and this (the world governed by the pagan empire) is now. So it is time to ask: exactly who and what is Israel in the sages' logic? How about a this-worldly, political definition? We have already addressed this matter. The secular sense of "Israel" and even "the Jews" occurs only very rarely in the rabbis' reading of the written Torah, mediated through the oral part. In all the rabbinic sages' authoritative writings in the formative age, for instance, I cannot point to the use of "Israel" to refer solely to the nation in the context of other nations of the same genus. To give a single example of what we do not find, the rabbinic sages do not undertake the comparison of Israel's kings and pagan kings; rather, what are compared are Israel's prophets and the pagan prophets. In the oral Torah "Israel" bears these three meanings, which we have already noted and have now to systematize: (1) holy family, that is, a social entity different from the nations because it is formed by a common genealogy; (2) holy nation among nations but holy among profane, a rose among thorns, sustained by a common root but yielding a different fruit; (3) unique Israel, sui generis, different not in contingent, indicative traits but categorically—that is to say, in its very category—from all other nations.

"Holy family" and "holy nation" do not wholly intersect and may well conflict, since one may accept the Torah of the holy nation, but how to acquire a past in a genealogy? In the ordinary world one may change one's opinion, but it is very difficult to change one's lineage. The fact that in the sages' Torah gentiles could enter "Israel" by accepting God's will in the Torah marks their "Israel" as other than ethnic, and the fact that by accepting the Torah the convert took over an entire genealogy, thus adopting a past for himself, underscores that judgment. The genealogy was supernatural, an identity that is put on, as much as the laws of the Torah were supernatural, a way of life that is taken over. Both then embody responses to God's call (as it were) to whom it may concern.[1]

The entire complex—Israel as holy people, Israel as extended family—found coherence in the story that was told to account for Israel, the story commencing with creation and Adam's fall, Noah's second chance, and Abraham's own conversion. For the sages, Scripture told the story of "Israel"—a man, Jacob. His children therefore are "the children of Jacob." That man's name was also "Israel," so that "the children of Is-

---

1. But, I hasten to add, the content of the story that the convert adopted could readily be read as an ethnic history, and it is not surprising that the category "Israel," by reason of its content, should be read, and not only by outsiders to the faith, as a fundamentally ethnic or national identification.

rael" comprised the extended family of that man. By extension upward, "Israel" formed the family of Abraham and Sarah, Isaac and Rebecca, Jacob and Leah and Rachel. "Israel" therefore invoked the metaphor of genealogy to explain the bonds that linked persons unseen into a single social entity; the shared traits were imputed, not empirical. That social metaphor of "Israel"—a simple one, really, and easily grasped—bore consequences in two ways. First, children in general are admonished to follow the good example of their parents. The deeds of the patriarchs and matriarchs therefore taught lessons on how the children were to act. Of greater interest is the use of "Israel" as a social metaphor whereby "Israel" lived twice: once in the patriarchs and matriarchs, a second time in the recapitulation by the heirs of those earlier lives. The stories of the family were carefully reread to provide a picture of the meaning of the latter-day events of the descendants of that same family. Accordingly, the lives of the patriarchs signaled the history of Israel.

While Israel was sufficiently like the gentiles to sustain comparison with them, Rome being treated as a correlative family to Israel but descended from the wrong side, Israel also was contrasted with the gentiles. In the end, despite all that has been said about Israel and the nations sharing a common genus, still Israel was to be seen as sui generis. Israel also found representation as beyond all metaphor. Seeing "Israel" as sui generis yielded a sustained interest in the natural laws governing "Israel" in particular, statements of the rules of the group's history viewed as a unique entity within time. The historical-eschatological formulation of a political teleology in that way moved from an account of illegitimate power to a formulation of the theory of the inappropriate victim, that is to say, of Israel itself. That explains why, as we have already seen, sentences out of the factual record of the past were formed into a cogent statement of the laws of this Israel's destiny, laws unique to the social entity at hand.

The teleology of those laws for an Israel that was sui generis focused upon salvation as resurrection and judgment for individual Israelites and upon redemption for all Israel at the end of history. This was an eschatological teleology formed for a social entity embarked on its own lonely journey through time. The gentiles pass from the scene at the last, when the dead are raised, the Land regained, and Eden restored. Then all the living will form one Israel, that is, all mankind will recognize the rule of the one and only God.

The conception of Israel as sui generis reaches expression in an implicit statement that Israel is subject to its own laws, which are distinct from the laws governing all other social entities. These laws may be discerned in the factual, scriptural record of Israel's past, and that past, by definition, belonged to "Israel" alone. It followed, therefore, that by discerning the regularities in Israel's history, implicitly understood as unique to "Israel," the sages recorded the view that "Israel," like God, was not subject to analogy or comparison. Accordingly, while not labeled a genus unto itself, Israel is treated in that way. The theory of Israel as sui generis produced a political theory in which Israel's sole legitimate ruler is God, and whoever legitimately governs does so as God's surrogate. The theory of legitimate sanctions then is recast into a religious statement of God's place in Israel's existence; but the theory retains its political valence when we recall that the sage, the man most fully "in our image, after our likeness," governs in accord with the law of the Torah. But how do the sages translate into concrete, practical terms the theory of the political order formed by Israel?

This brings us to the theology of politics contained within the image "kingdom of heaven." Here and now Israel forms the realm of God in this world, where God indwells synagogues and schoolhouses, prayers are recited, and the Torah is studied. God's kingdom, unlike the kingdoms of this world and this age, is neither tangible nor bound to a geographical location. One enters by adopting the right attitude and by undertaking to obey the commandments, which are its king's laws. To be Israel, in the sages' model, means to live in God's kingdom, wherever one is located and whenever in the sequence of the ages one lives. God's kingdom forms the realm of eternity within time. Death marks not an end but an interruption in life with God; the individual is restored to life at the end, within that larger act of restoration of Adam to Eden, meaning Israel to the Land, that Israel's repentance will bring about. Various religious activities represent a taste even now of what is coming, as the Sabbath, for example, affords a sixtieth of the taste of the world to come. Embodying God's kingdom by obeying God's will, Israel was created to carry out religious duties and perform good deeds. These differentiate Israel from the gentile idolaters. This blending of politics and theology emerges in the formula for reciting a blessing before carrying out a commandment or religious duty, "Blessed are you, Lord our God, king of the world, who has sanctified us by his commandments and commanded us to. . . ." This formula transforms an ordinary deed into an act of sanctification, a gesture of belonging to God's kingdom, accepting his rule—as Adam failed to do. The phrase "king of the world, who has commanded us" is essential:

> A. R. Zeira and R. Judah in the name of Rab, "Any blessing which does not include [a reference to] God's kingdom is not a valid blessing."
> B. Said R. Tanhuma, "I will tell you what is the basis [in Scripture for this rule]: 'I will extol thee, my God and King' [Ps.145:1]."

y. Berakhot 9:1 I:3

God is addressed in the political metaphor because God's kingdom is at hand not at one moment but at all times; the "us" then embodies all Israel even in a single individual, and the critical language then follows: "who has given commandments"—one of which is going to be carried out. That is how Israel is subject to the dominion of God and if properly motivated now lives in the kingdom of heaven. The kingdom of heaven is a phenomenon of this age as well as the world to come, and it involves tangible actions of everyday life, not only abstract existence. The doctrines in detail hold together in the conviction that God rules here and now, for those who, with a correct act of will and with proper conduct, accept his rule.

This is accomplished in various ways. First of all, it takes place through the declaration of the unity of God in the Shema: "Hear, O Israel, the Lord our God, the Lord is one." In so doing, the Israelite accepts God's authority, then the commandments that are entailed by that authority: a person should first accept upon himself the yoke of the kingdom of heaven by reciting the Shema and then take on the yoke of the commandments, e.g., the obligation to wear *tefillin* or phylacteries (*m. Berakhot* 2:2/I). The holy people has accepted God's kingship at Sinai and has no right to serve any other:

> On what account is the ear among all the limbs designated to be pierced? Because it heard from Mount Sinai, "For unto me are the children of Israel slaves, they are my slaves" [Lev. 25:55]. Yet the ear broke off itself the yoke of heaven and took upon itself the rule of the yoke of mortal man. Therefore Scripture says, "Let the ear come and be pierced, for it has not observed the commandment which it heard." (*t. Bava Qamma* 7:5)

Israel is God's slave and should be regarded as such.

In the following protracted exposition, we see how the conception of Israel forming God's kingdom plays itself out in the setting of Israel's current situation. Here we notice, therefore, the way in which the critical problematic—the anomaly of Israel's subordination to the idolatrous nations—governs discourse throughout:

> A. ["I am the Lord your God who brought you out of the land of Egypt to be your God"]:
> B. Why make mention of the exodus from Egypt in the setting of discourse on each and every one of the religious duties?

A parable makes the matter transparent:

> C. The matter may be compared to the case of a king whose ally was taken captive. When the king paid the ransom [and so

redeemed him], he did not redeem him as a free man but as a slave, so that if the king made a decree and the other did not accept it, he might say to him, "You are my slave."

D. When he came into a city, he said to him, "Tie my shoe-latch, carry my clothing before me and bring them to the bath house." [Doing these services marks a man as the slave of the one for whom he does them.]

E. The ally began to complain. The king produced the bond and said to him, "You are my slave."

F. So when the Holy One, blessed be he, redeemed the seed of Abraham, his ally, he redeemed them not as sons but as slaves. When he makes a decree and they do not accept it, he may say to them, "You are my slaves."

G. When the people had gone forth to the wilderness, he began to make decrees for them involving part of the lesser religious duties as well as part of the more stringent religious duties, for example, the Sabbath, the prohibition against consanguineous marriages, the fringes, and the requirement to don *tefillin*. The Israelites began to complain. He said to them, "You are my slaves. It was on that stipulation that I redeemed you, on the condition that I may make a decree and you must carry it out."

Sifre to Numbers CXV:V.4

Israel accepts God's rule as a slave accepts his redeemer's authority; that is, Israel owes God allegiance and obedience. By carrying out God's will through the commandments, Israel enters God's dominion.

As the passage unfolds, the urgent question presents itself: since Israel is governed by the nations of the world, does that not mean that God has given up his dominion over them? Then Israel no longer is subject to God's authority and need not keep the commandments.

A. "So you shall remember and do [all my commandments and be holy to your God. I am the Lord your God who brought you out of the land of Egypt to be your God.] I am the Lord your God" [Num. 15:37–41]:

B. Why repeat the phrase, "I am the Lord your God"?

C. Is it not already stated, "I am the Lord your God who brought you out of the land of Egypt to be your God"?

D. Why then repeat the phrase, "I am the Lord your God"?

E. It is so that the Israelites should not say, "Why has the Omnipresent given us commandments? Let us not do them and not collect a reward."

F. They do not do them, and they shall not collect a reward.

Now the precedent provided by Scripture shows the governing rule:

G. This is in line with what the Israelites said to Ezekiel: "Some of the elders of Israel came to consult the Lord [and were sitting with me. Then this word came to me from the Lord: 'Man, say to the elders of Israel, "This is the word of the Lord God: Do you come to consult me? As I live, I will not be consulted by you. This is the very word of the Lord God"'"]" [Ezek. 20:1–3].

H. They said to Ezekiel, "In the case of a slave whose master has sold him off, has not the slave left the master's dominion?"

I. He said to them, "Yes."

J. They said to him, "Since the Omnipresent has sold us to the nations of the world, we have left his dominion."

K. He said to them, "Lo, in the case of a slave whose master has sold him only on the stipulation that later on the slave will return, has the slave left the dominion of the master? [Surely not.]"

L. "When you say to yourselves, 'Let us become like the nations and tribes of other lands and worship wood and stone,' you are thinking of something that can never be. As I live, says the Lord God, I will reign over you with a strong hand, with arm outstretched and wrath poured out" [Ezek. 20:32–33].

M. ". . . with a strong hand": this refers to pestilence, as it is said, "Lo the hand of the Lord is upon your cattle in the field" [Exod. 9:3].

N. ". . . with arm outstretched": this refers to the sword, as it is said, "And his sword is unsheathed in his hand, stretched forth against Jerusalem" [1 Chron. 21:16].

O. ". . . and wrath poured out": this refers to famine.

P. "After I have brought against you these three forms of punishment, one after the other, then 'I will reign over you'—despite yourselves."

Q. That is why it is said a second time, "I am the Lord your God."

Sifre to Numbers CXV:V.5

God will not relinquish his rule over Israel, and he enforces his dominion despite Israel's conduct. The moral order then plays itself out within the inexorable logic of God's will.

The Commandments and the Presence of God

It follows that the kingdom of God is no abstraction. Within the sages' theory, sages' courts govern concrete cases on earth, but only within a larger system in which the heavenly court exercises jurisdiction over cases of another order. Certain concrete sins or crimes (the system knows no distinction between them) are referred to heaven for judgment. So Israel forms the this-worldly extension of God's heavenly kingdom—even now. Not only so, but this fact also bears material and tangible consequences in the governance of the social order. That is why the heavenly court is assigned tasks alongside the earthly one. The sages' court punishes murder when the rules of testimony, which are strict and rigid, permit; when not, there is always heaven to step in. Or when a man clearly has served as efficient and sufficient cause of death, the earthly court punishes him.

The kingdom of heaven above all was realized in the ordinary world in which Israel performed the commandments. When an Israelite carried out a positive commandment, or, more important, in obedience to heaven refrained from a deed prohibited by a negative commandment, that formed the moment of ultimate realization of God's rule on earth. Then Israel, through Israelites, may bring about God's rule on earth. The commandments, originally emerging in small groups, mark the appearance of God's kingdom on earth. But alone among the nations Israel finally got all of them, 248 positive ones, matching the bones of the body, 365 negative ones, matching the days of the solar year. So Israel alone within humanity has the possibility, and the power, to bring about God's rule, which, as we shall see, is fully realized in the restoration that marks the last things in the model of first things. Here the gradual delivery of the commandments is spelled out:

> A. R. Judah bar Simon commenced discourse by citing the following verse: "Many daughters show how capable they are, but you excel them all. [Charm is a delusion and beauty fleeting; it is the God-fearing woman who is honored. Extol her for the fruit of her toil and let her labors bring her honor in the city gate]" [Prov. 31:29–31].

We start with the six commandments assigned to Adam, as the facts of Scripture indicate:

> B. "The first man was assigned six religious duties, and they are: not worshiping idols, not blaspheming, setting up courts of justice, not murdering, not practicing fornication, not stealing.
> C. "And all of them derive from a single verse of Scripture: 'And the Lord God commanded the man, saying, "You may freely eat of every tree of the garden, [but of the tree of the knowledge of good and evil you shall not eat, for in the day that you eat of it you shall die]"' [Gen. 2:16–17].
> D. "'And the Lord God commanded the man, saying': this refers to idolatry, as it is said, 'For Ephraim was happy to walk after the command' [Hos. 5:11].
> E. "'The Lord': this refers to blasphemy, as it is said, 'Whoever curses the name of the Lord will surely die' [Lev. 24:16].

    F. "'God': this refers to setting up courts of justice, as it is said, 'God [in context, the judges] you shall not curse' [Exod. 22:27].

    G. "'The man': this refers to murder, as it is said, 'He who sheds the blood of man, by man his blood shall be shed' [Gen. 9:6].

    H. "'Saying': this refers to fornication, as it is said, 'Saying, will a man divorce his wife' [Jer. 3:1].

    I. "'You may freely eat of every tree of the garden': this refers to the prohibition of stealing, as you say, 'but of the tree of the knowledge of good and evil you shall not eat.'"

Noah inherited those six commandments and was given another:

    J. "Noah was commanded, in addition, not to cut a limb from a living beast, as it is said, 'But as to meat with its soul—its blood you shall not eat'" [Gen. 9:4].

Abraham got the seven and an eighth (though elsewhere it is alleged that Abraham in any event observed all the commandments):

    K. "Abraham was commanded, in addition, concerning circumcision, as it is said, 'And as to you, my covenant you shall keep' [Gen. 17:9].

    L. "Isaac was circumcised on the eighth day, as it is said, 'And Abraham circumcised Isaac, his son, on the eighth day'" [Gen. 21:4].

Jacob got a ninth, his son Judah a tenth:

    M. "Jacob was commanded not to eat the sciatic nerve, as it is said, 'On that account the children of Israel will not eat the sciatic nerve' [Gen. 32:33].

    N. "Judah was commanded concerning marrying the childless brother's widow, as it is said, 'And Judah said to Onan, "Go to the wife of your childless brother and exercise the duties of a *levir* with her"'" [Gen. 38:8].

But Israel got them all, matching the bones of the body to the days of the year, the whole of life through all time:

    O. "But as to you, at Sinai you received six hundred thirteen religious duties, two hundred forty-eight religious duties of commission [acts to be done], three hundred sixty-five religious duties of omission [acts not to be done],

    P. "the former matching the two hundred forty-eight limbs that a human being has.

Q. "Each limb says to a person, 'By your leave, with me do this religious duty.'

R. "Three hundred sixty-five religious duties of omission [acts not to be done] matching the days of the solar calendar.

S. "Each day says to a person, 'By your leave, on me do not carry out that transgression.'"

Pesiqta de Rab Kahana XII:I.1ff.

That Israel got them all is what requires explanation, and the explanation has to do with the union of the days of the solar year with the bones of man: at all time, with all one's being, one obeys God's commandments. The mode of explanation here does not require the introduction of proof-texts, appealing rather to the state of nature—solar calendar, human bone structure—to account for the facts. The kingdom of heaven, then, encompasses every day of the year and the components of the human body. The amplification in paragraphs R–S cannot be improved upon.

But the concrete realization of God's kingdom required constant encounter with the Torah, not only because the Torah was the source of the commandments that Israel was to carry out in obedience to its heavenly Father and King but also because, within it God's own "I," his self-manifestation, was eternally recorded and therefore always to be encountered. Torah study constituted the occasion for meeting God, because the words of the Torah convey whatever man knows with certainty about God. If Israel meets God in the Torah, God therefore is present when the Torah is opened and studied; then God is present within Israel:

A. Expounded Raba: What [is meant by what] is written, "Lord, you have been a dwelling place for us" [Ps. 90:1]?

B. These are the synagogues and academies.

C. Said Abbayye, "Initially I used to study at home and pray in the synagogue. After I heard what David said [namely], 'Lord, I loved the place of your house' [Ps. 26:8], I studied in the synagogue."

b. Megillah 4:4 I.14

There the Holy Spirit comes to rest. But that is not at all times or under every circumstance. The following powerful exposition invokes a metaphor to show the connection between Israel and God through the Torah as declaimed in synagogues and studied in schools. The point is that God is present in Israel when and where Israel meets God in the Torah. To separate God from Israel, the synagogues have to be boarded up, the schools closed. Then the chain forged at Sinai is broken:

D. R. Honiah in the name of R. Eleazar: "Why is he called 'Ahaz' [seize]?"

E. "Because he seized the synagogues and schools."

F. To what is Ahaz to be compared?

G. To a king who had a son, who handed him over to a governor. He wanted to kill him. He said, "If I kill him, I shall be declared liable to death. But lo, I will take his wet-nurse from him, and he will die on his own."

Now the parable is applied to the case of Ahaz. His reckoning contains the sages' entire theory of how God and Israel meet:

H. So did Ahaz say, "If there are no lambs, there will be no sheep; if there are no sheep, there will be no flock; if there is no flock, there will be no shepherd; if there is no shepherd, there will be no world, if there is no world—as it were. . . ."

I. So did Ahaz reckon, saying, "If there are no children, there will be no adults; if there are no adults, there will be no sages; if there are no sages, there will be no prophets; if there are no prophets, there will be no Holy Spirit; if there is no Holy Spirit, there will be no synagogues or schoolhouses—as it were. In that case, as it were, the Holy One, blessed be he, will not let his Presence rest upon Israel."

y. Sanhedrin 10:2 II:4

From the sages come the prophets, upon the prophets the Holy Spirit rests, and without the Holy Spirit there are no synagogues or schoolhouses, hence God's presence cannot come to rest in Israel.

What Israel must do then is to accept God's will, carry out God's commandments, above all, humbly take up its position in the kingdom of God. Israel's task is to accept its fate as destiny decreed by God, to be humble and accepting, and ultimately to triumph in God's time. Israel is similar to the dust of the earth, which is why Israel, like the dirt, will endure forever:

A. "I will make your descendants as the dust of the earth" [Gen. 13:16]:

B. Just as the dust of the earth is from one end of the world to the other, so your children will be from one end of the world to the other.

C. Just as the dust of the earth is blessed only with water, so your children will be blessed only through the merit attained by study of the Torah, which is compared to water [hence: through water].

D. Just as the dust of the earth wears out metal utensils and yet endures forever, so Israel endures while the nations of the world come to an end.

E. Just as the dust of the world is treated as something on which to trample, so your children are treated as something to be trampled upon by the government.

F. That is in line with this verse: "And I will put it into the hand of them that afflict you" [Isa. 51:23], that is to say, those who make your wounds flow.

G. Nonetheless, it is for your good that they do so, for they cleanse you of guilt, in line with this verse: "You make her soft with showers" [Ps. 65:11].

H. "That have said to your soul, 'Bow down, that we may go over' [Isa. 51:23]:

I. "What did they do to them? They made them lie down in the streets and drew ploughs over them."

J. R. Azariah in the name of R. Aha: "That is a good sign. Just as the street wears out those who pass over it and endures forever, so your children will wear out all the nations of the world and will live forever."

Genesis Rabbah XLI:IX.1

Israel will show acceptance and humility and so overcome the nations neither by power nor by its own might but by means of winning God's help through Torah study, obedience, and patience.

The Gentiles as Not-Israel

That brings us, in the end, to the matter of the nations and their idolatry. Just as the Torah teaches Israel to embody certain virtues, and just as an Israelite must be humble and maintain an attitude of forbearance and not arrogance, so Israel must find in its condition as subordinate a reason to hope for God's special favor. For, Scripture demonstrates, God prefers the pursued over the pursuer and favors the persecuted. The following collection of facts is arranged to prove that point, which contains ample consolation for Israel even in the here and now, before the last things have begun the restoration:

1. A. "God seeks what has been driven away" [Qoh. 3:15].

B. R. Huna in the name of R. Joseph said, "It is always the case that 'God seeks what has been driven away' [favoring the victim].

C. "You find when a righteous man pursues a righteous man, 'God seeks what has been driven away.'

> D. "When a wicked man pursues a wicked man, 'God seeks what
> has been driven away.'
> E. "All the more so when a wicked man pursues a righteous man,
> 'God seeks what has been driven away.'
> F. "[The same principle applies] even when you come around to
> a case in which a righteous man pursues a wicked man, 'God
> seeks what has been driven away.'"

Now, the general proposition in hand, we turn toward the evidence that
establishes it:

> 2. A.R. Yose b. R. Yudan in the name of R. Yose b. R. Nehorai says,
> "It is always the case that the Holy One, blessed be he, demands
> an accounting for the blood of those who have been pursued
> from the hand of the pursuer."

The cluster is formed of familiar players (Abel, Noah, Abraham, Isaac,
Jacob), and their enemies (Cain, Noah's contemporaries, Nimrod, Ishmael, Esau), and onward through the sequence, not bound by time, of
probative cases. They are all a living presence on that timeless plane
on which truth is established:

> B. "Abel was pursued by Cain, and God sought (an accounting for)
> the pursued: 'And the Lord looked (favorably) upon Abel and his
> meal offering' [Gen. 4:4].
> C. "Noah was pursued by his generation, and God sought (an ac-
> counting for) the pursued: 'You and all your household shall
> come into the ark' [Gen. 7:1]. And it says, 'For this is like the
> days of Noah to me, as I swore (that the waters of Noah should
> no more go over the earth)' [Isa. 54:9].
> D. "Abraham was pursued by Nimrod, 'and God seeks what has
> been driven away': 'You are the Lord, the God who chose Abram
> and brought him out of Ur' [Neh. 9:7].
> E. "Isaac was pursued by Ishmael, 'and God seeks what has been
> driven away': 'For through Isaac will seed be called for you'
> [Gen. 21:12].
> F. "Jacob was pursued by Esau, 'and God seeks what has been
> driven away': 'For the Lord has chosen Jacob, Israel for his
> prized possession' [Ps. 135:4].
> G. "Moses was pursued by Pharaoh, 'and God seeks what has been
> driven away': 'Had not Moses his chosen stood in the breach be-
> fore him' [Ps. 106:23].
> H. "David was pursued by Saul, 'and God seeks what has been
> driven away': 'And he chose David, his servant' [Ps. 78:70].

> I. "Israel was pursued by the nations, 'and God seeks what has been driven away': 'And you has the Lord chosen to be a people to him' [Deut. 14:2].
> J. "And the rule applies also to the matter of offerings. A bull is pursued by a lion, a sheep is pursued by a wolf, a goat is pursued by a leopard.
> K. "Therefore the Holy One, blessed be he, has said, 'Do not make offerings before me from those animals that pursue, but from those that are pursued: "When a bull, a sheep, or a goat is born"'" [Lev. 22:27].
>
> *Leviticus Rabbah* XXVII:V.1ff.:

In each case God explicitly prefers the pursued over the pursuer, and all of the cases together establish that point. What consequence might Israel anticipate from God's favor? What in the end made "being Israel" matter so much? To be Israel means to enjoy the promise of eternal life. There are no higher stakes.

That definition of who and what is Israel emerges in the following, through a simple manipulation of the opening statement: "All Israelites have a share in the world to come," meaning they will be resurrected, stand in judgment, and then live forever. This passage defines who fits into the category of "all Israelites":

> A. All Israelites have a share in the world to come,
> B. as it is said, "Your people also shall be all righteous, they shall inherit the land forever; the branch of my planting, the work of my hands, that I may be glorified" [Isa. 60:21].
>
> *m. Sanhedrin* 10:1

At the most profound level, therefore, to be "Israel" means to be those destined to rise from the dead and enjoy the world to come. Specifically, the definition of Israel is contained in the identification of "all Israel" as those who maintain that the resurrection of the dead is a teaching of the Torah and that the Torah comes from heaven. The upshot is, to be "Israel" is to rise from the dead to the world to come. Gentiles, by contrast, are not going to be resurrected when the dead are raised, but those among them who bear no guilt for their sins also will not be judged for eternal damnation:

> Gentile children who did not act out of free will and Nebuchadnezzar's soldiers who had no choice but to follow the orders of the evil king will not live after the resurrection of the dead but will not be judged for their deeds. (*y. Shevi'it* 4:10 IX)

If at the end of time Israel is comprised of those who will rise from the dead, in the interim "Israel" finds its definition in those who live the holy life and so imitate God. For Israel to be holy means that Israel is to be separate, and if Israel sanctifies itself, it sanctifies God:

1. A. "And the Lord said to Moses, Say to all the congregation of the people of Israel, You shall be holy [for I the Lord your God am holy]" [Lev. 19:1–2]:
2. A. "You shall be holy":
    B. "You shall be separate."
3. A. "You shall be holy, for I the Lord your God am holy":
    B. That is to say, "if you sanctify yourselves, I shall credit it to you as though you had sanctified me, and if you do not sanctify yourselves, I shall hold that it is as if you have not sanctified me."
    C. Or perhaps the sense is this: "If you sanctify me, then lo, I shall be sanctified, and if not, I shall not be sanctified"?
    D. Scripture says, "For I . . . am holy," meaning, "I remain in my state of sanctification, whether or not you sanctify me."

Sifra CXCV:I.2-3

The final trait of God's kingdom—the kingdom of heaven—then comes to the fore: its utopian character. To be "Israel" is personal and collective but utopian, not bound to place. The dead will rise wherever located. While the Land of Israel is elect along with the people of Israel, to be Israel does not mean to live in the Land but to live by the Torah.

The Theology of Classical Christianity

Augustine's conception of the city of God became the classical designation of the entire sweep of human anthropology and history from creation to redemption, as has already been indicated in chapter 1. Its range is so comprehensive that it extends to the resurrection of humanity. For that reason a consideration of the city of God will await us in chapter 7. In any case, making sense of the current human condition as a part of divine creation and compassion was imperative long before Augustine. Jesus focused on that issue in his preaching of the kingdom of God, a concept that was current in the early Judaism of his time;[2] Jesus made it the pivot of his preaching.

2. See Bruce Chilton, *God in Strength: Jesus' Announcement of the Kingdom* (Studien zum Neuen Testament und seiner Umwelt 1; Freistadt: Plöchl, 1979; repr., The Biblical Seminar, Sheffield: JSOT, 1987); and Bruce Chilton and J. I. H. McDonald, *Jesus and the Ethics of the Kingdom* (Biblical Foundations in Theology; London: SPCK; 1987; repr. Grand Rapids: Eerdmans, 1988).

The concept of the kingdom of God within the New Testament is foundational, and yet elusive. There is agreement among the Gospels and among scholars that the kingdom lay at the heart of the preaching of Jesus. Focus upon the kingdom also persisted as the Jesus movement survived his crucifixion and reached out to new followers, even gentiles, with the claim of his victory over death. But by the end of the first century, as we shall see, the emphasis upon the kingdom in its initial form had disappeared and was replaced by a fresh understanding.

It seems appropriate to approach the kingdom of God in the New Testament along the lines of a generative exegesis: after all, the underlying issue is how the sense of the concept was transformed as it passed through circles of Jesus' followers and different stages of the movement itself. Initially, we shall be concerned with the stage of evangelization and the stage of catechesis, as represented chiefly by the Synoptic Gospels. A complication of the study of the Synoptics is that within the texts as they stand we must distinguish diverse circles of tradition that differ over questions of meaning—sometimes sharply, as we have seen already in the crucial matter of the Eucharist. But the Synoptics will be treated very selectively here, in order to permit consideration of theological reflection upon catechesis (the third stage) as represented in John, the Pauline controversy concerning the kingdom (the fourth stage), and the attempted synthesis in the last of the Epistles (the fifth stage). As we observe these transformations, the kingdom will emerge as a consistent term of reference in the claim that God makes himself available through Christ in the form of ultimate and radical intervention on behalf of his people.

The Gospel of the Kingdom

No one who has read the relevant sources attentively is likely to deny that Jesus' preaching of the kingdom of God was rooted in the concept of the kingdom within early Judaism. That has been a matter of consensus since the end of the nineteenth century. The discovery of the importance of early Judaic theology as the foundation of Jesus' theology was nothing short of revolutionary in its impact.

What most struck scholars at the end of the nineteenth century was that the kingdom of God within early Judaism was a reference neither to an individual's life after death in heaven nor to a movement of social improvement upon the earth. Those had been dominant understandings, deeply embedded in the theology and preaching of the period, prior to the brilliant and incontrovertible assertions of Johannes Weiss and Albert Schweitzer.[3] They demonstrated that the kingdom of God in early Judaism and the preaching of Jesus referred to God's final judgment of the world; the concept was part and parcel of the anticipation of the last things (*eschata* in Greek, whence the term "eschatology"). Christian thought has been in some confusion ever since Weiss and Schweitzer made their point. Some deny that Jesus' focus was eschatological, although they can offer no convincing alternative to eschatology. Others accept that Jesus' thought was indeed eschatological but then try to argue that this idiom of theology was only designed to call attention to his own offer of salvation. But if Jesus' language was eschatological at all, what sort of Messiah can have been so mistaken? Once the challenge of eschatology has been appreciated, it is easy to understand why much Christian thought was in a retreat from its own Scriptures for most of the twentieth century. Typically, the retreat has taken one of two directions.

The less orderly withdrawal is that of what is usually called liberal Christianity. Rather than face what the Scriptures say, many liberal theologians have simply taken the vocabulary of the Bible and infused it with a meaning of their own. So, just when Weiss and Schweitzer were proving that the kingdom of God can only be understood as God's own intervention in human affairs, a school of thought in liberal Christianity called "the Social Gospel" tried to convince Americans that legislation and social action would bring about their understanding of society's perfection, which they called the kingdom of God. Instead of perfection, of course, what they got was Prohibition, and insofar as there has been confidence in the benign influence of government since that time, its basis has been pragmatic rather than theological. The Social Gospel is no longer a coherent agenda, although it has survived in the shape of engagement with issues of poverty, racism, and liberation. Whatever shape such engagement takes and however effective it might be, the liberal inattention to Scripture has become as obvious as liberals' widespread ignorance of the Bible.

The retreat of conservative Christians from the Scripture has been more strategic. They cite the Bible, and are often eager to instruct themselves in its contents, but they also restrict the number of meanings that they will accept from Scripture. The heart of Fundamentalism is a small body of "fundamentals" that the Bible is claimed to convey infallibly. Popularly, it is claimed that Fundamentalists are literalists, but that is a confusion that serves their own aims. The fact is that Fundamentalists ignore meanings that do not suit their theology: that is the only way to

---

3. For a history of discussion with selected readings, see Bruce Chilton, *The Kingdom of God in the Teaching of Jesus* (London: SPCK; Philadelphia: Fortress, 1984).

insist upon the inerrancy of Scripture. In the case of Jesus' preaching of the kingdom, some conservatives today assert that, although his understanding was eschatological, Jesus' teaching was nonetheless timeless, because it illustrated his personal hope in God as his Father.

This is a fascinating development, from the point of view of the history of theology. Albert Schweitzer made this argument at the beginning of the twentieth century. He wrote that Jesus' eschatological expectation was broken on the cross but the moral force of his hope in God was an abiding truth. When he applied to be sent as a Protestant missionary to Africa, his application was denied on the grounds that his theology was too radical. That is why Schweitzer trained as a medic, and Missions Evangéliques in Paris agreed to send him to Africa only if he agreed not to preach. He submitted to this stipulation but then over time quietly forgot it.[4]

Today scholars such as N. T. Wright take up a version of Schweitzer's argument as if it were an obviously Evangelical position.[5] In this construction, Jesus went to Jerusalem in order to take upon himself all the conditions of the covenant, including its hopes and fears for eschatological reward and judgment, so that the temporal side of eschatology was dissolved in his personal sacrifice. An oxymoron such as timeless eschatology is an interesting theological development, but it is not a scriptural oxymoron.

A generative exegesis can be bound by neither a "conservative" nor by a "liberal" agenda. The New Testament, as the canon of the system which is Christianity, may be neither ignored nor tamed by theological fashions. In the matter of the kingdom of God, moreover, cognizance must especially be taken of the milieu within early Judaism—represented by the Hebrew Bible, the Apocrypha, the Pseudepigrapha, and rabbinic sources including the *targumim*—that framed the conception Jesus developed and preached. Weiss and Schweitzer correctly focused on the kingdom as a systemic category of early Judaism rather than as a moral doctrine for modern Christians. But they assigned disproportionate importance to the issue of the time of the kingdom. The insistence of early Judaism that the kingdom represents the end of things as we know them is, no doubt, the most striking departure from most modern ways of conceiving of God and the world, but the temporal aspect is only one among several distinct emphases in the overall eschatology of the kingdom.

4. See Bruce Chilton, *Pure Kingdom: Jesus' Vision of God* (Studying the Historical Jesus 1; Grand Rapids: Eerdmans; London: SPCK, 1996), 2–6.

5. See N. T. Wright, *What Saint Paul Really Said: Was Paul of Tarsus the Real Founder of Christianity?* (Grand Rapids: Eerdmans, 1997), 178–83.

Five emphatic aspects of the kingdom of God will be cited here and then related to Jesus' conception of the kingdom. Each of the aspects will be illustrated by means of key passage from the book of Psalms, because psalmic usage was foundational for that early Judaism which was Jesus' milieu. In Psalms we must reckon with a much more variegated application of a language of kingship to God than the modern fixation upon temporal eschatology alone would allow. The assertion of God as king refers normally to his rule on behalf of his people, as present and to come, intervening and yet all-pervasive, demanding righteousness and anticipating perfection, requiring a purity cognate with God's sanctity, and extending from Israel so as to be inclusive of all peoples.

Five dimensions of the kingdom, then, all of them eschatological, play a paradigmatic role within the Psalms: (1) The temporally eschatological dimension: the kingdom is so near in time as to be present, and yet ultimate from the point of view of full disclosure:

> Say among the nations that the LORD reigns.
> The world is established, so as not to move:
> he shall judge the peoples with equity. (Ps. 96:10)

(2) The dimension of transcendence: the kingdom is forceful in its impact and will permeate all things:

> All your creatures will give you thanks, LORD, and your faithful will
>   bless you;
> they shall speak of the glory of your kingdom, and tell of your might,
> to make your mighty deeds known to the sons of men, and the glorious
>   splendor of his kingdom. (Ps. 145:10–12)

(3) The dimension of judgment: the kingdom is ever righteous, but attains to consummation:

> Break the arm of the wicked and evil;
> search out his wickedness until it cannot be found!
> The LORD is king for ever and ever;
> the nations perish from his earth! (Ps. 10:15–16)

(4) The dimension of purity: the kingdom is only consistent with what is clean, until all things are holy:

> Who will ascend the mount of the LORD,
>   and who will stand in his holy place?
> The innocent of hands and pure of heart,
>   who has not lifted up his soul to vanity,
>   and has not sworn deceitfully. (Ps. 24:3–4)

This passage is especially relevant here in view of the reference to God as king in vv. 7–10. (5) The dimension of radiance: although the kingdom is local (in Zion and in heaven), it is to include all peoples:

> God reigns over the nations;
> God sits upon his holy throne.
> The nobles of the peoples are gathered,
>   the people of the God of Abraham;
> for the shields of the earth are God's.
> He is highly exalted! (Ps. 47:8–9)

These five dimensions are so closely related within the language of the kingdom that one example from the Psalms might be used to illustrate more than one aspect. That tends to confirm that these are systemic dimensions of meaning for the kingdom, although a given speaker or circle of usage would of course develop a particular significance, appropriate to the historical conditions involved.

Within each dimension, the first pole designates the kingdom as it impinges upon those who might respond to it; for them, the kingdom appears (1) near, (2) powerful, (3) demanding, (4) pure, and (5) associated with Zion in particular. The second pole of each dimension designates the goal implicit within the kingdom, the (1) final, (2) immanent, (3) faultless, (4) holy, and (5) inclusive reality it promises to be. The kingdom of God, in other words, is not only a scandal for modern thinking because it purports to be final. It is indeed eschatological in respect of time, as Weiss and Schweitzer maintained, but also transcendent in respect of place (in Zion, heaven, everywhere), perfect in respect of action, sacred in its purity, and all-embracing in its choice of Israel.

Jesus' gospel of the kingdom distinctively developed dimensions of usage that had already been established. Perhaps his most signal innovation was the very act of announcing the kingdom: what was generally known as a promise of the Scripture was claimed by Jesus to be breaking in on the people he addressed in disparate towns and villages in Galilee. Within the résumé of the Petrine gospel from Acts 10 in the house of Cornelius, Peter speaks of the word of God that he sent to the sons of Israel, triumphantly preaching "peace through Jesus Christ" (Acts 10:36). Here is an example of a replacement of the concept of the kingdom, in this case by "peace." But the catechesis of the Petrine circle was unequivocal that the central focus of Jesus' preaching was the kingdom of God. Matthew (4:17), Mark (1:15), and Luke (4:43) use different wording to introduce the kingdom as the theme of Jesus' message, but that is only to be expected, since the Gospels are not simply literary copies one from another but portraits of Christian catechesis in churches of distinct places and times. Their typical variety, however, makes their consensus that the kingdom was the theme of Jesus' message all the more significant.

To promulgate the kingdom as a message was, at least implicitly, to claim God's forceful intervention along the lines of time, place, actions, objects, and people. Those dimensions in fact become explicit in Jesus' gospel, as when he states (in the mishnaic source known as Q):

> Many will come from east and west
> and recline in feasting
> with Abraham and Isaac and Jacob. . . . (Matt. 8:11; Luke 13:28, 29)

Clearly this statement envisions a future consummation involving a particular (though unnamed) place, the actions and material of festivity (including the luxurious custom of reclining, not sitting, at a banquet), and the incorporation of the many who will rejoice in the company of the patriarchs.

Jesus' use of the imagery of feasting in order to refer to the kingdom, a characteristic of his message, is resonant both with early Judaic kingdom discourse and his own ministry. The picture of God offering a feast on Mount Zion "for all peoples," where death itself is swallowed up, becomes an influential image from the time of Isaiah 25:6–8. Notably, the Targum of Isaiah refers to a divine disclosure on Mount Zion that includes the image of the feast as "the kingdom of the LORD of hosts" (24:23). Sayings such as the one cited from Q invoke that imagery, and Jesus' practice of fellowship at meals with his disciples and many others amounts to a claim that the ultimate festivity has already begun.

The dynamic of inclusion is not without its dark side, both in Isaiah and in Jesus' preaching. The Isaianic feast on Mount Zion is to be accompanied by the destruction of Moab (Isa. 25:10–12); the feast with the patriarchs includes the threat of exclusion for some in Israel (Matt. 8:12; Luke 13:28). Thus while the imagery may at first seem entirely festive, it turns out to involve judgment, as is natural within an expectation of the kingdom. The kingdom of God in the saying from Q is a feast for the future whose invitation is issued now by Jesus, so that response to the invitation is implicitly a condition of entry. The feast's location is related to Mount Zion, upon which Isaiah predicted a feast for all peoples. The judgment of the kingdom will exclude the wicked, and what is enjoyed in luxurious fashion will be pure. Finally, the kingdom's radiant power will include those from far away, all of whom are to be joined with the patriarchs. No wonder those who responded to Jesus' gospel asked him how to gain entry into this kingdom.

The Catechesis of the Kingdom

The movement of Jesus may be regarded has having started from the moment his preaching of the kingdom was accepted. Accepting his theme that the kingdom was dawning naturally involved a desire to enjoy the kingdom's light. How could one be among the "many" who were to feast in the kingdom, and not among those who were to be cast out? Jesus' own response to such issues within the movement is largely contained in the instruction for his disciples known as Q. In respect of social function, Jesus' instruction of his closest followers is to be distinguished from the catechetical program for beginners of which the Synoptic Gospels are an example, but the agenda of preparing adherents of the movement is shared by Q and the Synoptics.

The feast image in Matthew 8:11–12 and Luke 13:28–29 is developed along narrative lines in what is commonly known as the parable of the wedding feast, after the version in Matthew 22:1–10 (compare Luke 14:16–24). Within the parable, Jesus follows the rabbinic method of using narrative to teach ethics. The feast is prepared, but invitations must be accepted in order to be effective; and God is ready to drag outsiders in rather than permit his festivity to go unattended. Within the festal imagery we have just considered, the parable is an interesting development. Who would have expected invitees not to show up for the Isaianic feast? For the Jesus of this tradition, however, the kingdom is elusive enough that willful ignorance of it is possible. The narrative, that is to say, conveys the kingdom within a fresh perspective. The narrative is designed as a performance to show, without explaining, what the kingdom means for us.

The performance of meaning effected by the parable is not entirely a matter of reference to the imaginary. Precisely because the parable concerns God's activity as king, it makes a claim within the experience of anyone who knows what a king is. God, the parable claims, has been brought to act sovereignly but surprisingly. His present offer is out of the ordinary. The extraordinarily bad, even violent, behavior of those who should have been guests provides the impetus for a radical expansion in scope of an increasingly insistent invitation: leave your cares (however legitimate), and join the feast, take the opportunity of an invitation you could never have anticipated. The parabolic motif portrays divine action as begun but not perfected. The parabolic actions points towards the future as the locus of the kingdom's ultimate disclosure. Similarly, the ethical theme of the parable frames and encourages a wary, clever, even opportunistic response to this disclosure-in-progress.

The Petrine circle came increasingly to portray itself as a group apart from other sorts of Judaism (a self-portrait also readily apparent in the development of the parable of the wedding feast). Jesus' saying regarding wealth and the kingdom of God was transformed into a commendation of the peripatetic disciples whose support derived from those they taught (Matt. 19:16–30; Mark 10:17–31; Luke 18:18–30). Another, more subtle example of the Petrine transformation of the kingdom is the way in which an obscure saying of Jesus is presented. The statement "There are some standing here who will not taste death until they see the kingdom of God" is present and variously interpreted in each of the Synoptics (Matt. 16:28; Mark 9:1; Luke 9:27). An exegesis of the dictum will not be pursued here;[6] the relevant concern is rather the context of the saying within the Petrine tradition.

The statement occurs just after Jesus promises that everyone who denies himself, takes up his cross, and follows Jesus—even to the point of losing his life—will save his life (Matt. 16:24–27; Mark 8:34–38; Luke 9:23–26). So presented, the saying regarding those "standing here" would seem to be a promise of life until the *eschaton*. Then, however, the transfiguration follows (Matt. 17:1–9; Mark 9:2–10; Luke 9:28–36), when Peter, James, and John are taken up a mountain by Jesus, whose own appearance changes prior to the arrival of Moses and Elijah. The three privileged disciples, Peter at their head, have seen the promise of the kingdom in terms reminiscent of Moses' ascent of Sinai with three privileged followers (Exod. 24:1–11). Here are the emblems of the Petrine catechesis: Jesus is related to God as Moses once was, and Peter is his Aaron, a witness that the kingdom has been covenanted.

The signature of the Jacobean circle, by contrast, is detectable in Matthew 13:10–11, Mark 4:10–11, and Luke 8:9–10, where it is claimed that Jesus conveys the secret(s) of the kingdom to the larger group of twelve disciples, the precursor of what has come to be called the apostolic college in Jerusalem. The group concerned is not the select company around Peter, but those of Jesus' disciples who devote themselves to the authoritative interpretation of his teaching. Indeed, the passage occurs immediately prior to Jesus' explanation of the parable of the sower, which is the foundation of the parable collection in all three Synoptics. The message of the Jacobean group is that the company of James enjoys particular insight into the kingdom, and that the kingdom is essentially a didactic matter, into which Jesus' disciples offer initiation.

The circles of Peter and of James were able to control and transform the meaning of the kingdom by mastering the context of its presentation in sayings of and stories about Jesus. Each circle contextualized the

6. For my understanding of Jesus' initial meaning, see Bruce Chilton, "The Transfiguration: Dominical Assurance and Apostolic Vision," *New Testament Studies* 27 (1980): 115–24.

kingdom parables so as to support its own position of privilege. But at the same time the meaning of the kingdom shifted. What for Jesus was a divine intervention in the world (of time, space, action, objects, and humanity) became for the Petrine group the assurance of a particular, visionary experience (the transfiguration) and for the Jacobean group a method of authoritative interpretation (the explanation of parables).

Transformation by means of context is also evident in the other circles that fed the Synoptic Gospels, though with less dramatic impact. Reference has already been made to Jesus' promise of the inclusion of many from east and west in the patriarchal feast of the kingdom (Matt. 8:11–12; Luke 13:28–29). The mishnaic source (Q) including that saying tends to be pointed against the Jewish opponents of the movement. In the Matthean version, the saying appears as an addendum to the healing of the servant of the Roman centurion and includes an explicit warning against "the sons of the kingdom" (v. 12). In the Lukan version, the saying is presented as part of a discourse concerning salvation, in which hearers are warned that merely having enjoyed Jesus' company during his lifetime is no guarantee of fellowship with the patriarchs in the eschatological feast (13:22–30). The differences between the two versions make the supposition of a fixed, written Q appear less plausible than an instructional source susceptible of local variation.

Even at a later stage, context could result in variegated portrayals of the kingdom. Before we discuss contextualization in each Synoptic Gospel, however, it is necessary to explain that there is a commonly Synoptic transformation of the kingdom, a transformation plausibly associated with the circle of Barnabas in Antioch (whose power and influence is signaled by the letters of Paul). The transformation is general enough that the construal of each Synoptic Gospel may be described as a variation on a theme, but it is also distinctive enough that no other ancient document may be described as sharing it. It introduces the kingdom as preached by Jesus. This obvious feature of the Gospels' narratives is no less influential for being evident: the kingdom from this point onward is established as the burden of Jesus' message and no other's. Moreover, accepting Jesus involves embracing the characteristic understanding of the kingdom that unfolds.

The next major phase in the Synoptic transformation of the kingdom is pedagogical. The Jesus who is the kingdom's herald is also its advocate, explaining its features to those who hear but are puzzled (or even scandalized). The extent of the material each gospel devotes to this phase varies greatly, but in every case it is the largest phase. The distribution of this material also varies, but it is striking that none of the Synoptic Gospels invokes the term "kingdom" as a link to include all statements on the subject in a single complex of material. Such an association by catchword is indeed detectable over short runs of material, so that isolated sayings are the exception, not the rule, but in no case is subject matter or wording solely determinative of context. Rather, there is a narrative contextualization in which Jesus' preaching, teaching, and disputing activity becomes the governing framework for a given run of sayings. Those frameworks vary from gospel to gospel, of course, as do the logia presented; the distribution of sayings certainly cannot be explained by reference to some fixed historical or literary ordering. The point is rather that the typically Synoptic transformation of Jesus' preaching embeds the kingdom within his ministry, so that he and the kingdom approximate to being interchangeable. The particular textual moves that achieve this identification vary: the fact that it is achieved does not.

The last phase of the Synoptic transformation of the kingdom pursues the logic of the identification: Jesus' death and the kingdom are presented as mutually explicating. "I shall not drink of the fruit of the vine again until I drink it with you new in God's kingdom" (Matt. 26:29; Mark 14:25; Luke 22:18).[7] Whatever the sense of that saying was within the ministry of Jesus, within the Synoptics it serves to insist that the same Jesus who announced and taught the kingdom is also the sole guarantor of its glorious coming.

The Synoptic transformation of the kingdom essentially involves the distribution and narrative contextualization of the sayings within Jesus' ministry. The result is to focus upon Jesus as the herald, advocate, and guarantor of the kingdom in an innovative fashion. Arguably, the transformation explicates what is implicit within the sayings' tradition: an awareness that Jesus' ministry is a seal of the kingdom. The most obvious instance of such a claim within his sayings is Jesus' observation concerning his exorcisms and the kingdom (Matt. 12:28; Luke 11:20). But the emphasis even there falls more on the kingdom than on Jesus, so that the saying only heightens by contrast the Synoptic transformation, in which Jesus' preaching of the kingdom becomes the seal of his divine mission, not the principal point at issue. He who witnessed the kingdom is, within the Synoptics, attested as God's Son by virtue of his own message. Precisely because a signal adjustment of precedence between Jesus and the kingdom has taken place, the language of "transformation" is appropriate.

In view of its distinctiveness from the sense of the kingdom in other documents of early Judaism and Christianity, the Synoptic transforma-

---

7. See Bruce Chilton, *A Feast of Meanings: Eucharistic Theologies from Jesus through Johannine Circles* (Supplements to Novum Testamentum 72; Leiden: Brill, 1994) 38–45.

tion should be regarded as a particular framing of Jesus' sayings, not merely as a loose characterization of similar material in three gospels. How the transformation was effected, whether by literary borrowing from one document to another or by the sharing of a now lost antecedent, is a matter of conjecture.

Each of the Synoptic Gospels expresses the shared transformation of Jesus' kingdom teaching in a distinctive way. That is perhaps most easily appreciated by considering how Jesus' initial preaching is presented. In Matthew, Jesus says, "Repent, for the kingdom of heaven is at hand" (4:17), but he is not the first to do so. John is portrayed as delivering the same message (3:2). Part of the authority of the Matthean Jesus is that he is the climax of the prophetic witness which went before him; in Matthew alone, Jesus consciously decides to preach in Galilee, and his decision is held to fulfill a passage from the book of Isaiah (4:12–16). Mark has no such reference, but it does uniquely have Jesus say, "Repent, and believe in the gospel" (1:15c). That is an effective way to link Jesus' own preaching to the preaching about him, and Mark's Gospel alone commences, "The beginning of the gospel . . ." (1:1). As if to underline the point, Jesus' announcement of the kingdom is itself called "the gospel of God" (1:14). Luke offers the most confident equation between the kingdom and the one who preaches it. Although Luke assumes that Jesus preaches the kingdom (4:43), the instance of initial preaching which precedes that notice has Jesus quoting Scripture to the effect that he is God's anointed (4:16–21).

The narrative identification between the progress of the kingdom and Jesus' own ministry is of the essence of the transformation of traditions which the Synoptic Gospels reflect. Part of that transformation is the unequivocal belief that Jesus is to be the agent, along with God, in the final judgment of the kingdom. While Isaiah provided the principal image of kingdom festivity, the book of Daniel provided the principal image of Jesus' role in that judgment. Four beasts represent the great empires that were to rule from Daniel's time (Assyrian, Babylonian, Persian, and Seleucid). After the beasts are described, God appears on his throne (Dan. 7:9–10); "one like a son of man," a human being, is presented to God and receives total dominion (7:14). Within Daniel, this figure is essentially an agent of redemption and disclosure within the heavenly court. The faith of early Christians identified Jesus with that angelic vision. When the Temple authorities ask Jesus, with none of his disciples present, whether he is the Messiah, he replies unequivocally by citing Daniel 7 (see Matt. 26:63–64; Mark 14:61–62; Luke 22:66–69). Jesus, as the Danielic son of man, was not merely an angelic figure but was to return to earth to claim and vindicate his own. A complex of material within the Synoptics develops an apocalyptic scenario in which the most important elements are the destruction of the Temple and Jesus' coming as the triumphant son of man of Daniel 7 (see Matt. 25; Mark 13; Luke 21:5–36).[8] The Synoptic identification of Jesus with the kingdom is therefore coherent with the eschatological expectation of early Christians.

Royal Synthesis: The Kingdom of Christ

Even our brief consideration of the catechetical stage reveals its formative influence on the meaning of the kingdom within the New Testament. Transformations of the meaning of the kingdom at that stage—particularly in the commonly Synoptic phase, when the kingdom was integrated biographically with the preaching concerning Jesus—permitted the next developments to take place. Unless the catechetical transformations are appreciated, the paradox of the apparent disappearance of the kingdom of God as an emphasis within early Christianity will remain.

The Gospel according to John effects a radical reduction in focus on the kingdom: only one statement, about seeing (3:3) or entering (3:5) the kingdom, is ever made. Such explanation as is offered explicates the requirement for this experience: being born "from above" (anōthen) or "from water and spirit." The assumption is that no explanation of the kingdom itself is required. The passage is rather designed to insist that baptism in Jesus' name—birth from above by water and spirit—alone permits participation in the kingdom. The distinctively Johannine fashioning of Jesus traditions centers not on the kingdom but on receiving Jesus in such a manner as to become a child of God (1:12). That is, the Gospel's narratives and discourse are so consumed with the question of attaining eternal life (cf. 3:16) that the kingdom—the vision of what is actually achieved at the point where the eternal meets the temporal—is taken as a matter of course. The issue for John is means, not ends, because the Fourth Gospel is composed for those whose baptism is taken for granted.

Paul also communicates with those who have already been catechized, but he is not sanguine about his readers' conceptions of their own faith. His frequently controversial purposes comport well with his manner of reference to the kingdom, which is typically by way of correction. His insistence that the kingdom of God is not to be confused with food and drink (Rom. 14:17) is not the truism it may at first appear to be. Paul makes his statement in the midst of an argument against both maintain-

---

8. For an excellent study, see Walter Wink, *The Human Being: Jesus and the Enigma of the Son of Man* (Minneapolis: Fortress, 2002).

ing and blatantly flouting dietary purity regulations (14:13–23). Writing to the congregation at Rome near he end of his life (ca. 57 CE), Paul asserts that the kingdom is available as "righteousness and peace and joy in the Holy Spirit" to humanity as a whole (Rom. 14:17), whatever their views of purity. The primitive association of the kingdom and Eucharist, rooted in the practice of Jesus, here becomes the point of departure for insistence upon the inclusive reach of the kingdom. Paul claims that it would be better not to eat at all than to risk severing that association (14:21).

Because the kingdom is effective for those who attain to the promises of God through baptism into Christ, Paul views it as something that those who follow Christian ethics may "inherit." Even within the idiom of inheritance, however, Paul's formulation is typically negative, listing those who will not inherit the kingdom of God (so in Gal. 5:19–21; 1 Cor. 6:9–10). The foundational metaphor of inheritance is not an obvious development from earlier usage. Why should the kingdom now be inherited rather than entered? The transformation obviously has implications for eschatology in that Paul's construction of the kingdom is more consistently future than Jesus'. He ridicules those in Corinth who fancy themselves already regnant (1 Cor. 4:8) and explicitly portrays the kingdom as beyond the inheritance of flesh and blood (1 Cor. 15:50). But that moment of inheritance may be attained to, according to Paul, because Jesus—as life-giving spirit (15:45)—has prepared a spiritual people, fit for the resurrection of the dead (15:42–58).

By the reflective and controversial stages of John and Paul, then, the increasing focus of interest is preparation for the kingdom by means of baptism into Christ and the ethical performance of the baptismal spirit. There are evident differences in regard to the temporal emphasis of eschatology. The ultimacy of the kingdom may be expressed as "above" any concern for time or sequence (as in John 3:3, 5) or as keyed to that future moment when (as Paul puts it) Christ hands over the kingdom to God (1 Cor. 15:24). In either case, the issue of systemic importance is that Christ effects the transfer of the believer (at baptism, and thereafter) from his or her previous condition into the realm of God.

The stages of catechesis, reflection, and controversy added nothing, for all their variations of emphasis, to the dimensions implicit in the gospel of the kingdom. At the end of a generation of development, the kingdom remained God's realm: ultimate, transcendent, perfect, holy, inclusive. But he who had at first preached the kingdom was now at the forefront, explicitly and without compromise, as the means—and the only means—of access to the kingdom.

That development is starkly evident in the phrase "kingdom of Christ," used interchangeably with "kingdom of God." The earliest usage appears in Colossians 1:13, one of the letters attributed to Paul but emanating from the circle of Timothy (as the joint attribution to Paul and Timothy in 1:1–2 suggests) around 90 CE. The letter gives thanks to the Father for making believers worthy "of a share of the portion of saints in the light, who delivered us from the authority of the darkness and transferred us into the kingdom of the Son of his love . . ." (1:12–13). The continuity with Pauline emphases is obvious here, as in Ephesians 5:5, where the putative Paul speaks of those who do not have "an inheritance in the kingdom of Christ and of God."

In the present case the latest documents of the New Testament identify a systemic principle that had been active since at least the period of catechesis. Because baptism into Christ, prayer in the manner of Christ, the ethical imitation of Christ, and Eucharist in remembrance of Christ were the means of access into God's kingdom, functionally God's reign was also Christ's. All that could be said, then, of the kingdom of God in all its dimensions could also be said of what believers enjoyed as a result of their identification with Christ.

Comparing Theologies

Judaism on Christianity

The kingdom of heaven is an important category for both Christianity and Judaism. ("Heaven" routinely refers to God, so "kingdom of heaven" means "kingdom of God.") In Judaism God rules on earth, and Israel responds to God's rule by accepting the yoke of his dominion, carrying out various religious obligations of omission and commission. That, sum and substance, defines the category. In the halakhic context, accepting the yoke of God's kingdom is associated with putting on phylacteries and reciting the Shema—normative actions.

The kingdom of heaven, however, is no abstraction to be realized in individual consciousness alone. It is made concrete within the halakhic system. Thus God's court forms part of the system of enforcing the law of the Torah. So Israel forms the this-worldly extension of God's heavenly kingdom, and that is the fact even now. Not only so, but it is a fact that bears material and tangible consequences in the governance of the social order. That is why the heavenly court is assigned tasks alongside the earthly one. The sages' court punishes murder when the rules of testimony, which are strict and rigid, permit; when not, there is always heaven to step in. Or when a man clearly has served as efficient and sufficient cause of death, the earthly court punishes him. What are the consequences of Israel's humbly accepting the divine rule? What Israel must do is to accept God's will, carry out God's commandments, above all, humbly take up its position in the kingdom of God. Israel's task is to accept its fate as destiny decreed by God, to be humble and accepting, and ultimately to triumph in God's time.

What we see is that "kingdom of heaven" in Judaism is simply one way of referring to God's dominion. In the Christian system set forth in the Synoptic Gospels, it defines the heart of Jesus' message. Indeed, it is so systemically active that a particular literary form, the parable, is designated as principal medium for the message.

In Judaism God rules now, and those who acknowledge and accept his rule, performing his commandments and living by his will, live under God's dominion. To single out Israel, God sanctified the people by endowing them with numerous commandments. Carrying out these commandments, then, brings Israel into the kingdom of heaven, as they acknowledge the dominion of God. That merging of politics and theology emerges in the language of the blessing recited before the execution of a commandment or religious duty: "Blessed are you, Lord our God, king of the world, who has sanctified us by his commandments and commanded us to. . . ." That formula transforms an ordinary deed into an act of sanctification, a gesture of belonging to God's kingdom. The "kingdom of heaven" is atemporal. Whenever Israelites obeyed a commandment, God's rule on earth was realized.

Where is the difference with Christianity? The Christian heirs of Israelite Scripture subordinate much else to the kingdom of God, including sin, repentance, and atonement. The rabbinic heirs find sin, repentance, and atonement to be central. To that category they accommodate even the Israel-gentiles category and the kingdom of heaven.

Christianity on Judaism

The differences between Christianity and Judaism perhaps come out most clearly in their definitions of "Israel." According to St. Paul, God's Spirit defines Israel in a completely new way:

> For neither circumcision obtains, nor uncircumcision, but a new creation. And as many as walk by this standard, peace upon them and mercy, even upon the Israel of God. (Gal. 6:15–16)

The Spirit, received in baptism, takes the place of circumcision as the determinant of what constitutes the people of God. For that reason Paul comes to demand that Jewish followers of Jesus, once baptized, consistently abrogate their own rules of purity at meals for the sake of fellowship with non-Jewish followers (so Gal. 2).

Pauline rhetoric casts the issue in terms of whether circumcision can be demanded of non-Jewish followers, in addition to baptism, for inclusion in the movement. There were Christian teachers, described in Acts as Pharisees (Acts 15:5), who made just that demand. But James, Jesus' brother, simply instructed that non-Jewish Christians keep certain laws of purity for the sake of acknowledging Moses' authority (so Acts 15:13–21), while Peter was even more lenient (Acts 15:7–11). What really divided Paul from the others was not the practice of circumcision but his demand that the "Israel" of the "new creation" was to live apart from deeds (or "works") of the law. Finally, he argued that any definition of Israel needed to be subordinate to the revelation of God's kingdom, "because the kingdom of God is not food and drink, but righteousness and peace and joy in Holy Spirit" (Rom. 14:17). The gradual victory of Paul's thought in the church is best explained with reference to his insight that the "Israel" God chooses cannot be defined in terms of any human institution but is determined solely by the horizon of the kingdom.

In that the fundamental term of reference for Paul is "Israel," his systematic statement may still be described as a form of Judaism. But in that he openly and proudly flouts the accepted social markers of that Israel, he needs to explain his position. More especially, he needs to explain the role of the written law—Scripture—if Israel is in fact determined by means of identification with Christ.

The situation of Paul's argument in Galatians largely determines what he says on the basis of Scripture. Included in that situation, as we have seen, is his axiomatic assertion that the Spirit is released in baptism in an identification with Christ. For that reason, he can—without argument—say that the entire experience is commensurate with the righteousness of the primordial patriarch of Israel: "Just as Abraham believed in God, and it was reckoned to him as righteousness" (3:6). But how is the believer in baptism "just as" (kathōs) Abraham? Abraham in the book of Genesis is called righteous because he believed God's promise that his progeny was to thrive (see Gen. 15:5–6). What is the connection with belief in Christ at the moment of baptism?

Paul answers that question first by saying that faith itself links Abraham and the believer in the act of belief. Faith makes believers, as he says, "sons of Abraham," and even non-Jews who believe are blessed with the blessing promised to Abraham (Gal. 3:7–9). So Paul's initial claim is that faith in Christ is to be identified with the faith of Abraham. That is why he will claim, at the close of the letter, that faith makes "Israel" a "new creation" (6:15–16). This emergent Israel is not defined ethnically, or as a system of halakhah. The whole of any relation between God and people consists of their embrace of the Spirit of his Son—and of their own sonship—by faith.

5

The Body of Christ
and the Holiness of Israel

It was not enough for Judaic and Christian theologians to explain the division of mankind into "Israel" and "the gentiles." Nor was their work complete when they explained that "Israel" and the kingdom of God were not ethnic but theological categories, identified on the Judaic side with those who know God and will rise from the grave to recover Eden as their share in the world to come, and on the Christian side with the church as "the body of Christ." They also had to explain what everyday life in Israel (or the kingdom of God, or the body of Christ) entailed.

The faithful, the theologians recognized, live in the here and now of time and change, collision and conflict. If they really believed that man was made "in our image, after our likeness," then how were they to conduct themselves within that image, after that likeness? And what sort of corporate community took shape among those who undertook to embody the image and the likeness of God? Both responded with complex theories of deliberation and deportment, rules of intellect and of ethics. For Christian theologians, these are embodied in a systematic account of what it means to live with the transforming influence of God's Spirit, and for their Judaic counterparts, a coherent picture of the requirements of holiness. Here, then, we ask: when a Christian responded to Christ's words, "Take up your cross and follow me," and when Israel undertook to obey the commandment of God, "You shall be holy, for I the Lord your God am holy," what did he actually do? And in what settings of ordinary life did he hear those words?

The Theology of Classical Christianity

Paul saw the movement of God's Spirit through Christ as refashioning the world and its people, providing a "new creation" that joined people into an "Israel of God" transcending the categories of Israel's own Scriptures and the distinction between circumcision and uncircumcision (Gal. 6:15–16). He, more than any other thinker, provided increasingly non-Jewish Christianity with terms of reference for thinking socially. As his letter to the Galatians makes unmistakably plain, baptism is the moment at which one can address God as *Abba*, "Father," because the Spirit of God's own Son flows into one's heart (Gal. 4:6). By this point in the letter, it is clear that Paul conceives the spirit received in baptism as the Spirit of God himself (so 3:2, 3, 5, 14), which is here identified with the Spirit of Jesus. Paul can then assert, virtually without argument, that the Spirit is the principle of Christian identity. Reception of the Spirit came to be appreciated within primitive Christianity as the fundamental element of one's being in relation to God because it was also the foundation of understanding Jesus as the Messiah of God. Primitive Christian experience was correlated with Jesus' experience within baptism: because that was a matter of experience, it appears as an axiom shared by the Gospels and by Paul. Where Paul had to deploy his argumentative skills was in making the connection between receiving the Spirit of God and seeing those baptized as "Israel"—not as "new" Israel or "true" Israel, but simply as "the Israel of God," quite apart from the issue of circumcision (Gal. 6:15–16). That is the burden of his elaborate explanation, developed in chapters 3 and 4, for the proposition that embracing faith in baptism established one as a son of Abraham (Gal. 3:7).

Paul's radical definition was controversial in its time and it remains so now. The received view of Judaism in the Greco-Roman world, as today, was that it was the religion of a people, the Jews, and that circumcision was one of its principal markers. But from within Judaism the fundamental issue was solidarity with the patriarchs. The following Midrash shows how, long after Paul, the rabbinic sages portrayed Israel as those under God's dominion as laid out in the pattern of the Torah:

A. "On the third day Abraham lifted up his eyes and saw the place afar off" [Gen. 22:4]:

B "After two days he will revive us, on the third day he will raise us up, that we may live in his presence" [Hos. 6:2].

C. On the third day of the tribes: "And Joseph said to them on the third day, 'This do and live'" [Gen. 42:18].

D. On the third day of the giving of the Torah: "And it came to pass on the third day when it was morning" [Exod. 19:16].

E. On the third day of the spies: "And hide yourselves there for three days" [Josh. 2:16].

F. On the third day of Jonah: "And Jonah was in the belly of the fish three days and three nights" [Jonah 2:1].

G. On the third day of the return from the Exile: "And we abode there three days" [Ezra 8:32].

H. On the third day of the resurrection of the dead: "After two days he will revive us, on the third day he will raise us up, that we may live in his presence" [Hos. 6:2].

I. On the third day of Esther: "Now it came to pass on the third day that Esther put on her royal apparel" [Esth. 5:1].

J. She put on the monarchy of the house of her fathers.

K. On account of what sort of merit?

L. Rabbis say, "On account of the third day of the giving of the Torah."

Genesis Rabbah LVI:I

For these teachers, obedience to the dual Torah was the key to the pattern of divine redemption in every case. For Paul, however, the patriarchal pattern is realized when one believes in the way that Abraham believed:

> Just as Abraham believed in God, and it was accounted to him for righteousness, know therefore that those who are from faith, these are Abraham's sons. (Gal. 3:6–7)

Genesis Rabbah and Paul work out the patriarchal pattern in their characteristic ways, but the fact of the pattern is constitutive of Israel in both cases.

Although Paul was indeed profoundly creative, then, his creativity emerged on the basis of certain common features within primitive Christianity and early Judaism. Particularly, appeal to the pattern of the patriarchs is a typical element within Judaism and Christianity in the first century. Jesus himself made out the case that, because the patriarchs must be viewed as alive in the sight of God, resurrection as a general teaching should be accepted:

> But concerning the dead—that they are raised—have you not read in the
> book of Mosheh in the passage about the bush?—how God spoke to him
> saying, I am the God of Abraham and the God of Isaac and the God of
> Jacob? He is not God of the dead, but of the living. You are much deceived!
> (Mark 12:26–27)

In quite a different key, the *Genesis Apocryphon*, which was discovered
at Qumran, adds to the narrative of the book of Genesis an extensive
story concerning Abraham's prayer for (and against) the Egyptians, their
affliction (as a result of Sarah's abduction by Pharaoh), and then their
healing.[1] Whereas for Jesus Abraham and the patriarchs were a model
of the resurrection, in the *Genesis Apocryphon* Abraham models living
faithfully but compassionately with non-Jews. Appeal to the patriarchs
serves diverse ends.

Paul's teaching of the definition of Israel was grounded in a Christian
experience of the Spirit and a Judaic appeal to the patriarchs. Likewise,
his approach to Israel as reflected within the Scriptures, although as
radical as consistency with his basic definition of Israel demanded, was
grounded in what was emerging as a typically Christian approach to
interpretation. This is best seen in his correspondence with churches
in Corinth and in Rome.

From Purity to Spirit

In Corinth, a cosmopolitan city open to the many cultural influences
that trading brings, Paul found that his own teaching about the law was
being used against the ethical imperative that he believed was fundamental within the gospel. "All things are lawful" was the slogan of a group
in Corinth whose tendencies are obvious from Paul's rebuttal:

> All things are lawful to me, but all things are not advantageous. All things
> are lawful to me, but I will not be mastered by anyone. Foods are for the
> belly and the belly for foods, but God will do away with the one and the
> other. But the body is not for harlotry, but for the Lord, and the Lord
> for the body. Yet God both raised the Lord and will raise us through his
> power! Do you not know that your bodies are members of Christ? So
> shall I take the members of Christ and make them members of a harlot?
> By no means! Or do you not know that the one who joins to a harlot is
> one body? For the two, it states, will be as one flesh. But the one who is
> joined to the Lord is one spirit. (1 Cor. 6:12–17)

---

1. See the *Genesis Apocryphon*, column 20. For the Aramaic text and a translation,
see Joseph A. Fitzmyer and Daniel J. Harrington, *A Manual of Palestinian Aramaic Texts*
(Biblica et Orientalia 34; Rome: Biblical Institute, 1978).

What Paul has to face here is that his own position, worked out in Galatians—that the purity of foods should not be observed among the churches—is being used to indulge sexual impurity.

The pace and sequence of the events in Corinth is a matter of scholarly dispute, but it seems virtually certain that what is called 2 Corinthians joins at least two original letters.[2] But such issues pale in comparison with the importance of the fact that here Paul is wrestling with the consequences of his own position. Paul in Galatians had portrayed the law as a provisional guide to the reception of the Spirit by means of Christ; that was why he could insist, "For freedom Christ freed us, so stand and do not again be loaded again with slavery's yoke" (Gal. 5:1). But if the place of the law is relativized in that way, and if foods establish that purity also is no longer an autonomously binding category, how can Paul now object to sexual impurity?

The logical extension of Paul's conception was that all things are pure to the pure, precisely the formulation attributed to him in Titus 1:15. But Paul's actual *practice* turned out to be otherwise. In 1 Corinthians 8 he indeed departs from the policy of James by accepting that food offered to idols might be eaten, on the grounds that idols represent entirely fictional gods (1 Cor. 8:4–6). But he also warns against eating such food if some who believe in such gods are confirmed in their idolatry, so that "their conscience, being weak, is defiled" (1 Cor. 8:7–13, especially v. 7). The defilement here is internal and moral, rather than pragmatic, but it is nonetheless dangerous; Paul declares that he would rather not eat meat at all than cause a brother to sin (1 Cor. 8:13; see the restatement of the principle in Rom. 14:13–23). Because he is dealing here with matters of pragmatic action, there is no reason to take his statement as metaphorical: he here commends selective fasting for the sake of fellowship. By means of his own, characteristic argument, Paul approximates to what the rabbis would come to teach concerning the danger of idolatrous feasts (see *b. Avodah Zarah* 8a, instruction in the name of R. Ishmael).

Paul in this aspect reflects a more general tendency in Hellenistic Christianity. In his letters and in letters attributed to him there is an express connection between named vices (which are catalogued) and "impurity" (Rom. 1:24; Gal. 5:19; Eph. 4:19; 5:3; Col. 3:5). In early Christianity the medium of impurity came to be no longer foods themselves but moral intentions. And those intentions are as specifically identified in the New Testament as impure foods are discussed in rabbinic literature,

2. For a competent discussion and résumé of scholarship, see H. D. Betz's articles on both 1 Corinthians and 2 Corinthians in *The Anchor Bible Dictionary* (ed. D. N. Freedman et al.; Doubleday: New York, 1992), vol. 1, 1139–54.

because the danger in both cases was understood to be an impurity that made a real and dangerous separation from God.

The cataloguing of sins, and their classification with impurity, is scarcely a Christian invention. It is represented, for example, in Wisdom 14:22–31. But the genre is mastered to brilliant effect in Romans 1:24–32, Galatians 5:19–21, Ephesians 5:3–5, and Colossians 3:5–6 and is continued in the period after the New Testament (see *Didache* 5; *Shepherd of Hermas*, Mandate 8). What is striking in each case is not only the equation of impurity and sin, but a clear indication that impurity as such remains a fundamental category: sexual contact, a concern from at least the time of Leviticus 18, survives the declining significance of alimentary purity, even within Paul's thought. There is no question, therefore, of purity simply being abstracted into the realm of intention. Rather, intentionality of practice, together with bodily integrity, defines an ambit of purity. On such an understanding, one's body was indeed a temple of the Holy Spirit (see 1 Cor. 6:18–20; 3:16–17), and a rigorous attitude towards marriage is completely coherent with the emphasis that a new purity is required by God for the inheritance of his kingdom (see Matt. 5:27–28, 31–32; 19:3–12; Mark 10:2–12; Luke 16:18; 1 Cor. 7:10–16).

The success of the gospel of Jesus within the Hellenistic environment of primitive Christianity was in no small measure a function of its ability to frame a rational, practical, but stringent system of purity. The marketplace is declared pure in itself, provided it does not encourage the defilement of idolatry, and the requirements of James are largely forgotten. But moral, and especially sexual, requirements make it clear that purity has not been abandoned as a regulatory system, despite the efforts of Paul in regard to alimentary purity. In the passage from 1 Corinthians 6, the center of the argument is clearly marked as the possession of Spirit. Purity is now animated not by principles of inherent contagion but by actions that are (and are not) consistent with the reception of the Spirit of God in baptism.

Romans is the most systematic of Paul's works, because it was written to a community he had not yet visited but hoped to meet (see Rom. 15:22–25). The letter was written just after the Corinthians correspondence, in 57 CE, and represents a new (and obviously hard-won) maturity in Paul's thought. The passionately controversial style of Galatians and the tone of outraged dignity in the Corinthians letters are muted as Paul attempts to explain coherently how God's grace in Christ is both a confirmation of the covenantal promise to Abraham (see 1:18–4:25) and a powerfully ethical force (5:1–8:39).

On both fronts, Paul is much more lucid than in the earlier letters, largely because he is not responding to local issues (with which familiarity is assumed in Galatians and the two Corinthian letters), and also because he is not on the defensive. In the latter part of the letter, Paul offers crucial explanations of his position. In chapters 9 through 11, he makes clear his absolute fidelity to the promise of the covenant, even though he no longer regards the law as the means of fulfilling it. "All Israel will be saved" (Rom. 11:25–26), despite the rejection of Jesus by many Jews. Paul compares Israel to an olive tree (11:16b–24); though some of the branches have been cut off and replaced with wild gentile grafts, the natural branches can be grafted in again. By this operation, the fundamental election of Israel (the tree originally planted) is vindicated, and—despite the question of the law—Paul still does not imagine that Christianity and Judaism are separate plants. They have a single, holy root (11:16b). The one promise to Israel is in his mind fulfilled for all peoples in Christ (see 15:8–12). On the ethical front, Paul shows that he can think in positive terms, not only in response, as to those at Corinth. He develops, to some extent by means of his metaphor of Christ's body (12:3–8), a rather comprehensive recommendation to seek God's will (12:1–2) in the organization of the church (12:3–8), in the pursuit of caring relationships with others (12:9–21), in the acceptance of secular government (13:1–7), in the enactment of Christ's love to all (13:8–14), in regard for the conscience of others (14:1–23), and in whole-hearted generosity (15:1–13). It therefore becomes crystal clear that ethics belonged to the very essence of faith in Paul's understanding.

The engine of Paul's ethical thinking is, once again, his observation of what happens in baptism. In Romans he spells out the identification of believers with Christ even more clearly (6:3–11) than in his earlier letters. The pattern of Jesus' death and resurrection is repeated in the believer (6:3–4). Just as Jesus' faith involved dying, so we who were baptized, Paul says, were crucified in regard to sin (6:6–7). And Christ was raised from the dead so that we might conduct ourselves in "newness of life" (6:4). Our baptism means we accept a faith over which death's power has been broken (6:9); our life of faith through Jesus Christ is directed to the service of God alone, without regard for the constraints of sin (6:11).

In a daring analogy, Paul in 1 Corinthians had compared baptism and the exodus. We wish to specify the implications of that typology by looking at the passage first on its own and then in comparison with its companion exegesis is 2 Corinthians. Initially, Paul's comparison of baptism and exodus is straightforward:

> I do not want you to be ignorant, brothers: our fathers were all under the cloud, and all passed through the sea, and all were baptized into Moses in the cloud and in the sea. And they all ate the same spiritual food, and all drank the same spiritual drink. (For they drank from the spiritual rock

that was following, and the rock was Christ.) But God was not pleased with many of them, for they were brought down in the wilderness. These things became our examples (*typoi*), so that we might not be desirous of evil, as they desired. Neither must you become idolaters, as some of them did: as it is written, "The people sat down to eat and drink and arose to sport." Neither let us fornicate, as some of them fornicated, and in one day twenty-three thousand fell. Neither let us tempt Christ, as some of them tempted, and they were destroyed by serpents. Neither complain, just as some of them complained, and they were destroyed by the Devastator. All these things happened to them as examples (*typoi*), and they were written for our admonition—for us upon whom the final events of the ages have come. (1 Cor. 10:1–11)

Paul uses traditional, scriptural imagery to bring home the ethical imperative that is his principal concern in 1 Corinthians.

The reference in 1 Corinthians 10:7–8 to idolatrous eating and fornication is very much in Paul's interest within the letter as a whole. As we have seen, responsible eating and sexuality are basic among the concerns he addresses. In order to refer to them, he alludes to passages long after the story of the cloud and the sea from Exodus 13:20–14:31: the story of Aaron's idolatrous image (Exod. 32:1–6) and the story of Israelite harlotry with Moab (Num. 25 and 26:62). Various incidents associated with the exodus and the wandering in the wilderness are here united, and united without argument. Paul can rely upon the association of baptism with Passover within primitive Christian practice to invoke any materials relevant to the situation of the Corinthians within the traditions associated with Israel.

Paul cites two characteristic practices of primitive Christianity to interpret the Israel of the exodus as the Israel of faith: "All passed through the sea, and all were baptized into Moses in the cloud and in the sea. And they all ate the same spiritual food, and all drank the same spiritual drink" (1 Cor. 10:2–3). The passage through the sea (Exod. 14:16) is the type fulfilled by baptism, and the pillar of cloud and fire that guided the Israelites (Exod. 13:21–22; 14:19–24) is now the Spirit of God, into which every believer is also baptized. Likewise, the miraculous provision of food and drink in the wilderness (Exod. 16–17) is associated with the "spiritual" provision of Eucharist. Because the "rock" from which the water came is referred to more than once in the cycle of the exodus from Egypt (see Num. 20–21), Paul joins rabbinic tradition in imagining that the rock followed the Israelites, and he sees in Christ the fulfillment of the type.[3]

---

3. See *t. Sukkah* 3.11; and, for discussion, Gordon D. Fee, *The First Epistle to the Corinthians* (Grand Rapids: Eerdmans, 1987), 447–49.

The analogical thinking involved here is rather straightforward, but at every turn Paul emphasizes the tighter engagement between the believer and God than is the case of Israel during the exodus. One is baptized into the cloud, not merely guided by it, and the source of the "spiritual" food and drink is Christ himself. Implicitly, the fulfillment of the types involves a direct approach to God, not only the signs of God by means of miracle. Paul works out that implication to powerful effect in 2 Corinthians.

In 2 Corinthians, Paul works out an extensive justification of his own apostolate and at the same time spells out in classical terms how God's own Spirit in baptism quickens every believer:

> Are we beginning again to commend ourselves, or do we need (as some do) letters of recommendation to you or from you? *You are* our letter, written in our hearts, known and read by all humanity! Because you are evidently Messiah's letter, provided by us, written not by ink but by the living God's Spirit, not on stone tablets but on flesh tablets—hearts!
>
> We have such confidence through the Messiah towards God. Not that we are worthy from ourselves to account anything as from ourselves, but our worthiness is from God, who has made us worthy providers of a new covenant, not of letter but of Spirit. For the letter kills, but the Spirit makes alive. But if the provision of death, carved in stone letters, came with glory, so that the sons of Israel were unable to gaze into Moses' face on account of the glory of his face (which was fading) how will the provision of the Spirit *not* be in glory? For if there was glory for the provision of condemnation, how much more does the provision of righteousness exceed in glory! Indeed, what is glorified is not glorified in this respect: for the sake of the surpassing glory. For if what was fading was through glory, how much more is what remains in glory!
>
> So having such a hope, we employ much frankness, and not just as Moses put a veil upon his face, so the sons of Israel did not gaze on the end of what was fading. But their minds were hardened. For up until this very day, the same veil remains upon the reading of the old covenant, not disclosing that it is faded by Messiah. But until today whenever Moses is read, a veil lies on their hearts. "Whenever he turned to the Lord, he took off the veil" (Exod. 34:34). And "the Lord" is the Spirit, and where the Spirit of the Lord is: freedom! But we all—with uncovered face contemplating the Lord's glory—are transformed—from glory to glory—into the same image, exactly as from the Lord's Spirit. (2 Cor. 3:1–18)

The richness of this reading is as startling as the assurance with which Paul delivers it. Here he is writing to groups of predominantly non-Jewish Christians in the midst of a fractious debate, and Paul assumes their easy familiarity with the relevant scene from Exodus.

In that scene in Exodus 34 (vv. 29–35), Moses' direct encounter with God causes his face to shine, and the veil is used as a protection for the generality of Israel. In Paul's exegesis, however, the meaning of that gesture is transformed. Now Moses' veil is designed to cover the transience of the glory involved in the law, while the persistence of the Spirit among baptized Christians means they are being transformed into the image of the Lord who provides that Spirit.

That central transformation of the biblical image is used to reply to Paul's own critics, his apostolic competitors in Corinth. They may proffer letters of recommendation from other apostolic authorities, and they may seek such letters from the Corinthians themselves, but Paul insists that the only substance of authority is the Spirit of God. For that reason, he demotes all other forms of authority by comparison, including the law. Now he makes his most categorical statement of the position he had earlier developed in his letter to the Galatians: "Because the letter kills, but the Spirit makes alive." The problem of the legal "letter" is not so much what it says; indeed, Paul makes telling use—exactly at this point—of a precise passage from the Scripture. Its problem is rather that it is written at all, a mediated statement of the will of God.

Moses is not rightly considered to be a mediator at all. He is rather a paradigm of what is to occur as the result of faith on the part of every believer. When Moses is read, the reference to God is necessarily veiled, because it is mediated. When Moses is taken as a model of baptism, by contrast, the result is "new covenant," a phrase which enters the vocabulary of Christianity from this moment. At this point, however, what is "new" in the covenant is the fact of its direct revelation by means of the Spirit of God. It does not yet render the Scriptures of Israel "old," as will be the case in the Epistle to the Hebrews (probably written some thirty years after Paul's death). *Any* mediated revelation, any claim to authority aside from the fact of believers' reception of the Spirit, is here declared superseded.

Given the church as the revealed location of the Spirit, and his own association of those who accept baptism with the Israelites at the exodus, Paul in his correspondence with Corinth insists that belonging to the church amounts to membership in salvation. For reasons already explained, Paul held that sexual purity within the partnership with the Spirit was vitally important. The temple of the Spirit was no place for fornication (1 Cor. 6:18–20). That principle is not merely theoretical for Paul. Dealing with the issue of a member of the Corinthian congregation who has had sexual contact with his father's wife, Paul's judgment is explicit: such a one is to be handed over to Satan for destruction. "Satan" is the agent to whom one hands over a member of the community who has been expelled for final punishment:

I personally, while absent in body but present in spirit, have already judged, as though I were present, the person who has accomplished this thing in this way: in the name of the Lord Jesus, when you are gathered together, and my spirit with the power of the Lord, to deliver such a one to Satan for destruction of the flesh, so that the spirit might be saved in the day of the Lord. Your boast is not good. Don't you know that a little yeast leavens the whole dough? Cleanse out old yeast, so that you might be new dough, just as you are: unleavened. For Christ our Passover is sacrificed for us. Therefore let us keep the feast not with old yeast, neither with a yeast of depravity or wickedness, but with the unleavened bread of sincerity and truth. (1 Cor. 5:3–8)

Paul has the reputation of globally rejecting regulations of purity, and he does both set aside usual practices of restrictions on fellowship at meals and provide the guidance of intellectual reflection for the evolution of such policy. But here Paul insists that the book of Leviticus is correct: intercourse with one's stepmother is punishable by being cut off from the people (Lev. 18:8, 29), which is to say, by death (Lev. 20:11). In Paul's perspective, exclusion involves exposure to the eschatological travail which is to come, and there remains an element of hope (at least for the spirit), but the ferocity of his explicit commitment to purity in the church is quite remarkable. In this, he joins the mainstream of Hellenistic Christianity, which did not discount the importance of purity but conceived of the purity required by God as worked out in the medium of moral intention.[4]

Although Paul indeed portrays himself as supremely authoritative, the ground of that authority is the possession of God's Spirit by himself and the congregation, such that their joining together articulates divine judgment. He pursues that thought in what follows:

Do you not know that your bodies are members of Messiah? So taking the members of Messiah, shall I make them a whore's members? (1 Cor. 6:15)

Possession of the Spirit makes believers, collectively and individually, a new and literally corporate entity: the body of Messiah, Jesus Christ.

Eucharist, Baptism, and Body of Christ

Perhaps as a consequence of his association with Barnabas in the leadership of Hellenistic congregations (Antioch preeminently), Paul was

---

4. See Bruce Chilton, "Purity and Impurity," *Dictionary of the Later New Testament and Its Developments* (ed. R. P. Martin and P. H. Davids; Downers Grove: InterVarsity, 1997), 988–96.

quite familiar with the eucharistic meaning of the phrase "the body of Christ." As John A. T. Robinson pointed out in a study which remains valuable, "the words of institution of the Last Supper, 'This is my body,' contain the only instance of a quasi-theological use of the word which is certainly pre-Pauline."[5]

For Paul, Eucharist involved an active recollection of the passion: "For as many times as you eat this bread and drink the cup, you announce the Lord's death, until he comes" (1 Cor. 11:26). Paul repeats a key terms of reference within the eucharistic tradition in his own voice, and draws his conclusion ("for," *gar*), which is that the significance of the Eucharist is to be found in the death of Jesus. Drinking the cup is an act which declares that Jesus died and awaits his *parousia* at one and the same time.

Paul's assumption is that Jesus' last meal, the paradigm of the Lord's Supper, was of covenantal significance, a sacrificial "memorial" associated with the death of Jesus in particular. His wording, which refers to Jesus' cup as a new covenant in his blood (1 Cor. 11:25), agrees with the later version of Petrine tradition reflected in Luke (22:20), the Synoptic Gospel that has the strongest associations with Antioch.[6] It is likely that Paul's version of the Petrine tradition derived from his period in Antioch, his primary base by his own testimony (in Gal. 2) until his break with Barnabas.

Paul's development of the concept of "the body of Christ" was just that: a development rather than an original contribution. His commitment to the traditional theology was fierce, as he goes on in 1 Corinthians to indicate:

> So whoever eats the bread and drinks the cup of the Lord unworthily will be answerable to the body and blood of the Lord. Let a person examine oneself, and then eat from the bread and drink from the cup. For one who eats and drinks without discerning the body eats and drinks judgment against himself. For this reason, many are weak and ill among you, and quite a number have died. (1 Cor. 11:27–30)

Paul's last statement, which associates disease with unworthy participation in the Eucharist, shows how near the symbolic association of the bread and wine with Jesus' body and blood came to being a claim for the miraculous power of that food.

Long before the Johannine comparison of Jesus' flesh with the manna God gave his people in the wilderness (see John 6:32), Paul had arrived at

---

5. John A. T. Robinson, *The Body: A Study in Pauline Theology* (Studies in Biblical Theology; London: SCM, 1961), 56.

6. The wording of Matthew 26:28 and of Mark 14:24 is quite different.

the same thought. The analogy is developed in the material immediately preceding Paul's presentation of eucharistic tradition, as we have just seen (1 Cor. 10). Christ himself is presented as the typological meaning of Passover, as the entire complex of the exodus—including crossing the sea and eating miraculous food (Exod. 13–17)—is presented as "types" in 1 Corinthians 10:6. The cloud that led Israel, and the sea they crossed, correspond to baptism (vv. 1–2), while the food they ate and the water provided from the rock correspond to the Eucharist (vv. 3–4).[7] Typology also enables Paul to connect the idolatry in the wilderness and the fornication in Corinth which is one of his preoccupations (vv. 6–14), but the initial correspondence, between exodus and both baptism and Eucharist, is essential to his argument, and he labors the point with the introduction, "I would not have you ignorant, brethren . . ." (v. 1).

Within the order of Paul's exposition, the imagery begins with the cloud and the sea, proceeds through the food in the wilderness, and ends with the water from the rock; the correspondence is to the water (and Spirit) of baptism, the bread of Eucharist, and the wine of Eucharist respectively (1 Cor. 10:1–4). The typological key to the sequence is provided by Paul's own exposition of the rock from which drink flowed: "and the rock was Christ" (10:4).[8] Paul demonstrates that in Hellenistic Christianity a paschal reading of the Eucharist was an important element in a typology of Jesus himself as Passover.

It has frequently been objected that the eucharistic meaning of "the body of Christ" does not explain Paul's usage in general, because the concept of eating the body is quite different from being the body.[9] But the transition from the eucharistic meaning of the phrase to the corporate meaning of the phrase is not strained, as Paul himself indicates:

> The cup of blessing which we bless, is it not fellowship in the blood of Christ? The bread which we break, is it not fellowship in the body of Christ? Because there is one bread, we are one body, although we are many, because we all share from the one bread. (1 Cor. 10:16–17)

Paul goes on in his letters to develop that insight in many ways, and later writings in his name were to articulate the motif even further. But in the passage just cited, Paul shows us both the origin and the direction of his understanding of "the body of Christ." It begins with the Hellenistic

---

7. For a discussion, see Fee, *First Epistle to the Corinthians*, 443–50.

8. See Oscar Cullmann's article in *Theological Dictionary of the New Testament* (ed. G. Friedrich, trans. G. W. Bromiley; Grand Rapids: Eerdmans, 1979), vol. 6, 95–99, at 97.

9. See R. Y. K. Fung, "Body of Christ," *Dictionary of Paul and His Letters* (ed. Gerald F. Hawthorne, Ralph P. Martin, and Daniel G. Reid; Downers Grove: InterVarsity, 1993), 77.

theology of Eucharist, in which consuming the bread identifies the believer with Christ's death, and it consummates in the declaration that all who share that bread are incorporated into Christ, as into a single body.

The transition is natural for Paul, because he was familiar with the Hellenistic conception of a communal "body," the origin of the modern "corporation," which was especially popularized by Stoic writers. Jürgen Becker neatly summarizes the evidence:

> Agrippa M. Lanatus, for example, exhorted the plebeians not to break off fellowship with the city of Rome because, as in a human organism, all members need each other (Livy, *Ab urbe condita* 2.32–33). Plato also compares the state with an organism and, as in 1 Corinthians 12:26, emphasizes the suffering and rejoicing of the members together (Plato, *Republic* 462C–D). Seneca can see the state as the body of the emperor, who is the soul of the body (Seneca, *De clementia* 1.5.1).[10]

Becker claims that Paul "was probably the first to transfer this idea to a religious communion," but that is an incautious conclusion. Philo, after all, observes that the high priest's sacrifice welds Israel together "into one and the same family as though it were a single body" (Philo, *De specialibus legibus* 3.131).

Becker is on firmer ground in his observation that, for Paul, "the body of Christ" is not a mere metaphor but describes the living solidarity of those who share the Spirit of God by means of baptism and Eucharist. Again, Paul is the best commentator on his own thought. In 1 Corinthians 12, just after he has treated of the Eucharist, he explains in a fairly predictable way how diverse members belong to a single body. In the midst of that discussion, he puts forward the "body of Christ" as the principal definition of the church:

> For just as the body is one and has many members, and all the members of the body (being many) are one body, so is Christ. For in one Spirit we were all baptized into one body—whether Jews or Greeks, slave or free—and we all were given to drink of one Spirit. (1 Cor. 12:12–13)

By focusing on the "body" as the medium of eucharistic solidarity and then developing its corporate meaning, Paul turns the traditional, Petrine understanding of the Spirit (as received in baptism) into the single animating principle of Christian identity. His reply to any attempt to form discrete fellowships within the church will now always be, "Is Christ divided?" (so 1 Cor. 1:13).

---

10. Jürgen Becker, *Paul: Apostle to the Gentiles* (trans. O. C. Dean; Louisville: Westminster/John Knox, 1993), 428.

The further articulation of "the body of Christ" by Paul and his successors is easily traced. As in the case of 1 Corinthians 12 (and, by way of anticipation, 1 Cor. 6:15), the point in Romans 12:4–8 is that the society of those who are joined in Christ's body is itself a body which finds its unity in diversity and its diversity in unity. Two deutero-Pauline letters, Colossians and Ephesians, shift the application of the image of the body. Since in Colossians the church is seen as Christ's body (see Col. 1:18, 24), Christ himself is portrayed as the head of that body (Col. 1:18; 2:19) in order to stress his preeminence. That portrayal is extended in Ephesians (1:22–23; 4:15–16) to the point that Christ as "head" of the church can be thought of as distinct from her, as a husband is distinct from a wife (Eph. 5:21–33).

The startling thing about the Pauline conception of "the body of Christ" is not how it is developed within the Pauline and deutero-Pauline letters. That trajectory is a relatively consistent product of the interaction between the eucharistic theology of solidarity with Christ, which was common within Hellenistic Christianity, and the quasi-Stoic language of incorporation, which Paul had learned in Tarsus, his home town. The radical feature of Pauline usage is the claim that the church is defined *solely* in respect of this "body." For Jew and Greek alike, according to Paul, only incorporation into Christ mattered (1 Cor. 12:12–13). The consequence of that univocal definition is spelled out in Ephesians (after the motif of the body has been invoked): the dividing line between Jews and non-Jews had been set aside definitively in Christ (Eph. 2:11–22).

Paul's understanding of the body of Christ comports well with his definition of Israel. Just as he argued in Galatians that to believe in Christ was to fulfill the faith of Abraham, so he argued in 1 Corinthians that such faith made believers one body in Christ. The idiom of Galatians is biblical; that of 1 Corinthians is philosophical. But both letters in their differing ways implicitly raise the question of Israel. If belief fulfills the vocation of Abraham and incorporates the believer into Christ, what further value can be attached to what the Scriptures call Israel? Paul addresses that question at length in his letter to the Romans.

Paul argues carefully in Romans 9–11 that the promises of the Scriptures are fulfilled in Christ, in that "all Israel shall be saved" (Rom. 11:26). But in referring to Israel as "all" at the close of his argument, Paul makes an honest admission. That "all" includes both what he calls Israel "according to flesh" (Rom. 9:1–4), which bore the promise in advance of its fulfillment, and the Israel of faith, which is effected in baptism. His "all Israel" refers to Israel both according to the common definition and according to his own radical revision. So qualified, "Israel" designates those who are saved, but not the actual instrument of salvation. The instrument by which we are saved is incorporation into the body of

Christ, which faith effects by means of baptism and Eucharist. And in fact the commanding importance of the body of Christ frames Paul's presentation of his scriptural argument in Romans 9–11.

In Romans 6, Paul takes pains to insist upon the incorporating force of baptism:

> Or are you ignorant that as many of us as were baptized into Jesus Messiah were baptized into his death? So we were buried with him through baptism into death, in order that just as Messiah was raised from the dead through the glory of the Father, so we also might walk in newness of life. For if we have become grown together with him in the likeness of his death, yet we will also be in the likeness of his resurrection. Knowing this, that our old person was crucified together with him, so that the body of sin ceased—we no longer serve sin. For the one who has died has been justified from sin. But if we died with Messiah, we believe that we shall also live with him, knowing that Messiah raised from the dead dies no longer: death no longer has dominion over him. For what died, died to sin once for all; but what lives, lives to God. So you also, reckon yourselves dead to sin and living to God in Jesus Messiah. So do not let sin rule in your mortal body, to obey its desires, neither present your members to sin as weapons of unrighteousness, but present yourselves to God as living from the dead, and your members to God as weapons of righteousness. (Rom. 6:3–13)

Without here using the express language of "the body of Christ," Paul shows how deeply imbued he is with the thought. Baptism for him is the moment of identification with the pattern of Jesus' death and resurrection. What is received in baptism Paul goes on to call "the first fruit of the Spirit, such that believers "welcome sonship, the redemption of our bodies" (Rom. 8:23). Identifying with Christ means joining in his victory by life over death, and—at the same time—with his living triumph of the Spirit over the letter of the law.

In addition to providing insight into how Paul conceives of baptism's incorporative function, Romans also attests the astonishing range of that incorporation, as Paul understands it. One's individual bodily members are provided with a new nexus of identity. The physical estrangement from oneself that is the result of sin (elegantly depicted by Paul in Rom. 7) is overcome by dying to that constraint. The power of resurrection, effected by the Spirit in baptism, deploys one's body anew, so that one presents oneself to God as living. The emphasis in Romans 6 on being "buried with" Christ, "grown together with" Christ, "crucified together with" Christ, and the belief that one might "live with" Christ are all expressed by means of the characteristically Pauline idiom of prefixing "with" (*syn*) to various Greek verbs. They convey the deep sense of being embedded in Christ, so that the medium of one's bodily actions changes and one is "with" a new reality.

The extent of that new reality is not only individual but literally cosmic. The context in which Paul speaks of the reception of sonship in Romans 8 makes the cosmic dimension explicit and vivid:

> For the eager expectation of the creation welcomes the revelation of the sons of God. For the creation was subjected to vanity, not willingly but on account of the one who subjected it, in hope, because this creation also will be freed from the slavery of corruption for the freedom of the glory of the children of God. For we know that all creation sighs and travails together up until now. Not only so, but we ourselves have the first fruit of the Spirit, and we ourselves also sigh together in ourselves when we welcome sonship, the redemption of our bodies. (Rom. 8:19–23)

Paul's precise language is again redolent of his theology. Believers "sigh together," all creation "sighs and travails together," both expressed with the hallmark of prefixed "with" (*syn*), because what is happening individually and collectively to believers is also happening to the world at large. Christ is the secret of the universe as well as the key to human identity.

The focal point from which the transformation of individuals and the world is realized is the body of Christ. That is why Paul's entire apostolate is worked out in his service of communities of Christians. Only there, not in intellectual argument as such, can the body of Christ be realized. Once he has dealt with the question of Israel and the Scriptures in Romans 9–11, he turns to this preeminent theme:

> So I summon you, brothers, through the mercies of God, to present your bodies as a living sacrifice—holy, pleasing to God—your conscientious worship. And do not be conformed to this world, but be transformed in the renewal of the mind so that you test what the will of God is, good and pleasing and perfect. For through the grace given to me I say to everyone among you not to estimate oneself beyond what it is necessary to estimate, but to estimate oneself to think seriously, to each as God allotted a measure of faith. Because exactly as in one body we have many members, but all the members do not have the same function, so we many are one body in Messiah, each one members of one another. And we have different *charismata* according to the grace given to us, whether prophecy according to the correspondence to the faith, or service in the service, or one teaching in the teaching, or one summoning in the exhortation, the one imparting with generosity, the one leading with eagerness, the one who is compassionate with cheerfulness. (Rom. 12:1–8)

Although in Romans Paul is writing to a group of Christians with whom he had no firsthand familiarity beforehand, he assumes they understand where this sacrifice is to occur and what "the body of Christ" (which is not spelled out here as it is in 1 Corinthians) involves.

In the case of each theme—sacrifice and the body of Christ—Paul can rely on his readers' understanding. When Paul had reminded the Corinthians a year earlier of the basics of eucharistic teaching, he had said, "Because I received from the Lord what I also delivered over to you," and then he proceeded to speak of the fundamental tradition of the Lord's Supper, its sacrificial meaning, and the paramount importance of "discerning the body" in the Eucharist (1 Cor. 11:23–34). Now, in Romans 12, he truly takes for granted that his readers have received a basic catechesis (and, to judge from his argument from Scripture, something more than basic instruction, as well). The place where they are "to present your bodies as a living sacrifice" is the Eucharist, where, having been incorporated into Christ's body by baptism, and in discernment of that body, they are to offer themselves to God. Paul's words in 1 Corinthians stand as a commentary on his exhortation in Romans 12:1–2:

> For Christ our Passover is sacrificed for us. Therefore let us keep the feast, not with old yeast, neither with a yeast of depravity or wickedness, but with the unleavened bread of sincerity and truth. (1 Cor. 5:7c–8)

Eucharist is where the baptized body of Christ, individually and collectively, offers the conscientious worship of the Temple that has been created by the Spirit of God.

The discernment of that body within Eucharist is the connection that permits Paul, without apparent transition, to provide his succinct (and taken by itself, abbreviated) reference to the body of Christ in Romans 12:3–8. The brevity of his reference suggests that the theme was well established within Hellenistic Christianity, for reasons we have already discussed in our consideration of 1 Corinthians 12. The motif of the body of Christ therefore frames Paul's argument from Scripture in Romans 9–11, first in relation to baptism in chapters 6 through 8, and then in relation to Eucharist in chapter 12.

The structure of Paul's presentation, rather than an express argument, therefore signals a key transition in his theology. Although Israel was the conceptual focus of the promises of God, and remained as such throughout his thought, the body of Christ became the experiential and ethical focus of the activity of the Spirit of God within the believer, among believers, and in the world. In that regard, his thought is much less constrained by controversy than in the cases of his discussion of the covenant, Israel, or the law, because he articulated a matter of emerging consensus within the primitive church, a consensus that was to become classic.

The Theology of Rabbinic Judaism

Israel is commanded to be holy, like God. So precisely what does being holy as God is holy require? Among a variety of important and compelling responses, the following is the most germane to this context:

11. A. "You shall be holy to me, for I the Lord am holy":
    B. "Just as I am holy, so you be holy.
    C. "Just as I am separate, so you be separate."
13. A. R. Eleazar b. Azariah says, "How do we know that someone should not say, 'I do not want to wear mixed fibers, I don't want to eat pork, I don't want to have incestuous sexual relations.'
    B. "Rather: 'I do want [to wear mixed fibers, I do want to eat pork, I do want to have incestuous sexual relations.] But what can I do? For my Father in heaven has made a decree for me!'
    C. "So Scripture says, 'and have separated you from the peoples, that you should be mine.'
    D. "So one will turn out to keep far from transgression and accept upon himself the rule of heaven."

Sifra CCVII:II.11, 13

To be "Israel" is to be holy, like God, and that means to separate oneself from the world that ignores God and its ways. The positive side of sanctification comes to expression in the teaching of Rabbi Eleazar ben Azariah: to be holy is to follow the commandments neither instinctively nor on the basis of reasonable persuasion but because one accepts the rule of heaven—even if one finds God's demands unreasonable or uncomfortable. In the language of the Gospels, the corresponding terms speak of the kingdom of heaven. Here Eleazar explains what we must do to enter the kingdom of heaven: accept God's sovereignty over our lives and God's rule over the Israel—the community framed by the Torah of Sinai.

The boundaries of sanctification overspread all of life, both individual and corporate, penetrating every chapter of ordinary existence. Certainly ethical conduct took priority. Christ and Aqiba concurred that the great commandment, the encompassing principle of the Torah, is Leviticus 19:18:

A. ". . . but you shall love your neighbor as yourself: [I am the Lord]" [Lev. 19:18]:

B. R. Aqiba says, "This is the encompassing principle of the Torah."

C. Ben Azzai says, "'This is the book of the generations of Adam' [Gen. 5:1] is a still more encompassing principle."

Sifra CC:III

And so too, in an equally famous tale, the opinion of Hillel, the founder of the paramount household or school of sages:

A. There was another case of a gentile who came before Shammai. He said to him, "Convert me on the stipulation that you teach me the entire Torah while I am standing on one foot." He drove him off with the building cubit that he had in his hand.

B. He came before Hillel: "Convert me."

C. He said to him, "'What is hateful to you, to your fellow don't do.' That's the entirety of the Torah; everything else is elaboration. So go, study."

b. Shabbat 2:5 I.12/31a

It follows that ethical conduct formed the foundations of the vast construction, encompassing conduct and conviction, that accommodated holiness.

Reason and the Image of God

But to begin with, the sages addressed the most fundamental question that monotheism had to address. If, as monotheism maintained, God is wholly other, transcendent, creator but not created, then how can man hope to be like God? The sages understood the statement in Torah that man is created in God's image to mean that God and man correspond, bearing comparable traits. To begin with, God and Israel relate. They think alike. That is why Israel can grasp the Torah. They feel the same sentiments. That is why God can be represented as sharing man's attitudes and emotions, as he is throughout the Torah. Like God, man—Israelite man—is in command of, and responsible for, his own will and intentionality and consequent conduct. The very fact that God reveals himself through the Torah in terms and categories that man grasps shows how the characteristics of God and man prove comparable.

Because theology in its later, philosophical mode has long insisted on the incorporeality of God, we take up in some detail the oral Torah's explicit claim that God and man look exactly alike, sharing even corporeal traits, and are distinguished only by actions performed by the one but not the other:

> A. Said R. Hoshayya, "When the Holy One, blessed be he, came to create the first man, the ministering angels mistook him [for God, since man was in God's image,] and wanted to say before him, 'Holy, [holy, holy is the Lord of hosts].'
>
> B. "To what may the matter be compared? To the case of a king and a governor who were set in a chariot, and the provincials wanted to greet the king, 'Sovereign!' But they did not know which one of them was which. What did the king do? He turned the governor out and put him away from the chariot, so that people would know who was king.
>
> C. "So too when the Holy One, blessed be he, created the first man, the angels mistook him [for God]. What did the Holy One, blessed be he, do? He put him to sleep, so everyone knew that he was a mere man.
>
> D. "That is in line with the following verse of Scripture: 'Cease you from man, in whose nostrils is a breath, for how little is he to be accounted' [Isa. 2:22]."
>
> *Genesis Rabbah* VIII:X.1

Man—Adam—is in God's image, interpreted in a physical way, so the angels did not know man from God. Only the fact that man sleeps distinguishes him from God.

Then how does man perceive God? Beyond the words of the Torah, God makes himself manifest to man in many ways. It is quite proper, in the sages' view, to imagine God in human form; God makes himself accessible to man in ways that man can comprehend. Moreover, God may show diverse faces to various individuals. The reason for diverse understandings or descriptions of God is made explicit. People differ, and God, in the image of whom all mortals are made, must therefore sustain diverse images—all of them formed in the model of human beings:

> 3. A. Said R. Yose bar Hanina, "And it was in accord with the capacity of each one of them to listen and understand what the Word spoke with him.
>
> B. "And do not be surprised at this matter, for when the manna came down to Israel, each and every one would find its taste appropriate to his capacity, infants in accord with their capacity, young people in accord with their capacity, old people in accord with their capacity.
>
> C. "Infants in accord with their capacity: just as an infant sucks from the breast of his mother, so was its flavor, as it is said, 'Its taste was like the taste of rich cream' [Num. 11:8].
>
> D. "Young people in accord with their capacity: as it is said, 'My bread also which I gave you, bread and oil and honey' [Ezek. 16:19].

E. "Old people in accord with their capacity: as it is said, 'The taste of it was like wafers made with honey' [Exod. 16:31].

F. "Now, if in the case of manna, each and every one would find its taste appropriate to his capacity, so in the matter of the Word, each and every one understood in accord with capacity."

The same holds for God's voice:

G. "Said David, 'The voice of the Lord is [in accord with one's] in strength' [Ps. 29:4].

H. "What is written is not 'in accord with his strength in particular' but rather 'in accord with one's strength,' meaning, in accord with the capacity of each and every one.

I. "Said to them the Holy One, blessed be He, 'It is not in accord with the fact that you hear a great many voices, but you should know that it is I who [speaks to all of you individually]: 'I am the Lord your God who brought you out of the land of Egypt' [Exod. 20:2]."

Pesiqta de Rab Kahana XII:XXV

The individuality and particularity of God rest upon the diversity of humanity. But, it must follow, the model of humanity—"in our image"—dictates how we are to envisage the face of God.

But how is man most like God? It is in the capacity to know. First come shared rules of intellect, which render God and man consubstantial. God and man intellectually correspond in the common logic and reason that they share. That is in two aspects. First, like Abraham at Sodom, the sages simply took for granted that the same rationality governs. God is compelled by arguments man finds persuasive, so that man can effectively appeal: "Will not the Judge of all the world do right?" Second, meeting God through the study of the record of God's self-revelation, the Torah, the sages worked out their conviction that man's mind corresponded to God's, which is why man can receive the Torah to begin with. That man can study the Torah proves that man has the capacity to know God intellectually. That explains why they maintained that God is to be met in the study of the Torah, where his presence will come to rest. God's presence, then, came to rest with those who, in an act of intellect, took up the labor of Torah-learning:

A. R. Halafta of Kefar Hananiah says, "Among ten who sit and work hard on Torah the Presence comes to rest,

B. "as it is said, 'God stands in the congregation of God' [Ps. 82:1].

C. "And how do we know that the same is so even of five? For it is said, 'And he has founded his group upon the earth' [Amos 9:6].

> D. "And how do we know that this is so even of three? Since it is said, 'And he judges among the judges' [Ps. 82:1].
> E. "And how do we know that this is so even of two? Because it is said, 'Then they that feared the Lord spoke with one another, and the Lord hearkened and heard' [Mal. 3:16].
> F. "And how do we know that this is so even of one? Since it is said, 'In every place where I record my name I will come to you and I will bless you' [Exod. 20:24]."
>
> *m. Avot 3:6*

Here is the point at which the correspondence of man and God bears profound theological meaning. The sages took as their task not only passive learning of the Torah but also active and thoroughly critical inquiry into the meaning of the Torah. Everyone can acquire information to some extent, and most people can memorize and repeat, but the capacity to understand, perceive, even intuit—that is rare! Likewise, it is one thing to absorb the Torah, quite another to form in oneself the intellectual habits that sustain the Torah—but this is what the sages set out to do. They deliberately adopted categories of thought and patterns of argument that they saw as providing the intellectual substructure of Torah, and rejected others, because (given the premise that the Torah was written by God and dictated by God to Moses at Sinai) to do so was to enter into the very mind of God. But in discerning how God's mind worked, the sages claimed for themselves a place in that very process of thought that had given birth to the Torah, which is to say, God's plan for creation. They could debate about the Torah because, knowing how the Torah originally was written, they too could write the Torah—though, unlike God, they could not reveal it. That is, man is like God, but God is always God.

That view of man's capacity to join his mind with God's is not left merely implicit. God not only follows and joins in the sages' argument concerning the laws of the Torah conducted by sages but subjects himself to the ruling formed by their consensus—and says so. God not only participates in the debate but takes pride when his children win the argument over him. The miracles of nature cast God's ballot—which does not count over man's reason. God's judgment, as at Sodom, is outweighed by reason, which man exercises, and which takes priority in the reading of the Torah's laws even over God's judgment! The following famous story, repeated in every account of rabbinic theology, explicitly affirms the priority of reasoned argument over all other forms of discovery of truth:

> A. There we have learned: If one cut [a clay oven] into parts [so denying it its normal form as an oven] but put sand between the parts [so permitting it to function as an oven]

B. Eliezer declares the oven [broken-down and therefore] insusceptible to uncleanness. [A utensil that is broken and loses the form
in which it is useful is deemed null, and so it cannot receive the
uncleanness that pertains to whole and useful objects.]

C. And the sages declare it susceptible [because while it is formally
broken it is functionally useful, and therefore retains the status
of an ordinary utensil].

D. And this is what is meant by the oven of Akhenai [*m. Kelim*
5:10].

Up to this point we have examined only the statement of the issue, which,
as we see, concerns in practical terms the theoretical problem of what
defines an object, form or function. When an object loses its ordinary
form, it ceases to belong to its category—so the one side. But so long as
an object accomplishes that for which it is made, its teleology, it remains
within its category—so the other side. No philosopher will have found
the dispute a difficult problem to follow. But what has God to do with
all this? Now comes the answer:

E. Why [is it called] the oven of Akhenai?

F. Said R. Judah said Samuel, "It is because they surrounded it
with argument as with a snake and proved it was insusceptible
to uncleanness."

G. It has been taught on Tannaite authority:

Here come God's ballots, the miracles, and the sages' rejection of them
in favor of arguments devised by man:

H. On that day R. Eliezer produced all of the arguments in the
world, but they did not accept them from him. So he said to
them, "If the law accords with my position, this carob tree will
prove it."

I. The carob was uprooted from its place by a hundred cubits—
and some say, four hundred cubits.

J. They said to him, "There is no proof from a carob tree."

K. So he went and said to them, "If the law accords with my position, let the stream of water prove it."

L. The stream of water reversed flow.

M. They said to him, "There is no proof from a stream of water."

N. So he went and said to them, "If the law accords with my position, let the walls of the school house prove it."

O. The walls of the school house tilted toward falling.

P. Joshua rebuked them, saying to them, "If disciples of sages are
contending with one another in matters of law, what business
do you have?"

Q. They did not fall on account of the honor owing to R. Joshua, but they also did not straighten up on account of the honor owing to R. Eliezer, and to this day they are still tilted.

R. So he went and said to them, "If the law accords with my position, let the heaven prove it!"

S. An echo came forth, saying, "What business have you [contending] with R. Eliezer, for the law accords with his position under all circumstances!"

T. Joshua stood up on his feet and said, "'It is not in heaven' [Deut. 30:12]."

Here is the point at which God is told the rules of engagement: sages' reason rules, and miracles do not matter. How does God take it? The answer forms the climax of the story:

U. What is the sense of, "'It is not in heaven' [Deut. 30:12]"?

V. Said R. Jeremiah, "[The sense of Joshua's statement is this:] For the Torah has already been given from Mount Sinai, so we do not pay attention to echoes, since you have already written in the Torah at Mount Sinai, 'After the majority you are to incline' [Exod. 23:2]."

W. Nathan came upon Elijah and said to him, "What did the Holy One, blessed be he, do at that moment?"

X. He said to him, "He laughed and said, 'My children have overcome me, my children have overcome me!'"

b. Bava Metzia 59A–B

Here man is not only like God but, in context, man is equal to God because both are subject to the same logic. God is bound by the same rules of logical argument, of relevant evidence, of principled and proportionate exchange, as is man. So man can argue with the mere declaration of fact or opinion—even God's, beyond the Torah, must be measured against God's own reason, set forth, we see, within the written part of the Torah. That is why the (mere) declaration of matters by heaven is dismissed. Why? Because God is bound by the rules of rationality that govern in human discourse, and because humanity in the person of the sage thinks like God, as God does; so right is right, and nature has no call to intervene, nor even God to reverse the course of rational argument.

As the sages read the declaration of man "in our image, after our likeness," man has the capacity to imitate God. But that conviction freed the sages to represent God as doing the deeds that they know characterize man. The God in whose image and likeness man is made does what man does. Here we find how, by reason of that conviction, the sages impute to God profoundly human actions and concerns. God's deeds amply characterize the divinity as familiar by reason of man's image and likeness: here God does the deeds of man, deeds of compassion and service to those in need:

> C. Said R. Simlai, "We have found that the Holy One, blessed be he, says a blessing for bridegrooms, adorns brides, visits the sick, buries the dead, and says a blessing for mourners.
>
> D. "What is the evidence for the fact that he says a blessing for bridegrooms? As it is said, 'And God blessed them' [Gen. 1:28].
>
> E. "That he adorns brides? As it is written, 'And the Lord God built the rib . . . into a woman' [Gen. 2:22].
>
> F. "Visits the sick? As it is written, 'And the Lord appeared to him' [Gen. 18:1].
>
> G. "Buries the dead? As it is written, 'And he buried him in the valley' [Deut. 34:6]."
>
> H. R. Samuel bar Nahman said, "Also he concerns himself for the mourner. It is written, 'And God appeared to Jacob again, when he came from Paddan-aram, and blessed him' [Gen. 35:9].
>
> I. "What was the blessing that he said for him? It was the blessing for mourners."

Genesis Rabbah VIII:XIII.1

But it should be said, in the sages' own words, that the deeds of God like the deeds of man in fact should be seen in the opposite way: deeds man does in imitation of God. The particular ethical actions emphasized by sages therefore follow the model that God has provided, hence, just as rites are (merely) natural, so acts of supererogatory virtue fostered by sages, acts that produce merit, are treated as divine. What is stunning is the clear notion that God does the things virtuous mortals do, and these things are spelled out in homely terms indeed. But matters go still further. God not only acts like a human being. God also takes the form of a human being. God is incarnate in that God and mortals look exactly alike. God and man correspond; the virtuous deeds that God values in man God himself carries out.

Where are God and man consubstantial? It is, above all, in mind and at heart. They intersect not only in intellectual but also in affective capacities. A systematic statement of the matter comes to us in tractate *Avot*, ca. 250 CE, a compilation of rabbinic sages' sayings, which presents the single most comprehensive account of religious affections. These turn out to pertain to God's as much as to man's feelings. The reason is that, in that document above all, how we feel defines a critical aspect of virtue. A simple catalogue of permissible feelings comprises humility, generosity, self-abnegation, love, a spirit of conciliation, and eagerness to please. A list of impermissible emotions is made up of envy, ambition, jealousy, arrogance, sticking to one's opinion, self-centeredness, a grudging spirit, vengefulness, and the like. People should aim at eliciting from others acceptance and goodwill and should avoid confrontation, rejection, and humiliation of the other. This they do through conciliation and giving up their own claims and rights. So both catalogues form a harmonious and uniform whole, aiming at the cultivation of the humble and malleable person, one who accepts everything and resents nothing. Time and again, the compilation tractate *Avot* underscores, one who conciliates others is favored by God. God respects and honors those who freely give up what no one can demand:

> A. He would say, "Make his wishes into your own wishes, so that he will make your wishes into his wishes.
> B. "Put aside your wishes on account of his wishes, so that he will put aside the wishes of other people in favor of your wishes."
>
> *m. Avot* 2:4

If a man makes God's wishes his own, he will make the man's wishes his, and if one gives way to others, God will protect the man from the ill-will of others. God further favors those who seek to please others:

> A. He would say, "Anyone from whom people take pleasure—the Omnipresent takes pleasure.
> B. "And anyone from whom people do not take pleasure, the Omnipresent does not take pleasure."
>
> *m. Avot* 3:10

Aqiba at *t. Berakhot* 3:3 goes over the same ground: "One in whom mankind delights, God delights. One in whom mankind does not delight, God does not delight. One who is content with his own portion, it is a good sign for him. One who is not content with his own portion, it is a bad sign for him." A sequence of paradoxes—strength is marked by weakness, wisdom by the capacity to learn, wealth by making do, honor by the power to honor others—yields the picture of traits that man should cultivate and to which God will respond:

> 1. A. Ben Zoma says, "Who is a sage? He who learns from everybody,
>   B. "as it is said, 'From all my teachers I have gotten understanding' [Ps. 119:99].
>   C. "Who is strong? He who overcomes his desire,
>   D. "as it is said, 'He who is slow to anger is better than the mighty, and he who rules his spirit than he who takes a city' [Prov. 16:32].

E. "Who is rich? He who is happy in what he has, as it is said, 'When you eat the labor of your hands, happy will you be, and it will go well with you' [Ps. 128:2].

G. "('Happy will you be in this world, and it will go well with you in the world to come.')

H. "Who is honored? He who honors everybody,

I. "as it is said, 'For those who honor me I shall honor, and they who despise me will be treated as of no account' [1 Sam. 2:30]."

18. A. R. Simeon b. Eleazar says, "Do not try to (1) make amends with your fellow when he is angry,

B. "or (2) comfort him when the corpse of his beloved is lying before him,

C. "or (3) seek to find absolution for him at the moment at which he takes a vow,

D. "or (4) attempt to see him when he is humiliated."

19. A. Samuel the Small says, "Rejoice not when your enemy falls, and let not your heart be glad when he is overthrown, lest the Lord see it and it displease him, and he turn away his wrath from him [Prov. 24:17]."

m. Avot 4:1, 18, 19

These virtues derive from knowledge of what really counts, which is what God wants. But God favors those who—like God—aspire to please others. The point of correspondence then is clear: virtues appreciated by human beings prove identical to the ones to which God responds as well. And what single virtue of the heart encompasses the rest? Restraint, the source of self-abnegation, humility, serves as the antidote for ambition, vengefulness, and, above all, for arrogance. Restraint of self-interest enables us to deal generously with others; humility generates a liberal spirit towards others.

So the emotions prescribed in tractate *Avot* turn out to provide variations of a single feeling, which is the sentiment of the disciplined heart, whatever affective form it may take. And where does the heart learn its lessons, if not in relationship to God? So: "Make his wishes yours, so that he will make your wishes his" (*m. Avot* 2:4). Applied to the relationships between human beings, this inner discipline of the emotional life will yield exactly those virtues of conciliation and self-abnegation, humility, and generosity of spirit that the framers of tractate *Avot* spell out in one example after another. Imputing to heaven exactly those responses felt on earth—e.g., "Anyone from whom people take pleasure, God takes pleasure" (*m. Avot* 3:10)—makes the point at the most general level.

Do the sages mean that man and God correspond, or do they present some sort of figurative or poetic usage that represents relationships of a less tangible character than I have suggested? I should claim that the entire system of theology, with its account of world order based on God's pervasive justice and rationality, means to portray exactly how things actually are—or, with man's correct engagement, can be made to be. For the sages, we deal with the true picture of the reality that this world's corruption obscures. What we see therefore is an application of a comprehensive exercise in analogical thinking—something is like something else, stands for, evokes, or symbolizes that which is quite outside itself. It may be the opposite of something else, in which case it conforms to the exact opposite of the rules that govern that something else. The reasoning is analogical or it is contrastive, and the fundamental logic is taxonomic. The taxonomy rests on comparisons and contrasts that we should call parabolic. In that case what lies on the surface misleads, just as we saw how the sages deem superficial the challenges raised by private lives to God's justice. Conceding the depth of human suffering, the sages also pointed out that sometimes suffering conveys its own blessing. Therefore what lies beneath or beyond the surface is always the true reality. People who see things this way have become accustomed to perceiving more—or less—than is at hand.

God and man correspond in the call from the One to the other for forbearance, patience, humiliation, self-abnegation. God, disappointed with creation and challenged by gentile idolatry, corresponded with Israel, which was defeated and subjugated by the worldly dominance of those who rejected the Torah. Both, the sages maintained, dealt with failure, and both had to survive defeat. But we cannot remind ourselves too often: if God and man correspond, God is always God and man, man; they are Creator and creature. We conclude the matter of theological anthropology exactly where we ended our account of the ultimate anomaly, man's condition in the world order of justice, with the insistence that, all things having been said, man's ultimate task is silence in the face of the tremendum:

5. A. Said R. Judah said Rab, "At the time that Moses went up on high, he found the Holy One in session, affixing crowns to the letters [of the words of the Torah]. He said to him, 'Lord of the universe, who is stopping you [from regarding the document as perfect without these additional crowns on the letters]?'

   B. "He said to him, 'There is a man who is going to arrive at the end of many generations, and Aqiba b. Joseph is his name, who is going to interpret on the basis of each point of the crowns heaps and heaps of laws.'

   C. "He said to him, 'Lord of the Universe, show him to me.'

   D. "He said to him, 'Turn around.'

   E. "He went and took a seat at the end of eight rows, but he could not grasp what the people were saying. He felt faint. But when the discourse reached a certain matter, and the disciples said, 'My lord, how do you know this?' and he answered, 'It is a law given to Moses from Sinai,' he regained his composure.

F. "He went and came before the Holy One. He said before him, 'Lord of the Universe, How come you have someone like that and yet you give the Torah through me?'

G. "He said to him, 'Silence! That is how the thought came to me.'

H. "He said to him, 'Lord of the Universe, you have shown me his Torah, now show me his reward.'

I. "He said to him, 'Turn around.'

J. "He turned around and saw his flesh being weighed out at the butcher-stalls in the market.

K. "He said to him, 'Lord of the Universe, "Such is Torah, such is the reward?"'

L. "He said to him, 'Silence! That is how the thought came to me.'"

b. Menahot 3:7 II.5/29b

The sages had in mind to construct man in God's image, not God in man's.

Holiness through Halakhah

So much for the aggadic definition of what it means to be holy like God. But rabbinic theology takes normative shape in the halakhah, the concrete rules of inner life of Israel. So we ask, how does the halakhah frame in the dimensions of interiority the same conception of holiness? The goal of the system of civil law is set forth in the three "gates": *Bava Qamma* (the first gate), *Bava Metzi'a* (the middle gate), and *Bava Batra* (the last gate). These continuous expositions spell out the practical rules of the holy society of Israel in the recovery of the just order that characterized Israel upon entry into the Land, recalling the goal of the Sabbatical year *(Shevi'it)* and of the halakhah that governs land owner-ship and utilization in general.

The exposition is acutely particular, using concrete cases to set forth principles pertinent to all times and places. Through its episodic prob-lems the halakhah sets forth its main points. These aim at the preserva-tion of the established wholeness, balance, proportion, and stability of the social economy. This idea is powerfully expressed in the organization of the three tractates that comprise the civil law, each of which is com-posed of ten chapters. The first fifteen chapters (*Bava Qamma* and the first half of *Bava Metzi'a*) focus upon abnormal transactions, that is, repairing damage done to the social order. Here the framers deal with damages done by chattels and by human beings, thefts, and other sorts of malfeasance against the persons and the property of others. The civil law in both aspects pays closest attention to how the property and person of the injured party are, so far as possible, restored to normality. The second fifteen chapters (the second half of *Bava Metzi'a* plus *Bava Batra*) focus upon normal transactions, that is, acts preserving the balance and perfection of the social order. These include labor relationships, rentals and bailments, real-estate transactions, and inheritance. So attention to torts focuses upon penalties paid by the malefactor to the victim rather than upon penalties inflicted by the court on the malefactor for what he has done. Thus Israel, in its interior relationships, is governed by halakhah that establishes and maintains a perfect state in which all things are in their place and all persons and property secure.

The contents of these three tractates may also be analyzed in terms of human intentionality in the ordering of Israel's inner life. The whole of *Bava Qamma*, with its focus on damages and torts, takes up the results of wicked intentionality in the form of willful acts stemming either from malice or from flagrant neglect of duty. The rules of *Bava Metzi'a* address situations in which intentionality plays a role, is excluded as irrelevant, or may or may not enter into the adjudication of a situation of conflict. And the topics treated in *Bava Batra* take account of the idiosyncrasy of intentionality and exclude private interest from intervening in customary arrangements.

All topics covering illicit transactions involve righting the wrongs done by people on their own account. When free will is taken into account, encompassing negligence and malice, the social order requires forceful intervention to right the balance upset by individual aggression. Some licit transactions permit individual intentionality to register, specifically, those freely entered into and fairly balanced among contracting parties. And some licit transactions leave no space for the will of the participants and their idiosyncratic plans. Considerations of fairness take over and exclude any engagement with the private and the personal. It follows that Israel's social order takes account of intentionality, especially controlling for the damage that ill will brings about.

The first half of the civil law then treats intentionality as a critical factor in assessing damages, negligence representing a chapter therein. But normal licit transactions are carried forward in accord with rules of balance, proportion, and coherence that yield a society that is stable and enduring, fair and trustworthy. In the second fifteen chapters, intentionality forms only one consideration in the process of preserving the status, as to value, of parties to transactions and exchanges; it may make all the difference, no difference, some difference; it may not enter into consideration at all. That underscores the judgment of the halakhah that, when it comes to righting wrongs against chattels and persons, the malefactor has acted willfully and has therefore to be penalized in an equitable manner. By his act of will, he has diminished the property or person of the victim; he must then restore the property or person to its prior value, so far as this is possible, and may not benefit from what he has done.

In accord with the halakhah of *Bava Qamma*, man undertakes to assume responsibility for what he does, always in just proportion to causation. Within Israel's social order what God wants a man to do is take responsibility for his own actions, for the results of what he or his chattel has done—no more, no less. And that pervasive point of insistence transforms our view of the halakhic category before us. True, it forms an exercise in restoration and stasis of the just society. But in the details of the law is worked out a chapter of theological anthropology, an answer to the question, what, in the formation of the just society, can a man do? And the answer is, a man can and must take responsibility for not only what he does but also—and especially—what he brings about, the things he may not do but does cause to happen. Viewed in this way, the laws of *Bava Qamma* form a massive essay upon the interplay of causation and responsibility: what one could have prevented but through negligence (in varying measure depending on context) has allowed to take place, one is deemed (in that same measure) to have caused. And for that, one is required (in that same measure) to make amends.

Responsibility begins in right attitude. Man must form the intentionality of taking responsibility for his actions; this he must do by an act of will. That is why the whole of *Bava Qamma* plays itself out as an exercise in the definition of the valid intentionality in transactions involving damage and conflict. Where one has diminished another, he must willingly take responsibility for his deed of omission or commission. The message of the halakhah on man's taking responsibility cannot be missed in the ringing opening words of the Mishnah tractate, which link causality and responsibility:

> What they [generative causes of damages] have in common is that they customarily do damage and taking care of them is your responsibility. And when one of them has caused damage, the [owner] of that which causes the damage is liable to pay compensation. . . . In the case of anything of which I am liable to take care, I am deemed to render possible whatever damage it may do. If I am deemed to have rendered possible part of the damage it may do, I am liable for compensation as if [I have] made possible all of the damage it may do. (*m. Bava Qamma* 1:2)

That remarkably eloquent, decisive formulation contains the entire message of *Bava Qamma* and the first half of *Bava Metzi'a*.

The halakhah of *Bava Qamma,* then, portrays man in all of his dignity as possessing both free will to assume responsibility and the power to take action in consequence of responsibility. And that principle assumes religious status in two steps. First, in the words of the written Torah God himself has framed the laws that link causation and responsibility—negligence and culpability, for instance. In the very portrayal of the holy society that Israel at Sinai is commanded to realize, God's stake in man's framing of the social order is made explicit. Consequently, Israel—in the workaday transactions of one person with another—acts out in this-worldly terms the governing principle of its transactions with heaven. The one in palpable terms shows the character of the other in intangible ways.

The halakhah holds that we are responsible for what we do and what we cause, but we are not responsible (or not responsible in the same degree) for what we cannot control. So the law asks how our action or lack of action relates to consequences. If we do not know that an act has caused a result, we cannot hold the acting person responsible for the consequences. The law thus works out gradations between total culpability and total absolution from culpability: (1) responsibility for all damages done, because the event that caused loss and damage was voluntary, foreseeable, not the result of overwhelming external force, or preventable, and brought about not through mere negligence but through willful action, culpable knowledge, or deliberate choice; (2) responsibility for the greater part of the damages, because the damage was foreseeable, not resulting from overwhelming external force, and preventable, but brought about not voluntarily but through culpable ignorance; (3) responsibility for the lesser part of the damages, because the damage was foreseeable but resulted from overwhelming external force and was not preventable, involuntary, but the result of culpable ignorance and negligence; (4) no responsibility at all, the event being involuntary, the result of overwhelming external force, unforeseeable, hence coming about through inculpable ignorance, e.g., pure chance.

We therefore identify in the working out of the halakhah three operative criteria: (1) whether the action that produced an event was voluntary or involuntary; (2) whether or not the event, or the consequence of an action, was foreseeable; (3) whether the event was preventable or not; or an action necessary (and therefore blameless) or not. Thus we may construct a grid of three layers or dimensions, one grid formed of considerations of what is voluntary vs. involuntary, the second, of what is foreseeable vs. not foreseeable, the third, of what is preventable vs. not preventable. That permits us to identify an efficient cause that is voluntary, foreseeable, and preventable; voluntary, foreseeable, and not preventable; involuntary, foreseeable, and preventable; involuntary, not

foreseeable, and not preventable; and so on. These points of differentiation in the analysis of events and the actions that produce them form a
three-dimensional grid with, in theory, eight gradations of blame and
responsibility and consequent culpability.

The social order then forms an exercise in man's accepting responsibility for what he does or causes. What, in Israelite context,
marks that statement as critical to the theology of the halakhah?
To answer that question, we revert to the initial point at which the
world order of justice was disrupted by an act of man. Israel relates
to God in one way above all, namely, by exercising the God-given
power of free will in ways that show love for God and acceptance
of God's dominion. Correct the error of Eden—that time and again
turns out to form the religious statement of the halakhah, just as we
noted in connection with the halakhah of *Orlah*. The story of man's
disobedience in Eden (Gen. 3:11–13) tells why man's accepting responsibility for what he causes forms the center of the halakhah of
damages and misappropriation. Here is the original version of man's
denial of responsibility:

> *God:*   Did you eat of the tree from which I had forbidden you to eat?
> *Man:*   The woman you put at my side—she gave me of the tree
> and I ate.
> *God:*   What is this you have done?
> *Woman:* The serpent duped me and I ate.

At the center of the story of the human condition in the tragedy of Eden
is man's and woman's denial of responsibility for the deed each did, and,
implicitly, rejection of responsibility for the consequent loss of Eden.
At the heart of the halakhah of damages and misappropriation is the
opposite: Israelite man's explicit acceptance of responsibility for what
he causes. If Israel wants to show God that it is regenerate, how better
to do so than act out in cases of damages and injury the requirement
to bear responsibility for what one does and causes to happen? Here
in its everyday conduct of the inner affairs of the community, Israel
shows how, unlike Adam and Eve, Israel has through the instruction
of the Torah learned what it means to take responsibility for injury and
damage to others.

In its workaday life, in the practicalities of conflict and conflict-
resolution, Israel conducts an ongoing exercise aimed at restoring
and preserving the perfection of the status quo. The exercise makes
explicit one's responsibility for what one has caused, then apportions
damages in proportion to one's negligence or malfeasance. What is

voluntary, foreseeable, and preventable imposes maximum liability for restoration. Man can neither blame his ox nor impose upon passersby the responsibility to accommodate the obstacles he has set up in the public way. The premise of the exercise is that Israel's inner affairs, the transactions between and among Israelites, in the most practical terms, are conducted as a test of whether regenerate man—Israelite man—can bear responsibility for his own actions, now viewed in the broadest context of causation, and, if so, what it means to match levels of compensation to degrees of responsibility. No excuses ("the woman you put at my side," "the snake duped me") exculpate when one has caused damage, because Israelite man assumes the burden of his actions and takes responsibility so far as possible to restore the world to its original condition, before some deed or act of negligence of his disrupted it. I can think of no more direct response to "the woman . . . the snake . . ." than the language, "In the case of anything of which I am liable to take care, I am deemed to render possible whatever damage it may do."

In the myriad of individual transactions for which the law provides, Israel shows it has learned the lesson of Eden and applied that lesson to the social order of the Land. Why in the interiorities of relationships at home? Because it is not among strangers but within the community that workaday actions matter most. In intimacy, responsibility registers. In Eden it was before God that man was ashamed, and, in Israel, it is with one's fellow Israelite that one shows one has learned the lesson of Adam's denial. That is what is at stake in those eloquent, implacable words, which Adam should have said but Israel now does say: "In the case of anything of which I am liable to take care, I am deemed to render possible whatever damage it may do." And, in the language of the Mishnah itself: man is perpetually an attested danger whether what is done is done inadvertently or deliberately, whether man is awake or asleep. If he blinded the eye of his fellow or broke his utensils, he pays the full value of the damage he has caused. Would that Adam had said of himself to God what Israel affirms day by day and, as we see in the spinning out of the halakhah, in every way as well.

Sin, crime, torts and damages—these carry forward bad attitudes; differentiating types and degrees of intentionality when addressing how the social order is disrupted yields nothing of interest. By contrast, in treating ordinary exchanges and transactions, the halakhah turns out to form an essay on when intentionality matters and when it does not. Intentionality or attitude matters in situations of conflict. Then the attitude of both parties makes all the difference, since to resolve conflicting claims, we have in the end to conciliate all parties to a common outcome; there, intentionality or attitude forms the critical medium for restoring and sustaining balance and order. Parties to an exchange are now responsible to one another, and they must intend the outcome to be a proportionate and equal exchange of value. Both parties must accept the outcome, that is, form at the end the same attitude toward the transaction. A claim of ownership ends in an act of despair. Responsibility is proportionate to the attitude of the bailee, that is, to the degree of accountability that he has accepted to begin with. So much for the uses of intentionality in the restoration and maintenance of the social order. The upshot is clear. Sanctification means regaining the condition of Eden.

Comparing Theologies

Judaism on Christianity

Paul forthrightly addressed the issue of the this-worldly embodiment of that otherworldly, supernatural, and transcendent social entity that would everywhere and always be called by the name "Israel." He solved the problem of entering Israel without adhering to the requirements of the Torah in such a way as to adumbrate the solution to a peculiarly modern problem that has faced the Jews as a social entity: can a person be "Jewish" without being "Judaic," that is, form part of the ethnic group ("the Jewish people," or in received language, "Israel") without believing in or practicing Judaism, the religion?

Paul's solution to the identity of Israel emerges as peculiarly modern. He wants to distinguish Israel as an ethnic group from Israel as a transcendental, or supernatural community. Gentiles do not join an ethnic group when they become part of the Israel that inherits the promises of prophecy and the fulfillment of Jesus, whom Paul knew as the Christ (the Messiah), now risen from the dead and transcendent over the Torah. Paul's distinction between the ethnic character of the children of the flesh and the transcendental or supernatural character of the children after the promise has no standing in the Torah. "Israel" is, and can only be, that eternal Israel that God through the Torah at Sinai called into being.

On behalf of the authorities of Judaism who produced those documents that authoritatively interpret Scripture and set forth the whole Torah of Sinai, oral and written, I argue that in the Torah "Israel" stands for a transcendental community, a congregation formed in response to God's call and defined by God's special love: the Israel that came into being at Sinai. This Israel knows no distinction between the ethnic and the religious. The child of a Jewish mother at birth and by reason of birth belongs to this Israel. But in the case of a male, the same child is circumcised into the covenant of Abraham, our father, and becomes responsible, in due course, at maturity for carrying out the provisions of that covenant. Men and women of Israel may sin, but never lose their place in that "Israel" of which the Torah speaks. And that conception of who and what Israel is profoundly differs from Paul's, since it makes no provision whatsoever for an ethnic Israel that is distinguished from a religious one: an Israel after the flesh but not after the promise. To be Israel is to be Israel both after the flesh and after the promise, and gentiles through time find their place within that same Israel by accepting the Torah and becoming responsible to the covenant.

Christianity on Judaism

To hear God and humanity described as consubstantial, both intellectually and emotionally, is startling, since in the Christian tradition this adjective is used of the divine nature as shared by Father, Son, and Holy Spirit. The Torah's teaching of the deep affinity between God and human beings is therefore deeply resonant with Christian faith. Salvation involves becoming "participants in divine nature" (2 Peter 1:4); the influence of God's kingdom takes us beyond the conventions of this world. For that reason, when Christians explore and adapt the customs of Judaism of other religions, they are not merely dabbling or trying to ingratiate themselves. In principle, every religion might teach us about levels of engagement with God of which we would otherwise be unaware.

That is because faith goes beyond what we learn and involves the discovery of our true nature. The pattern of creation is set out in the *logos* or "Word" of God, the divine architect of all that is. The Word's architecture is fully human and the Gospel according to John in a famous passage (John 1:1–18) identifies it with Jesus Christ, who makes God fully known. Christ, the universe, and the human heart all mirror the image of God to one another.

During the second century, Justin articulated just this understanding. He describes his own development from Platonism to Christianity as a result of a conversation with an old man. The sage convinced him that the highest good which Platonism can attain, the human soul, should not be confused with God himself, since the soul depends upon God for life (*Dialogue with Trypho* 6). Knowledge of God depends rather upon the revelation of God's Spirit, as we saw in the passage quoted from *Dialogue with Trypho* 7.[11] Here is a self-conscious Christianity, which

11. See pp. 105–6 above.

distinguishes itself from Judaism and proclaims itself the true and only adequate philosophy.

Justin's account of the truth of the *logos* depends upon two sources of revelation, resonant with one another: the prophetic Scriptures, which attest the Spirit, and the wise reader, who has been inspired by the Spirit. Writing somewhat later than Justin, Clement of Alexandria also spoke of the power of the *logos* to save in terms that invoke a principle of inspiration:

> Therefore, the all-loving Word, anxious to perfect us in a way that leads progressively to salvation, observes an order well adapted to our development; at first, he persuades, then he educates, and after all this he teaches.
>
> Our Educator, you children, resembles his Father, God, whose Son he is. He is without sin, without blame, without passion of soul, God undefiled in form of man, accomplishing his Father's will. He is God the Word, who is in the Father, and also at the right hand of the Father, with even the form of God. . . .
>
> Both as God and as man, the Lord renders us every kind of service and assistance. As God, he forgives sin; as man, he educates us to avoid sin completely. Man is the work of God; he is naturally dear to him. Other things God made by a simple word of command, but man he fashioned by his own direct action and breathed into him something proper to himself.[12]

Clement sets out a precise and influential account of how the eternal Word, having been revealed to and within humanity, is in the process of transforming human nature. The God who creates also re-creates, as Clement spells out what it is to become "participants in divine nature."

The key to Clement's account, and an irreducible difference between Judaism and Christianity, is conveyed in his almost laconic remark, "Other things God made by a simple word of command, but man he fashioned by his own direct action. . . ." To Clement's mind, this means that "man, whom God made, is desirable in himself," and that leads to the climax of this section of his argument: "Man is, then, an object of his love; indeed, man is loved by God." In searching for the connection between God and humanity beyond the relationship of command and obedience, Christian thinkers drew from St. Paul's dichotomy between "works" and "faith," and provided a more precise definition of "grace" than Paul himself did. In contrast to creatures that have no awareness of God, human consciousness involves knowing God, and Christ the Educator permits us to feel how and why God loves us. That relation extends to actions, emotions, and thoughts, but the transformation oc-

12. See *Paidagōgos* 1.1.1–6 as translated in Bruce Chilton and Jacob Neusner, *Trading Places Sourcebook* (Cleveland: Pilgrim, 1997).

curs affectively in the first instance. Christianity develops the realm of grace and emotional response, where in Judaism command and will are the analogues. Christians in antiquity and today have tended to dismiss as "legalistic" any concern with the rational defense of divine commandments in the Scriptures. Their impatience is natural, once one appreciates that their entire system of religion replaces divine commandment as the center of revelation with the belief that God "breathed" into humanity "something proper to himself."

6

Sin and Atonement

"Sin" may stand for many things, but in rabbinic Judaism and classical Christianity it conforms to a single definition. It is one that, by this point, we may readily surmise. For the shared story that they tell concerning man's origins and destiny—the system and logic governing both theological constructions—dictates their definition in common of "sin." Sin can only stand for rebellion against God. And atonement then entails overcoming the effects of sin by remorse for rebellion. In rabbinic Judaism, atonement takes two forms, responding to two classifications of sin. (1) Sin may come about inadvertently, not as an act of rebellion, but without intention. That is to be expiated through an act of service, in Temple times, a sin offering for the Temple altar. Such an offering expiated unintentional sin. The Mishnah expresses this conception very clearly:

> For those [thirty-six classes of transgressions listed in the prior paragraph] are people liable, for deliberately doing them, to the punishment of extirpation, and for accidentally doing them, to the bringing of a sin offering, and for not being certain of whether or not one has done them, to a suspensive guilt offering [Lev. 5:17]. (*m. Keritot* 1:2)

(2) Sin may embody a deliberate and willful act of defiance of God. When the sinner has rebelled but then repented, atonement comes about, depending upon the seriousness of the transgression, either through the advent of the Day of Atonement, which through the very power of the Sabbath accords to creation a second chance, or through death, which atones for all sin, deliberate or otherwise. It follows that at death nearly all sinners are reconciled with God.

In Christianity the capacity of Jesus to deal with the origin and consequences of human sin puts him in a unique category. Christology is an obvious feature that distinguishes Christian theology from Judaism. The purpose and motivation of this Christological development only come into focus, however, when the plight of humanity, its inherent sinfulness, comes into view. Sin, along with Christology, becomes more a matter of nature than of function, just as the nature of Christ comes into unique focus. In the Epistle to the Hebrews, Christ's nature in relation to sin comes to its clearest expression within the New Testament. With the destruction of the Temple in 70 CE, cultic atonement was lost on the ground just as the theology of the *imitatio Christi*, already well established, was coming to maturity. As a result, Hebrews effects the replacement of the Temple by Christ—along with every other major term of reference of early Judaism.

The Theology of Rabbinic Judaism

The category *sin* serves a very particular systemic purpose. Sin explains the condition of Israel. The governing theory of Israel—that had Israel kept the Torah from the beginning, the Holy People would never have had any history at all but would have lived in a perfect world at rest and balance and order—is now invoked. There would have been nothing to write down, no history, had Israel kept the Torah. I can imagine no more explicit statement of how the world order is disrupted by sin, and, specifically, sinful attitudes, than the following:

I. 18 A. Said R. Ada b. R. Hanina, "If the Israelites had not sinned, to them would have been given only the Five Books of the Torah and the book of Joshua alone, which involves the division of the Land of Israel. How come? 'For much wisdom proceeds from much anger' [Qoh. 1:18]."

b. Nedarim 3:1 I.14–18 / 22a–b

Adam ought to have stayed in Eden. With the Torah in hand, Israel, the new Adam, ought to have remained in the Land, beyond the reach of time and change, exempt from the events of interesting times. Sin ruined everything for Adam and also for Israel, bringing about the history recorded in Scripture.

That the theology of the oral Torah spins out a simple but encompassing logic makes the character of its treatment of sin entirely predictable. God is one, omnipotent, just, and merciful. Yet where is the justice in a world governed by those who do not acknowledge God but worship idols? And what accounts for the circumstance that God's people has lost its Land and become subjugated to the gentiles? First, the system must account for imperfection in the world order of justice; sin supplies the reason. Second, it must explain how God remains omnipotent even in the face of imperfection. The cause of sin, man's free will corresponding to God's, tells why. Third, it must allow for systemic remission. Sin is so defined as to accommodate the possibility of regeneration and restoration. And, finally, sin must be so presented as to fit into the story of the creation of the perfect world. It is.

Sin and Intentionality

Defined after the model of the first sin, the one committed in Eden, sin is an act of rebellion against God. Rebellion takes two forms. As a gesture of omission sin embodies the failure to carry out one's obligation to God set forth in the Torah. As one of commission, it constitutes an act of defiance. In both cases sin comes about by reason of man's intention to reject the will of God, set forth in the Torah. However accomplished, whether through omission or commission, an act becomes sinful because of the attitude that accompanies it. That is why man is responsible for sin, answerable to God in particular, who may be said to take the matter personally, just as it is meant. The consequence of sin is death for the individual, exile and estrangement for holy Israel, and disruption for the world. That is why sin accounts for much of the flaw of creation.

When we recall that man is "in our image, after our likeness," all else follows. I have emphasized that man is like God in intellect, but there is a trait that is still more characteristic of both man and God: free will or intentionality. The climax of the unfettered intellect comes with the formation of one's own will or intentionality. If the one power in all of creation that can and does stand against the will of God is man's will or intentionality, then man bears responsibility for the flawed condition of creation, and God's justice comes to its fullest expression in the very imperfection of existence, a circularity that once more marks a well-crafted, severely logical system. But free will also forms the source of remission; God's mercy intervenes when man's will warrants. Specifically, God restores the perfection of creation through his provision of means of atonement through repentance. But that presents no anomaly but conforms to the encompassing theory of matters. For repentance represents yet another act of human will that is countered with a commensurate act of God's will. The entire story of the world from start to finish therefore records the cosmic confrontation of God's will and man's freedom to form and carry out an intention contrary to God's will. The universe is not animate but animated by the encounter of God and—in his image, after his likeness—man. This is the one story told in the oral Torah's recapitulation and completion of the written Torah.

Since sin is deemed not personal alone but social and even cosmic, explaining sin carries us to the very center of the theology that animates the oral Torah. What is at stake in sin is succinctly stated: it accounts for the deplorable condition of the world, defined by the situation of Israel. But sin is not a permanent feature of world order. It is a detail of an orderly progression, as God to begin with had planned, from chaos, which gave way to creation, to the Torah, which after the flood through Israel restored order to the world, and onward to the age of perfection and stasis. To understand that doctrine, we have first to examine the place of sin in the unfolding of creation. In the oral Torah the history of the world is divided into these three periods, indicated by Israel's relationship with God:

A. The Tannaite authority of the household of Elijah [stated], "The world will last for six thousand years:
B. "two thousand years of chaos, two thousand years of Torah,
C. "two thousand years of the time of the Messiah.
D. "But because of the abundance of our sins, what has passed [of the foreordained time] has passed."

b. Avodah Zarah 1:1 II.5/9a
[= *b. Sanhedrin* 1:1 I.89/97a]

The "two thousand years of chaos" mark the period prior to the giving of the Torah at Sinai, as God recognized the result of creating man in his image and the consequence of the contest between man's will and God's. Then come the two thousand years of Torah, which is intended to educate man's will and endow man with the knowledge to want what God wants. Then comes the time of the Messiah, of which we shall hear more in chapter 7. Now the persistence of sin has lengthened the time of the Torah and postponed the advent of the Messiah. It follows that, to understand how the sages account for the situation of the world in this age, revealing God's justice out of the elements of chaos in the here and now, we have to pay close attention to the character of their doctrine of sin.

What has already been said about sin as an act of rebellion implies that an act may or may not be sinful, depending upon the attitude of the actor, a view that our inquiry into intentionality has adumbrated. In fact, only a few actions are treated as sinful by definition. Chief among them are, specifically, murder, fornication, and idolatry. Under all circumstances a man must refrain from committing such actions, even at the cost of his own life. These represent absolute sins:

> A. Another matter: "For the earth is filled with violence" [Gen. 6:13]:
> B. Said R. Levi, "The word for violence refers to idolatry, fornication, and murder.
> C. "Idolatry: 'For the earth is filled with violence' [Gen. 6:13].
> D. "Fornication: 'The violence done to me and to my flesh be upon Babylonia' [Jer. 51:35]. [And the word for 'flesh' refers to incest, as at Lev. 18:6].
> E. "Murder: 'For the violence against the children of Judah, because they have shed innocent blood' [Joel 4:19].
> F. "Further, the word for 'violence' stands for its ordinary meaning as well."

> *Genesis Rabbah* XXXI:VI.1

Since these were the deeds of the generation that so outraged God as to bring about mass destruction through the flood, they form a class of sin by themselves. The children of Noah, not only the children of Israel, must avoid these sins at all costs. But there is a sin that Israel may commit that exceeds even the cardinal sins. Even those three are forgivable, but rejection of the Torah is not:

> A. R. Huna, R. Jeremiah in the name of R. Samuel bar R. Isaac: "We find that the Holy One, blessed be he, forgave Israel for idolatry, fornication, and murder. [But] for their rejection of the Torah he never forgave them."
> B. What is the scriptural basis for that view?
> C. It is not written, "Because they practiced idolatry, fornication, and murder," but rather, "And the Lord said, 'Because they have forsaken my Torah.'"
> D. Said R. Hiyya bar Ba, "'If they were to forsake me, I should forgive them, for they may yet keep my Torah. For if they should forsake me but keep my Torah, the leaven that is in [the Torah] will bring them closer to me.'"
> E. R. Huna said, "Study Torah [even if it is] not for its own sake, for, out of [doing so] not for its own sake, you will come [to study it] for its own sake."

> *y. Hagigah* 1:7/I:3

The intentionality or attitude of the actor determines the classification of an action even of the most severe character.

An Israelite's rejection of not God but the Torah is forthwith set into the context of will or intentionality. God does not object to insincerity when it comes to study of the Torah, because the Torah itself contains the power to reshape the will of man (as framed succinctly by sages elsewhere, "The commandments were given only to purify the heart of man," "God craves the heart," and similar formulations). The very jarring intrusion at D, developing C but making its own point, underscores that conviction. God can forgive Israel for forsaking him, because if they hold on to the Torah, they will find their way back. The Torah will reshape Israel's heart. And then, amplifying that point but moving still further from the main proposition, comes Huna's sentiment, E, that studying the Torah does not require proper intentionality, because the Torah in due course will effect the proper intentionality. Two critical points emerge. First, intentionality plays a central role in the discussion of principal sins. Second, sin ordinarily does not form an absolute but only a relative category: an action that is sinful under one set of circumstances, when the intent is wicked, is not sinful under another set of circumstances.

The variable of sin is man's intentionality in carrying out the action, not the intrinsic quality of most sinful actions (though, as we saw, not all). That fact emerges in a striking formulation of matters. Here we find a position that is quite remarkable, yet entirely coherent with the principal stresses of the theology of the oral Torah. The sages maintain that it is better sincerely to sin than hypocritically to perform a religious duty; to "sin boldly," the sages would respond, "No, rather, sincerely!" It would be difficult to state in more extreme language the view that all things are relative to attitude or intentionality than to recommend sincere sin over hypocritical virtue:

11. A. Said R. Nahman bar Isaac, "A transgression committed for its own sake, in a sincere spirit, is greater in value than a religious duty carried out not for its own sake, but in a spirit of insincerity.
     B. "For it is said, 'May Yael, wife of Hever the Kenite, be blessed above women, above women in the tent may she be blessed' [Judg. 5:24].
     C. "Now who are these women in the tent? They are none other than Sarah, Rebecca, Rachel, and Leah." [The murder she committed gained more merit than the matriarchs' great deeds.]

The saying shocks and is immediately challenged:

D. But is this really true, that a transgression committed for its own sake, in a sincere spirit, is greater in value than a religious duty carried out not for its own sake, but in a spirit of insincerity? And did not R. Judah say Rab said, "A person should always be occupied in study of the Torah and in practice of the commandments, even if this is not for its own sake [but in a spirit of insincerity], for out of doing these things not for their own sake, a proper spirit of doing them for their own sake will emerge"?

E. Say: it is equivalent to doing them not for their own sake.

Now we revert to the view that insincere Torah study and practice of the commandments still have the power to transform a man:

12. A. Said R. Judah said Rab, "A person should always be occupied in study of the Torah and in practice of the commandments, even if this is not for its own sake [but in a spirit of insincerity], for out of doing these things not for their own sake, a proper spirit of doing them for their own sake will emerge."

Now comes a concrete case of blatant insincerity's producing a reward; the Messiah himself is the offspring of an act of hypocrisy on the part of Balak, the king of Moab, the ancestor of Ruth, from whom the scion of David, the Messiah, descends:

B. For as a reward for the forty-two offerings that were presented by the wicked Balak to force Balaam to curse Israel, he was deemed worthy that Ruth should descend from him.

C. For said R. Yose b. R. Hanina, "Ruth was the granddaughter of Eglon, the grandson of Balak, king of Moab."

b. Horayot 3:1–2 I.11/10b

The upshot is, as we already realize, intentionality is everything; sin is rarely absolute but ordinarily conditioned upon the attitude of the actor; and sincerity in sin exceeds in merit hypocrisy in virtue.

Since the sages identify emotions and feelings, attitudes and intentions, as the source of both virtue and sin, we may hardly find surprising their explanation of sin as the result of emotions that generate wrong attitudes. For the sages do not suppose that man is a creature only of reasoned reflection; rebellion comes about not only after intellection but also by reason of wrong emotions, which yield sin. Chief among these are losing one's temper and losing composure. The composite on losing one's temper sets forth the basic theory that people who lose their temper take vows. That is regarded as a sin.

I. 14 A. Said R. Samuel bar Nahman said R. Yohanan, "Whoever loses his temper—all the torments of Hell rule over him: 'Therefore remove anger from your heart, thus will you put away evil from your flesh' [Qoh. 11:10], and the meaning of 'evil' is only Hell: 'The Lord has made all things for himself, yes, even the wicked for the day of evil' [Prov. 16:4]. Moreover, he will get a belly ache: 'But the Lord shall give you there a trembling heart and failing of eyes and sorrow of mind' [Deut. 28:65]. And what causes weak eyes and depression? Stomach aches."

The explicit involvement of God's presence in the situation is stated as follows:

I. 16 A. Said Rabbah bar R. Huna, "Whoever loses his temper—even the Presence of God is not important to him: 'The wicked, through the pride of his countenance, will not seek God; God is not in all his thoughts' [Ps. 10:4]."

Sages lose their knowledge of the Torah by reason of ill temper:

I.17 A.R. Jeremiah of Difti said, "[Whoever loses his temper]—he forgets what he has learned and increases foolishness: 'For anger rests in the heart of fools' [Qoh. 7:9], and 'But the fool lays open his folly' [Prov. 13:16]."
   B. R. Nahman bar Isaac said, "One may be sure that his sins outnumber his merits: 'And a furious man abounds in transgressions' [Prov. 29:22]."

b. Nedarim 3:1 I.14ff./22a–b

Losing one's temper marks a man as unlettered, an indication that, if he knew the Torah, he has forgotten it. But, we should not find surprising, the sages deemed even ill temper to be subject to remissions. Losing composure in general is deplorable, but doing so when a sage dies is praiseworthy.

The rabbinic sages formulate the theology of sin within a larger theory of the character of man. If man is like God, then theological anthropology must explain how it is that man's will does not correspond with, but rebels against, the will of God. Here man's free will requires clarification. Man and God are possessed of free will. But man's free will encompasses the capacity to rebel against God, as we know, and that comes about because innate in man's will is the impulse to do evil, *yetser hara* in Hebrew. Man then corresponds to God but is complex, comprised as he is of conflicting impulses, whereas God is one and unconflicted.

That impulse within man to do evil struggles with man's impulse to do good, *yetser hattov*. The struggle between the two impulses in man then corresponds with the cosmic struggle between man's will and God's word. But creation bears within itself the forces that ultimately will resolve the struggle. That struggle will come to an end in the world to come, which itself comes about by an act of divine response to human regeneration, as we shall see in due course.

> G. [The answer] is in accord with the exposition of R. Judah:
>   "In the world to come, the Holy One, blessed be he, will bring the evil inclination and slay it before the righteous and before the wicked.
> H. "To the righteous the evil inclination will look like a high hill, and to the wicked it will appear like a hair-thin thread.
> I. "These will weep, and those will weep.
> J. "The righteous will weep, saying, 'How could we ever have overcome a hill so high as this one!'
> K. "The wicked will weep, saying, 'How could we not have overcome a hair-thin thread like this one!'
> L. "And so too the Holy One, blessed be he, will share their amazement, as it is said, 'Thus says the Lord of Hosts. If it be marvelous in the eyes of the remnant of this people in those days, it shall also be marvelous in my eyes' [Zech. 8:6]."
>
> *b. Sukkah* 5:1D II.3–4/52a

The stress on the relative, not absolute, character of sin finds its counterpart here.

> 4. A. Said R. Assi, "The inclination to do evil to begin with is like a spider's thread and in the end like cart ropes.
>   B. "For it is said, 'Woe to them who draw iniquity with cords of vanity and sin as with cart ropes' [Isa. 5:18]."

Everything, therefore, depends upon man himself. Since the sages explain large and small things in the same way, encompassing within their theology both the condition of Israel and the character of the individual Israelite, we may not find surprising the dimensions of activity of the impulse to do evil, individual persons, sages in particular, Israel in general.

What about the gentiles—why do they sin? What is striking in the following is that the impulse to do evil does not attack the nations of the world but only Israel, and, within Israel, predictably, sages of the Torah are a prime target, or, in other language, are possessed of a greater *yetser hara* than ordinary folk:

7. A. Our rabbis have taught on Tannaite authority:
    B. "But I will remove far away from you the hidden one" [Joel 2:20] speaks of the impulse to do evil, which is ready and hidden away in a man's heart.
    C. "And I will drive it into a land barren and desolate" [Joel 2:20] speaks of a place in which are found no men against whom it may make an attack.
    D. "With his face toward the eastern sea" [Joel 2:20]: For it set its eyes against the first sanctuary and destroyed it and killed the disciples of sages who were there.
    E. "And his hind part toward the western sea" [Joel 2:20]: For it set its eyes against the second sanctuary and destroyed it and killed the disciples of sages who were there.
    F. "That its foulness may come up and its ill-savor may come up" [Joel 2:20]: For he neglects the nations of the world and attacks only Israel.

b. Sukkah 5:1D II.7/52a

That is not to say the nations do not sin; but when they sin against God, it is through idolatry; their sins are scarcely differentiated, except in relationship to Israel.

Here is the crux of the matter: man by nature is sinful but only by encounter with the Torah knows how to do good. That explains why the gentiles, with idolatry in place of the Torah, in the end cannot overcome their condition but perish, while Israel, with Torah the source of life, will stand in judgment and enter eternal life, as we shall see fully spelled out in chapter 7. The key to man's regeneration lies in the fact that Israel, while part of humanity and by nature sinful, possesses the Torah. That is how and where Israel may overcome its natural condition. Herein lies the source of hope. Gentiles enjoy this world but have no hope of regeneration in the world to come. Here three distinct components of the theology of the oral Torah—theological anthropology, the doctrine of sin, and eschatology—intersect to make a single coherent statement accounting for the destiny of the whole of humanity.

Repentance and Atonement

From the definition of sin, both public and personal, we turn to its consequences, once more noting the correspondence between the costs of sin to the individual and those exacted from holy Israel all together. In both cases sin exacts a two-sided penalty. The sinner, acting out of arrogance, is diminished; the sinner, defying God, is cut off from God. That applies, in so many words, to both the private person and all Israel. So what the person sought—aggrandizement through rebellion against God's will—he does not gain, but what he did not want—diminution—is what he gets. Thus with regard to seeking to feed one's arrogance: before a person sins, people pay reverence and awe to him, but once the person sins, he must subjugate himself and so pay reverence and awe to others:

> 3. A. R. Ishmael taught on Tannaite authority, "Before a man has sinned, people pay him reverence and awe. Once he has sinned, they impose on him reverence and awe."

This is spelled out in the case of Adam:

> B. "Thus, before the first man had sinned, he would hear [God's] voice in a workaday way. After he had sinned, he heard the same voice as something strange. Before he had sinned, the first man heard God's voice and would stand on his feet: 'And they heard the sound of God walking in the garden in the heat of the day' [Gen. 3:8]. After he had sinned, he heard the voice of God and hid: 'And man and his wife hid' [Gen. 3:8]."
> C. Said R. Aibu, "At that moment the height of the first man was cut down and he became a hundred cubits high."

Now we turn to Israel, which found itself diminished:

> D. [Ishmael continues:] "Before the Israelites sinned, what is written in their regard? 'And the appearance of the glory of the Lord was like a consuming fire on the top of the mountain before the eyes of the children of Israel' [Exod. 24:17]."
> E. Said R. Abba bar Kahana, "There were seven veils of fire, one covering the next, and the Israelites gazed and did not fear or take fright."
> F. "But when they had sinned, even on the face of the intercessor [Moses] they could not look: 'And Aaron and all the children of Israel feared . . . to come near' [Exod. 34:30]."

We turn next to David, then Solomon, and finally Saul:

> 5. A. "Before the deed of David [with Bath Sheba] took place, what is written? 'For David: The Lord is my light and my salvation, of whom shall I be afraid?' [Ps. 27:1].
> B. "But after that deed took place, what is written? 'I will come upon him while he is weary and weak-handed' [2 Sam. 17:2].
> 6. A. "Before Solomon sinned, he could rule over demons and demonesses: 'I got for myself . . . Adam's progeny, demons and demonesses' [Qoh. 2:8].

    B. "What is the sense of 'demons and demonesses'? For he ruled over demons and demonesses.

    C. "But after he had sinned, he brought sixty mighty men to guard his bed: 'Lo, the bed of Solomon, with sixty mighty men around it, all of them holding a sword and veterans of war' [Song 3:7–8].

7. A. "Before Saul had sinned, what is written concerning him? 'And when Saul had taken dominion over Israel, he fought against all his enemies on every side, against Moab, against the Ammonites, against Edom, against the kings of Zobah, and against the Philistines; wherever he turned he put them to the worse' [1 Sam. 14:47].

    B. "After he had sinned what is written concerning him? 'And Saul saw the camp of the Philistines and was afraid' [1 Sam. 28:5]."

Pesiqta de Rab Kahana V:III.3ff.

The cases validate the proposition that sin weakens the sinner; various figures are shown to have been strong prior to sin but afterward weak. The composition of the list—Adam, Israel, David, Solomon, Saul—does not on its own suggest that the point common to the entries is the one that is made. But a second look shows that joining these particular names yields the proposition at hand.

If the sages' theology builds upon the foundation of God's justice in creating a perfect world and accounts for the imperfections of the world by appeal to the conflict of man's will and God's plan, then, we must ask ourselves, what is the logical remedy for the impasse at which Israel and the world find themselves in the present age? How, specifically, is sin to be overcome? The sages' explanation for flaws and transience in creation, sin brought about by the free exercise of man's will, contains within itself the systemic remission—that required, logical remedy for the human condition and creation's as well. It is an act of will to bring about reconciliation between God and Israel, God and the world. And that act of will on man's part will evoke an equal and commensurate act of will on God's part. When man repents, God forgives, and Israel and the world will attain that perfection that prevailed at Eden. And that is why death will die. So we come to the account of restoring world order. Here we begin to follow the unfolding of the restorationist eschatology that completes and perfects the sages' theology set forth in the documents of the oral Torah. All begins with the act of will embodied in repentance, leading to atonement and reconciliation.

The logic of repentance is simple and familiar. It is a logic that appeals to the balance and proportion of all things. If sin is what introduces rebellion and change, and the will of man is what constitutes the variable in disrupting creation, then the theology of the oral Torah makes provision for restoration through the free exercise of man's will. That requires an attitude of remorse, a resolve not to repeat the act of rebellion, and a good-faith effort at reparation: in all, a transformation from rebellion against God's will to obedience. So with repentance we come once more to an exact application of the principle of measure for measure—here, will for will—each comparable to, corresponding with, the other. World order, disrupted by an act of will, regains perfection through an act of will that complements and corresponds to the initial, rebellious one. That is realized in an act of willful repentance (Hebrew *teshuvah*).

In the oral Torah repentance, a statement of regret and remorse for the sin one has committed and hence an act of will, effects the required transformation of man and inaugurates reconciliation with God. Through a matched act of will, now in conformity with God's design for creation, repentance therefore restores the balance upset by man's act of will. So the act of repentance, and with it atonement, takes its place within the theology of perfection, disruption, and restoration, that all together organizes—shows the order of—the world of creation.

Apology does not suffice; an atoning act also is required. That is why repentance is integral to the categories atonement and Day of Atonement. The one in the cult, the other in the passage of time, respond to the change of will with an act of confirmation, on God's part, that the change is accepted, recognized, and deemed affective. That is because, through the act of repentance, a person who has sinned leaves the status of sinner but must also atone for the sin and gain forgiveness, so that such a person is no longer deemed a sinner. Self-evidently, within a system built on the dialectics of competing wills, God's and man's, repentance comes first in the path to reconciliation. That is because the act of will involves a statement of regret or remorse, a resolve never to repeat the act, and, finally, the test of this change of heart or will (where feasible). Specifically, it is a trial of entering a situation in which the original sin is possible but is not repeated. Then the statement of remorse and voluntary change of will is confirmed by an act of omission or commission, as the case requires.

Repentance then is a declaration and act of will, proclaiming that an act of rebellion brings remorse, an effort to show goodwill in place of bad will. Followed by atonement, therefore, repentance commences the work of closing off the effects of sin: history, time, change, inequity. It marks the beginning of the labor of restoring creation to Eden: the perfect world as God wants it and creates it. Since the Hebrew word *teshuvah* is built out of the root for "return," the concept is generally understood to mean "returning to God from a situation of estrangement." The turning is not only from sin but toward God, for sin serves as an indicator of a deeper pathology, which is utter estrangement from God—man's will alienated from God's.

Teshuvah then involves not humiliation but reaffirmation of the self in God's image, after God's likeness. It follows that repentance forms a theological category encompassing moral issues of action and attitude: wrong action, arrogant attitude. Repentance forms a step in the path to God that starts with the estrangement represented by sin: doing what I want, instead of what God wants, thus rebellion and arrogance. Sin precipitates punishment, whether personal for individuals or historical for nations; punishment brings about repentance for sin, which in turn leads to atonement for sin and consequently reconciliation with God. That sequence of stages in the moral regeneration of sinful humanity, individual or collective, defines the context in which repentance finds its natural home.

True, the penitent corrects damage actually inflicted on his fellow man. But apart from reparations, the act of repentance involves only the attitude, specifically substituting feelings of regret and remorse for the arrogant intention that lead to the commission of the sin. If the person declares regret and undertakes not to repeat the action, the process of repentance gets under way. When the occasion to repeat the sinful act arises and the penitent refrains from doing it again, the process comes to a conclusion. So it is through the will and attitude of the sinner that the act of repentance is realized; the entire process is carried on beyond the framework of religious actions, rites, or rituals. The power of repentance overcomes sins of the most heinous and otherwise unforgivable character. The following is explicit that no sin overwhelms the transformative power of repentance:

> A. A Tannaite statement:
> B. Naaman was a resident proselyte.
> C. Nebuzaradan was a righteous proselyte.
> D. Grandsons of Haman studied Torah in Bene Beraq.
> E. Grandsons of Sisera taught children in Jerusalem.
> F. Grandsons of Sennacherib taught Torah in public.
> G. And who were they? Shemaiah and Abtalion.

b. Gittin 5:6 I.26/57b

Shemaiah and Abtalion are represented as the masters of Hillel and Shammai, who founded the houses dominant in many areas of the halakhah set forth in the Mishnah and related writings. The act of repentance transforms the heirs of the destroyers of Israel and the Temple into the framers of the redemptive oral Torah. A more extreme statement of the power of any attitude or action defies imagining—even the fact of our own day that a distant cousin of Adolph Hitler has converted to Judaism and serves in the reserves of the Israel Defense Army.

That to such a remarkable extent God responds to man's will, which time and again has defined the dynamics of complementarity characteristic of the oral Torah's theology, accounts for the possibility of repentance. As much as mercy completes the principle of justice, so repentance forms the complement to sin; without mercy, represented here by the possibility of repentance, justice as God defines justice cannot endure. For were man to regret sin and see things in God's way without a corresponding response from God, God would execute justice but not mercy, and, from the sages' perspective, the world would fall out of balance. To them, therefore, it is urgent that God have his own distinctive message to the sinner, separate from the voices of Wisdom, of Prophecy, and even of the Pentateuch (the Torah narrowly defined):

> A. Said R. Phineas: "'Good and upright [is the Lord; therefore he instructs sinners in the way]' [Ps. 25:8].
> B. "Why is he good? Because he is upright.
> C. "And why is he upright? Because he is good.
> D. "'Therefore he instructs sinners in the way'—that is, he teaches them the way to repentance."

Now we interrogate the great compendia of God's will—Wisdom and Prophecy—then turn to God himself, and ask how to treat the sinner:

> E. They asked wisdom, "As to a sinner, what is his punishment?"
> F. She said to them, "Evil pursues the evil" [Prov. 13:21].
> G. They asked prophecy, "As to a sinner, what is his punishment?"
> H. She said to them, "The soul that sins shall die" [Ezek. 18:20].
> I. They asked the Holy One, blessed be he, "As to a sinner, what is his punishment?"
> J. He said to them, "Let the sinner repent, and his sin will be forgiven for him."
> K. This is in line with the following verse of Scripture: "Therefore he instructs sinners in the way" [Ps. 25:8].
> L. "He shows the sinners the way to repentance."

> *y. Makkot* 2:6 I:4/10a

The response of wisdom presents no surprise; it is the familiar principle of measure for measure, and prophecy concurs, but God has something more to say. Accordingly, the proposition concerns the distinctive mercy of God, above even the Torah. The data for the composition, lines E–L, respond to the question that is addressed to the components of the Torah, that is, what does prophecy say about the punishment of the sinner? But the question is prior, and the question forms part of the systemic plan: to demonstrate the uniquely merciful character of God, the way in which God is God.

But the power of repentance is disproportionate, out of all balance with sin in a way in which the penalty for sin never exceeds the gravity of the sin. We may say that, while, when it comes to sin, God effects exact justice, when it comes to repentance, God accords mercy out of all proportion to the arrogance of the act of rebellion, an idea already familiar. The act of will that is represented by repentance vastly outweighs in effect the act of will that brings about sin. That is because one may commit many sins, but a single act of repentance encompasses them all and restores the balance that those sins all together have upset. So repentance makes sense, in its remarkable power, only in the context of God's mercy. It follows that any account of repentance and atonement must commence with a clear statement of God's mercy, the logical precondition for the act of repentance.

Now as to the matter of divine mercy, God's mercy vastly exceeds his justice, so when God metes out reward, he does so very lavishly, thus *t. Sotah* 4:1: "I know only with regard to the measure of retribution that by that same measure by which a man metes out, they mete out to him [*m. Sotah* 1:7A]. How do I know that the same is so with the measure of goodness?" God's power to forgive sin, however formidable, and to reward virtue, however slight, is expressed in his acts of mercy. And the mercy of God comes to expression in his deeds:

A. "The Lord is good to all, and his tender mercies are over all his works" [Ps. 145:9]:

B. Said R. Joshua b. Levi, "'The Lord is good to all, and his tender mercies are over all, for they are his works.'"

C. Said R. Samuel bar Nahman, "'The Lord is good to all, and his tender mercies are over all, for lo, by his very nature, he extends mercy.'"

D. R. Joshua in the name of R. Levi: "'The Lord is good to all, and out of his store of tender mercy he gives [mercy] to his creatures.'"

E. R. Abba said, "Tomorrow a year of scarcity will come, and people will show mercy to one another, on account of which the Holy One, blessed be he, is filled with mercy for them."

Genesis Rabbah XXXIII:III.1f.

The attitude of mercy that characterizes God must shape man's will, and that comes about when man needs mercy from heaven and learns out of necessity to show mercy to other men. When God sees men treating one another mercifully, then God responds with an act of mercy of his own.

Repentance is the precondition of atonement; there is no atonement without the statement of remorse and appropriate confirming action.

But atonement on its own must follow. Atonement comes about through diverse means, but the principal ones are the Day of Atonement, Yom Kippur—"For on this day atonement shall be made for you to cleanse you of all your sins" (Lev. 16:30)—and the death of the sinner. The former, the Day of Atonement, is explicitly designated for its purpose by Moses. But an attitude, an act of will, still forms a precondition. One may not "atone preemptively," that is, sin in full intention that the Day of Atonement will make things up. That is stated in so many words, as follows:

> A. He who says, "I shall sin and repent, sin and repent"—
> B. they give him no chance to do repentance.
> C. [If he said,] "I will sin and the Day of Atonement will atone,"—the Day of Atonement does not atone.
> D. For transgressions done between man and the Omnipresent, the Day of Atonement atones.
> E. For transgressions between man and man, the Day of Atonement atones, only if the man will regain the good will of his friend.

> *m. Yoma* 8:9

The Day of Atonement itself does not work *ex opere operato* but only within the framework of qualifying (or at least not disqualifying) intentionality. And that fact generates another. If one rebels against God's rule and does not repent, no atonement is possible. But if he does repent, then the Day of Atonement effects atonement for him, so

> D. Rabbi says, "For all of the transgressions that are listed in the Torah, whether one has repented or not repented, the Day of Atonement attains atonement, except for one who breaks the yoke [of the kingdom of heaven from himself, meaning, denies God] and one who treats the Torah impudently, and the one who violates the physical mark of the covenant. In these cases if one has repented, the Day of Atonement attains atonement, and if not, the Day of Atonement does not attain atonement."

Now come the facts to validate the proposition:

> E. What is the scriptural basis for the position of Rabbi?
> F. It is in line with that which has been taught on Tannaite authority:
> G. "Because he has despised the word of the Lord": This refers to one who is without shame in interpreting the Torah.
> H. "And broken his commandment": This refers to one who removes the fleshly marks of the covenant.

I. "That soul shall utterly be cut off." "Be cut off"—before the Day of Atonement. "Utterly"—after the day of atonement.

J. Might one suppose that that is the case even if he has repented?

K. Scripture says, "his iniquity shall be upon him" [Num. 15:31]—I say that the Day of Atonement does not effect atonement only when his iniquity is still upon him.

The contrary view invokes the same facts but interprets them differently:

L. And rabbis?

M. "That soul shall utterly be cut off." "Be cut off"—in this world. "Utterly"—in the world to come.

N. "His iniquity shall be upon him" [Num. 15:31]—if he repented and died, death wipes away the sin.

b. Shevu'ot 1:1ff. XVI.2/13A

What is reconciled is the atoning power of the Day of Atonement with the intransigence of the sinner. How to explain the limits of the one in the face of the other? The answer lies in the power of repentance or of failure to repent, which explains when the Day of Atonement atones or fails. When faced with the possible conflict between the power of the Day of Atonement and the enormity of sins against heaven itself, the resolution lies in invoking the matter of intentionality, expressed through the act of repentance or the failure to perform that act.

So much for the Day of Atonement, which is, as we say, contingent. But death is something else; it happens willy-nilly. Death marks the final atonement for sin, which bears its implication for the condition of man at the end. Because one has atoned through sin (accompanied at the hour of death by a statement of repentance, "May my death be atonement for all my sins," in the liturgy in due course), when he is raised from the dead, his atonement for all his sins is complete. The judgment after resurrection becomes for most a formality. That is why "all Israel has a portion in the world to come," with the exception of a few whose sins are not atoned for by death, and that is by their own word. The Day of Atonement provides atonement, as the written Torah makes explicit, for the sins of the year for which one has repented, and that accounts for the elaborate rites of confession that fill the day.

Here is how the media of atonement through death (for a lifetime) and the Day of Atonement (for the year just past) are sorted out:

A. A sin offering and an unconditional guilt offering atone.

B. Death and the Day of Atonement atone when joined with repentance.

C. Repentance atones for minor transgressions of positive and negative commandments.

D. And as to serious transgressions, [repentance] suspends the punishment until the Day of Atonement comes along and atones.

m. Yoma 8:8

The first statement sorts out the workings of repentance, death, the Day of Atonement, and atonement. We see that repentance on its own serves for the violation of commandments, for that involves God; when another man is involved in a man's sin, then the this-worldly counterpart to repentance, which is reparation and reconciliation, is required. The formulation underscores the tight weaving of the several components of a single tapestry. The beginning of the definition of repentance lies in the contrasting means of atonement for unintentional and intentional sin. For unintentional sin, an offering at the Temple in Jerusalem suffices. For deliberate sin, the necessary first step is a change of attitude: *teshuvah*, repentance.

So by "atonement" the sages understand an act or event (death or the Day of Atonement in particular) that removes the effects of sin by bringing about God's forgiveness of sin. The forms of the Hebrew based on the root KPR do not exhaust the category, for any action that produces the result of removing the effect of a sin will fit into that category, whether or not labeled an act of *kapparah*. The written Torah speaks of atoning offerings in the Temple. Atonement in this age, without the Temple and its offerings, is accomplished through charity:

And said R. Eleazar, "When the Temple stood, someone would pay off his sheqel-offering and achieve atonement. Now that the Temple is not standing, if people give to charity, well and good, but if not, the gentiles will come and take it by force. And even so, that is still regarded for them as an act of righteousness: 'I will make your exactors righteousness' [Isa. 60:17]." (*b. Bava Batra* 1:5 IV.23/9a)

The principal categorical component is the atonement brought about by the advent of the Day of Atonement. So, for instance, on that day the high priest, representing all Israel, brings about atonement through the rites of the Day of Atonement, beginning with the confession. Scripture presents diverse facts on a given sin, the penalty thereof, and the media of remission of the penalty, and reason and exegesis then make possible the classification of those facts into a coherent whole:

4:6 A. R. Ishmael says, "There are four kinds of atonement.

B. "[If] one has violated a positive commandment but repented, he hardly moves from his place before they forgive him,

    C. "since it is said, 'Return, backsliding children. I will heal your backsliding' [Jer. 3:22].

4:7 A. "[If] he has violated a negative commandment but repented, repentance suspends the punishment, and the Day of Atonement effects atonement,

    B. "since it is said, 'For that day will effect atonement for you' [Lev. 16:30].

4:8 A. "[If] he has violated [a rule for which the punishment is] extirpation or death at the hands of an earthly court, but repented, repentance and the Day of Atonement suspend [the punishment], and suffering on the other days of the year will wipe away [the sin],

    B. "since it says, 'Then will I visit their transgression with a rod' [Ps. 89:32].

    C. "But he through whom the Name of Heaven is profaned deliberately but who repented—repentance does not have power to suspend [the punishment], nor the Day of Atonement to atone,

    D. "but repentance and the Day of Atonement atone for a third, suffering atones for a third, and death wipes away the sin, with suffering,

    E. "and on such a matter it is said, 'Surely this iniquity shall not be purged from you until you die' [Isa. 22:14]."

t. Kippurim 4:6–8

The four kinds of atonement are worked out in their own systematic and logical terms, but the verses of Scripture then contribute to the validation of the classification scheme. There is a grid established by positive and negative commandments, intersecting with the matter of repentance; then there is the grid established by the kind of penalty—extirpation or the earthly court's death sentence; here repentance and the Day of Atonement form the intersecting grid; and then there is the matter of the profanation of the divine name, in which case repentance and the Day of Atonement come into play along with suffering and death. So the point of differentiation is established by appeal to the type of sin, on the one side, and the pertinent penalties, on the second, and the effects of media of atonement—repentance, death, Day of Atonement, suffering. The entire complex exhibits the traits of mind that we have met many times: systematic classification by indicative traits, an interest in balance, order, complementarity, and commensurate proportionality.

Clearly, then, what is at stake in repentance and atonement vastly transcends issues of this world. Time and again we have noted that repentance, along with atonement, forms the condition of the restoration of world order. Even in the here and now, Israel is able through repentance to reconcile itself with God, and in God's own time, the reconciliation—Israel's will now voluntarily conforming to God's word—will mark the end of the world as man knows it and the beginning of the time of restoration. That is why repentance forms the bridge between the analysis of the imperfection of world order and the account of the restoration of world order at the last. In so many words repentance is linked to the salvation of the individual Israelite and the redemption of Israel, for these mark the return to Eden.

And so we find that repentance is required if one is to be resurrected at the end of time and gain a portion in the world to come:

> A. Said R. Jonah in the name of R. Hama bar Hanina, "One who dies during the seven year [battle of] Gog [Ezek. 38–39] [so as not to suffer fully the troubles of the nation] does not have a portion in the coming world.
> B. "The mnemonic sign for this is: 'One who takes part in the wedding preliminaries will [also] have a share in the wedding feast.'" [But whoever is not involved in the preliminaries does not have a part in the feast.]
> C. R. Yose heard [this] and said, "Now, is this really true?
> D. "[For] there is always repentance [as a method of earning a place in] the world to come." [This applies even if the individual has not suffered along with the Israelite nation.]
>
> _y. Shevi'it_ 4:10 VI
> [Translation by Alan J. Avery-Peck]

The act of repentance joined to atonement, whether by the Great Sabbath (as the Day of Atonement is called, a clear reference to the Sabbath of creation, since man now enjoys a new beginning) then serves to secure the victory over death represented by resurrection and consequent entry into the world to come—a considerable result.

The Theology of Classical Christianity

The Epistle to the Hebrews has long stood as an enigma within the New Testament. "Who knows who wrote the Epistle?" asked Origen in the third century; he answered the question himself, "God knows!" But the enigma of Hebrews goes beyond the question of who wrote it; when and where it was written, as well as to whom, are also issues of lively debate. But all those issues become vital, because Hebrews sets out the classical teaching of sin and atonement in Christianity.

It is natural to wish to answer the historical and literary questions the Epistle raises as clearly as possible, but it is even more vital not to permit them to obscure the essential clarity of Hebrews' contribution. Origen himself valued the Epistle as the work of a follower of Paul's (such as

Luke or Clement of Rome). In North Africa, Tertullian described it as having been written by Barnabas, not Paul, but reported it was "more widely received among the churches than the *Shepherd [of Hermas],*" one of the most popular works among Christians of the second century. B. F. Westcott, perhaps the greatest commentator in English on Hebrews, provides the key to why the Epistle was accepted as canonical, doubts regarding its authorship aside, "no Book of the Bible is more completely recognised by universal consent as giving a divine view of the facts of the Gospel, full of lessons for all time, than the Epistle to the Hebrews."[1] "A divine view of the facts of the Gospel" is just what Hebrews purports to deliver, and by understanding its purpose and achievement, the Epistle comes into a clear focus.

The Christological Environment of Hebrews

Hebrews takes a great deal for granted in the development of Christology. Christianity by its time could see no mystery about the messiah, the Christ. Although many categories are used to understand Jesus within the New Testament, "Christ" predominated and was so naturally associated with Jesus (and Jesus alone) that "Christ Jesus" and "Jesus Christ" indistinguishably refer to the church's Lord. And so one mystery of the Messiah—who he might be—is no mystery. His identity may be specified in a way which would satisfy the curiosity of anyone who is not obsessed with outdated notions of historical verification. A second potential mystery—what the Messiah is to do—is also no mystery. Christ releases a Spirit in baptism which becomes available to the believer, such that prayer to God as Father is natural, behavior in the manner of Jesus is performed, and public thanksgiving with other Christians in eucharistic worship becomes a joy. He who proclaimed God's kingdom provides access to that kingdom, so we are transferred into that realm which is final in respect of time, transcendent in respect of space, perfect, holy, and inclusive of all those who enter its narrow gate. The entire system of Christian faith presupposes a familiarity with Christ Jesus, at least in narrative terms, and an awareness of the range of what he offers in the practice of the church and in the divine realm.

The mystery which the New Testament does not resolve, but in which it finds itself implicated, is: how can Jesus be Christ? What makes it possible for him, given his historical identity as a rabbi from Galilee during the first century, to provide full access to the power of God's Spirit and gracious inclusion within the divine kingdom? That is the systematic

1. B. F. Westcott, *The Epistle to the Hebrews* (London: Macmillan, 1889), xxi.

question of Christology. Frequently, attempts are made to answer that question by tabulating Christological titles in the New Testament and identifying their common denominator. By such a method, the term "prophet" is frequently isolated as the origin of Christology. Such exercises only prove in their results what should have been obvious from the outset: early Christians could agree on no single title which they felt conveyed the identity of Jesus. "Prophet" puts Jesus in a category that was not widely used during his period and in any case must be redefined in order to be applied to him, just as "Christ" itself, "son of man" (inspired by Dan. 7), "Son of God," "lord," "teacher," or "rabbi."

The number of such titles undermines the attempt to identify any one of them as the origin of Christology. Each can in fact be applied to Jesus in a misleading way. He is no prophet in the manner of Moses, in that Jesus was never a figure of truly national stature. If by "Messiah" we have in mind only the wise, forceful ruler of the *Psalms of Solomon* who subdues all comers with the word of his mouth (17:21–46), it is difficult to see how that term should be applied to Jesus at all. "Son of man," as referred to in Daniel 7, is a purely heavenly figure whose precise connection with Jesus is not immediately obvious. "Son of God," on the other hand, seems almost too flexible to be informative: it might refer to an angel (Gen. 6:2), to all Israel (Exod. 4:22), to a righteous person (Wis. 2:18). "Lord," "teacher," and "rabbi" might similarly be titles of relative honor, or allusions to God's own attributes as master, instructor, and judge. If the history of research has shown plainly how much there might be in a name, it has also demonstrated that the welter of titles and allusions makes precision regarding Jesus' identity within Christianity problematic.

The story of Peter's confession of Jesus (Matt. 16:13–20; Mark 8:27–30; Luke 9:18–21) is a classic of primitive Christology. The Petrine account has Jesus ask who people say he is. Common identifications are given (John the Baptist, Elijah, one of the prophets). Jesus then asks who the disciples say he is, and Peter answers that he is the Christ.

The direction of the questioning leads away from the notion that a prophetic Christology is adequate; the disciples are implicitly encouraged by Jesus to try another category, which is precisely what Peter attempts. The response of Peter occasions a signal variation within the Synoptic tradition. Mark (8:30) and Luke (9:21) have Jesus admonish his disciples not to speak concerning his identity. Matthew (16:17–19), on the other hand, has Jesus praise Peter as the bearer of special revelation; the admonition to silence then follows (16:20). The peculiarly Matthean narrative makes explicit what the Synoptic Gospels generally presuppose: "Christ" is the designation which will ultimately triumph. Even so, Peter's confession is immediately qualified by Jesus' own prediction, the first in the Synoptics, that—as "the son of man"—he is about to suffer, be condemned, and be executed (Matt. 16:21–23; Mark 8:31–33; Luke 9:22). The pericope as a whole is a magisterial demonstration that no single term, not even "Christ," may be accurately used of Jesus unless it is redefined in the light of knowledge of Jesus himself.

The method of seeking a response to the issue of who Jesus might be is also evident in the instructional source of Jesus' sayings. One dictum in particular has long attracted critical attention:

> I warrant to you, Father, Lord of heaven and of earth, because you hid these things from wise and understanding people, and uncovered them to infants! Yes, Father, because so it became pleasing before you. Everything has been delivered over to me by my Father, and no one recognizes the Son except the Father, nor does anyone recognize the Father except the Son and one to whom the Son elects to uncover (Matt. 11:25b–27; Luke 10:21–22).

The setting in the instructional source is a series of denunciations against those who have rejected the message of Jesus and his followers (Matt. 11:20–24; Luke 10:12–15, compare vv. 16–20). The saying contrasts those whose arrogance blinds them to a simple truth to the "infants" (*nēpioi*).

The metaphor builds upon the axiom, well established within the Petrine catechesis, that in order to enter the kingdom one must receive it as a child receives: without inhibition, completely absorbed by the vision of what is sought (Matt. 19:13–15 and 18:3; Mark 10:13–16; Luke 18:15–17). What is commended in such sayings is not the innocence of children (a romantic theme that ill accords with the skepticism of antiquity); rather, their naive, single-minded desire is commended as a good model for how to enter the kingdom. A due sense of proportion is precisely what causes the wise and intelligent to reject the revelation that naifs may enjoy.

The relationship between Father and Son is the generative point of the saying. Within that circle of intimacy, each is defined in terms of the other, and "infants" are only included by incorporation, because the Son reveals the truth to them. By the time we come to the end of the saying, "infants" is no longer even a metaphor of human temperament but a way of speaking of how believers are related to God the Father through Christ.

The whole of the teaching turns, then, around the circular relationship of mutual knowledge between Father and Son. In a manner even more radical than in the pericope concerning Peter's confession, any established category by which to measure Jesus (however exalted) is refused. Father and Son are only truly intelligible to one another; anyone else is (at best) a fledgling adopted into the family circle. The pericope underscores its method by the lack of specification even as to whether the "Son" is "of God" or "of man." The hearer is left to decide, and then to see that a decision between the alternatives is beside the point, because titles are deliberately transcended here. The instructional source joins the Petrine catechesis in insisting upon the priority of a way of thinking about Jesus over any title that may be used of him. Both passages proceed from an insight concerning Jesus' relationship with God, which then becomes the basis upon which categories that might be applied to him are rejected or qualified.

The new radicalism of the instructional source is its insistence upon the mutuality of the relationship. One might have predicted, on the basis of the story concerning Peter's confession, that Jesus would say that no one knows the Son truly except the Father. God can be the only valid standard of his own emissary. But the instructional source introduces what is not a corollary but a statement of equivalent weight, that no one knows the Father truly except the Son. The Jesus of John's Gospel will say to his disciples (by way of a response to a question from Thomas):

> I am the way and the truth and the life; no one comes to the Father except through me. If you knew me, you will know my Father, and from this moment you do know him and have seen him. (John 14:6–7)

The inescapable implication, that seeing Jesus is seeing the Father, is spelled out in an exchange with Philip (vv. 8–9). The Fourth Gospel has picked up and expanded upon the symmetrical and mutual relationship of Father and Son which is a feature of Q.

The instructional saying manifests what is commonly regarded as a "high" Christology, precisely in that the relationship is fully mutual, and not a matter of the subordination of Jesus to the Father. Commentators for better than a century have come to call the passage the "Johannine meteorite," as if it were unexpected so early within the traditions behind the Gospels. But John and Q together show that the close, mutual relationship between Jesus and God was well established during the same period that Hebrews was written, and the Epistle developed the understanding of that relationship to include Jesus' relationship to sinful humanity.

The Argument of Hebrews

The Epistle has been compared to a homily and calls itself a "word of exhortation" in 13:22. "Word" here (*logos*, as in John's Gospel) bears the meaning of "discourse," and the choice of diction declares Hebrews' homiletic intent. It is a sustained argument on the basis of authoritative tradition that intends to convince its readers and hearers to embrace a fresh position and an invigorated sense of purpose in the world. Hebrews engages in a series of scriptural identifications of Jesus: both Scripture (in the form of the Septuagint) and God's Son are the authoritative point of departure.

Scripture is held to show that the Son, and the Son's announcement of salvation, are superior to the angels and their message (1:1–2:18, see especially 2:1–4). Jesus is also held to be superior to Moses and Joshua, who did not truly bring those who left Egypt into the rest promised by God (3:1–4:13). Having set up a general assertion of the Son's superiority on the basis of Scripture, the author proceeds to his main theme:

> Having, then, a great high priest who has passed into the heavens, Jesus the Son of God, let us hold the confession fast. (Heb. 4:14)

That statement is the key to the central argument of Hebrews, and therefore to an understanding of the Epistle.

Two terms of reference in the statement are used freshly and—on first acquaintance with the Epistle—somewhat unexpectedly. Jesus, whom we have known as Son, is now "great high priest." The term "high priest" is in fact used earlier, to speak of his having expiated sin (2:17). This introduces the vital link between Christ's nature and his way of coping with sin. The Epistle states here that Jesus was "made similar" to people "so he might become a compassionate and faithful high priest of what relates to God for expiating the sins of the people." The language of similarity immediately implies that the category of humanity alone cannot contain Jesus: evidently, the opening reference to him as "Son" is meant to establish a different category of existence as compared to humanity as a whole. In that vein Jesus is also called the "apostle and high priest of our confession" (3:1). But now, in 4:14, Jesus is the "great high priest," whose position is heavenly. Now, too, the single confession of his heavenly location is the only means to obtain divine mercy.

Jesus' suffering is invoked again in 4:15 in order to make the link to what was said earlier, of Jesus' expiation. But then 4:16 spells out the ethical point of the entire epistle: "Let us then draw near with assurance to the throne of grace, so that we might receive mercy and find grace in time of need." With bold calculation, Jesus is presented as the unique means of access to God in the only sanctuary that matters, the divine throne in heaven.

The portrayal of Jesus as great high priest, exalted in heaven (Heb. 4–7), proves to be the center of the Epistle. At first, the argument may seem abstruse, turning as it does on Melchizedek, a relatively obscure figure in Genesis 14. In Genesis, Abram is met by Melchizedek after his defeat of the king of Elam. Melchizedek is identified as king of Salem and as priest of God Most High (Gen. 14:18). He brings bread and wine, and blesses Abram; in return, Abram gives Melchizedek one tenth of the spoils of war (Gen. 14:18–20).

The author of Hebrews hammers out a principle and a corollary from this narrative. First, "It is beyond all dispute that the lesser is blessed by the greater" (Heb. 7:7). From that straightforward assertion, the superiority of Melchizedek to Levitical priests is deduced. Levi, the founding father of the priesthood, was still in Abram's loins at the time Abram paid his tithe to Melchizedek. In that sense, the Levitical priests who were to receive tithes were themselves tithed by the greater priest (Heb. 7:8–10).

The importance of Melchizedek to the author of Hebrews, of course, is that he resembles Jesus, the Son of God. His very name means "king of righteousness," and he is also "king of peace," Salem. He does not bear a genealogy, and his birth and death are not recorded (Heb. 7:2b–4). In all these details, he adumbrates Jesus, true king of righteousness and peace, descended from a line that is not priestly in a Levitical sense, of whom David prophesied in the Psalms, "You are a priest for ever, after the order of Melchizedek" (Heb. 7:11–25, citing Ps. 110:4 at 7:11, 15, 17, 21). Jesus is the guarantor by God's own promise of a better, everlasting covenant (7:22). His surety is linked to Melchizedek's as clearly as the bread and wine which both use as the seal of God's promise and blessing.

The superiority of the better covenant is spelled out in what follows through chapter 9, again relying on the attachment to Jesus of God's promise in Psalm 110:

> For the law appoints men having weakness as high priests, but the word of the oath which is after the law appoints a Son for ever perfected. (Heb. 7:28)

Perfection implies that daily offerings are beside the point. The Son was perfect "once for all, when he offered himself up" (7:26–27). The author leaves nothing to implication: Moses' prescriptions for the sanctuary were a pale imitation of the heavenly sanctuary that Jesus has actually entered (8:1–6). Accordingly, the covenant mediated by Jesus is "better," the "second" replacing the "first," the "new" replacing what is now "obsolete" (8:6–13).

Chapter 9 simply puts the cap on an argument that is already clear. In its elaboration of a self-consciously Christological interpretation,

Hebrews turns the Synoptic approach to the relationship between Jesus and Scripture into an actual theory with a devotion to detail that attests the concern to develop that relationship fully. The chapter begins with the "first" covenant's regulations for sacrifice, involving the Temple in Jerusalem. Specific mention is made of the menorah, the table and presented bread in the holy place, with the holy of holies empty except for the gold censer and the ark. The reference to the censer as being in the holy of holies fixes the point in time of which the author speaks: it can only be the Day of Atonement, when the high priest made his single visit to that sanctum, censer in hand.

That precise moment is only specified in order to be fixed, frozen forever. For Hebrews, what was a fleeting movement in the case of the high priest was an eternal truth in the case of Jesus. The movement of ordinary priests in and out of the holy place, the "first tabernacle" (9:6), while the high priest could enter "the second tabernacle," the holy of holies (9:7), only once a year, was designed by the Spirit of God as a parable: the way into the holy of holies could not be revealed while the first Temple, the first tabernacle and its service, continued (9:8–10). That way could only be opened after the Temple was destroyed in the presentation of Hebrews, which conflates Jesus' death with the destruction of the Temple. Christ became high priest and passed through "the greater and more perfect tabernacle" of his body (9:11) by the power of his own blood (9:12) so that he could accomplish eternal redemption in the sanctuary.

Signal motifs within the Gospels are developed in the passage. The identification of Jesus' death and the destruction of the Temple, which the Gospels achieve in narrative terms, is assumed to be complete. Moreover, the passage takes it for granted that Jesus' body was a kind of "tabernacle," an instrument of sacrifice (9:11), apparently because the Gospels speak of his offering his body and his blood in the words of institution. "Body" and "blood" here are Jesus' self-immolating means to his end as high priest. John, of course, actually has Jesus refer to "the temple of his body," 2:21, and Paul conceives of Jesus as a place of expiation (hilastērion, Rom. 3:25) because he provides the occasion on which God may be appeased, an opportunity for the correct offering of sacrifice in Jerusalem. But in contrast to these earlier parallels between Temple and Christ, Hebrews develops an argument of direct replacement. In Hebrews, the Jerusalem Temple has been replaced by a purely ideological construct, referring to the "tabernacle" of the Pentateuch rather than to the physical building. The true high priest has entered once for all (9:12) within the innermost recess of sanctity, so that no further sacrificial action is necessary or appropriate.

In Hebrews the interpretative conviction of the Gospels, that Scripture finds its purpose in Jesus, is elevated to the status of a theory. The hermeneutics that had attested the resurrection (for example, in Luke 24:25–27) has now become the hermeneutics of preexistence. Jesus lives because he was always alive, and in the light of his activity one can finally understand what Scripture was speaking of. The destruction of the Temple in 70 CE was an advantage, because it enables us to distinguish the image from the reflection.

In the conception of Hebrews, the Temple on earth was a copy and shadow of the heavenly sanctuary, of which Moses had seen "types." A type (*typos* in Greek) is an impress, a derived version of a reality (the antitype). Moses had seen the very throne of God, which was then approximated on earth. That approximation is called the "first covenant" (9:1), but the heavenly sanctuary, into which Christ has entered (9:24), offers us a "new covenant" (9:15), which is the truth that was palely reflected all along.

The concluding three chapters of Hebrews point to what has preceded in order to influence the behavior of those who hear and read the Epistle. Literal sacrifice is to be eschewed (10:1–18) because the approach to God in purity is now by means of Jesus (10:19–22). The confession is to be maintained, love and good works are to be encouraged, communal gatherings are to continue as the day of the Lord approaches (10:23–25).

Above all, there is to be no turning back, no matter what the incentives (10:26–40). Faith in that sense is praised as the virtue of the patriarchs, prophets, and martyrs of old, although they were not perfected (11:1–39). Jesus alone offers perfection, as "the pioneer and perfecter of our faith" (12:1–3). Many ancillary commandments follow: do not be afraid of shedding your blood (12:4); do not become immoral or irreligious in leaving old ways behind (12:16); give hospitality and care for prisoners and those who are mistreated (13:1–3); honor marriage and do not love money (13:4–5); respect leaders and beware false teaching (13:7, 9, 17); remember to share and to pray (13:16, 18). Interesting as those commands are individually (especially in drawing a social profile of the community addressed), the overriding theme is evident and carries the weight of the argument: "Pursue peace with all, and sanctification, apart from which no one will see God" (12:14). Divine vision, the sanctification to stand before God, is in Hebrews the goal of human life, and the only means to such perfection is loyalty to Jesus as the great high priest.

The sense of finality, of a perfection from which one must not defect, is deliberately emphasized:

But you have come to Mount Zion and the city of the living God, the heavenly Jerusalem, and to myriads of angels in festal gathering, and to the assembly of first-born enrolled in heaven, and to a judge—God of all—and to the spirits of the just who are made perfect, and to Jesus the mediator of a new covenant, and to sprinkled blood which speaks better than the blood of Abel. (Heb. 12:22–24)

Jesus, the only mediator of perfection, provides access to that heavenly place which is the city of the faithful, the heart's only sanctuary.

The themes of Hebrews were to become the themes of catholic, orthodox Christianity. The Son of God would be understood as inherently and obviously superior to the angels, to Moses and Joshua, as the great high priest who alone provides access to the only sanctuary which matters. Framing a single confession of his heavenly location in relation to the divine throne was to require literally centuries of discussion within the church, but the necessity of such a confession was axiomatic.

Because Hebrews' themes became widespread, their development in the Epistle will strike many Christian readers as needlessly elaborate. But those themes were only discovered because the author maintained his rigorously Christological focus on Melchizedek, so that the bread, the wine, and the blessing he gave Abraham became the key to Jesus' superiority in the bread and the wine of a new and better covenant. Moses' prescriptions are shadows, imitations of the heavenly sanctuary that Jesus has actually entered. The Temple in Jerusalem has in Hebrews been replaced by a conception of the divine throne in heaven and the faithful congregation on earth, and Jesus' perfect sacrifice is the unique and perfect link between the two.

Hebrews does not entertain the question of how Jesus, as the perfect link between the heavenly sanctuary and a world in need of forgiveness, can relate to both God and people. In one breath, the author portrays Jesus as learning and perfected by his suffering (Heb. 5:7–10); indeed, here his suffering obedience is held to be the precedent of his designation by God as a high priest after the order of Melchizedek. But in another breath, even as he assures us that "we do not have a high priest who is unable to sympathize with our weaknesses," the author cannot resist observing that in Jesus we have a high priest who was "tempted in everything in the same way, apart from sin" (Heb. 4:15). Jesus is both like people and not like people, because he is the great high priest in the divine sanctuary.

So is Jesus human, divine, or some combination of the two natures? And did Jesus' human experience actually teach him anything he did not already know? Catholic, orthodox Christianity, in councils, creeds, persecutions, and more councils, addressed just such issues. Commentators, usually functioning as theologians, have naturally taken them up in discussing Hebrews, but in so doing they overlook the achievement of the Epistle. Hebrews so centrally locates Jesus as the locus of revelation that it became inevitable to ask new questions about his nature(s) and his consciousness. Hebrews develops a religious system which derives completely from Jesus.

Jesus himself had insisted upon a policy of treating all of Israel as Israel, pure by means of its customary practice to accept and enter the kingdom of God. For Peter, that made Jesus a new Moses: just as there is an implicit analogy between the followers of Jesus and the Israel that followed Moses out of Egypt, the prophetic covenant of Moses and the divine sonship of Jesus stand side by side. James's point of departure was David rather than Moses (see Acts 15:13–21). Here, the belief of gentiles achieves not the redefinition of Israel but the restoration of the house of David, which is committed to preserve Israel in its purity. But Paul began with Abraham, who in his theology embodied a principle of believing which was best fulfilled by means of faith in and through Jesus Christ. The Synoptic Gospels, in their variety, posit an analogy between Jesus and the figures of the Hebrew Bible: Christ becomes the standard by which Israel's Scripture is experienced, corrected, and understood to have been fulfilled. John's nuance is sophisticated but plain: Jesus is the true Israel, attested by the angels of God, by whom all the families of the earth will be blessed.

All such options are brushed aside in Hebrews. The author understands Israel, literally, as a thing of the past, the husk of the first, now antiquated, covenant. He says the word "Israel" just three times. Twice in chapter 8 he refers to Israel, but simply as part of his quotation of Jeremiah 31:31–34, where to his mind a completely new covenant is promised (Heb. 8:8, 10). The point of that citation, as elaborated by the author, is that the new covenant makes the former covenant obsolete (8:13). Accordingly, when the author speaks of Israel in his own voice, it is simply to refer to "the sons of Israel" in the past, at the time of the exodus from Egypt (11:22). Melchizedek is a positive, theological category. Israel is no longer, and remains only as a cautionary tale from history.

The ability of the author of Hebrews to relegate Israel to history is related to the insistence, from the outset of the Epistle, that the Son's authority is greater than that of the Scripture. Previously God spoke in many and various ways through the prophets; now, at the end of days, he speaks to us by a Son (Heb. 1:1–2). The comparative judgment is reinforced when the author observes that if the word delivered by angels (that is, the Torah) carried with it retribution for transgression, how much more should we attend to what we have heard concerning the Son (Heb. 2:1–4). The implication of both statements is clear: Scripture is only authoritative to the extent that it attests the salvation mediated by the Son (1:14; 2:3–4). The typology that is framed later in the Epistle between Jesus and the Temple derives directly from the conviction of the prior authority of the Son of God in relation to Scripture.

The dual revaluation, of Israel and Israel's Scripture, is what permits Hebrews to trace a theology in which Christ replaces every major institution, every principal term of reference, within the Judaism of its time. Before Hebrews, various Christian Judaisms conceived of Christ in various ways as the key to the promises to Israel. Hebrews' theology proceeds from those earlier theologies, and it remains a Christian Judaism in the sense that all of its vocabulary of salvation is drawn from the same Scriptures that were axiomatic within the earlier circles. But the Christian Judaism of Hebrews is also and self-consciously a system of autonomous Christianity, because all that is Judaic is held to have been provisional upon the coming of the Son, after which point it is no longer meaningful. There is a single center with the theology of Hebrews. It is not Christ with Moses, Christ with Temple, Christ with David, Christ with Abraham, Christ with Scripture, Christ with Israel. In the end, the center is not really even Christ with Melchizedek, because Melchizedek disappears in the glory of his heavenly archetype. Christ is the beginning, middle, and end of theology in Hebrews, just as he is the same yesterday, today, and forever (Heb. 13:8). Everything else is provisional—and expendable—within the consuming fire which is God (12:29).

From Christian Judaism to Christianity

The intellectual achievement of Hebrews may be gauged by comparing its insistence upon Christ as the unique center of faith with the presentations of previous circles of thought and practice. The care with which the Petrine circle has presented Jesus with Moses in the Transfiguration (see Mark 9:4) is simply abandoned when the author of Hebrews remarks, as if in passing, that Jesus was counted worthy of more glory than Moses (Heb. 3:2–6). Similarly, James's emphasis on the Davidic promise in Jesus is all but ignored in Hebrews, as David appears only as the author of Psalms (Heb. 4:7) and as one of a string of heroes from the past (11:32). And chapter 9 of Hebrews, of course, sets aside any continuing interest in the Temple in Jerusalem, where James's authority was centered (see Acts 21:17–26).

Comparison between Paul and Hebrews is natural. Paul presented Jesus as the fulfillment of God's promises to Abraham (Gal. 3:6–9), and argued that the fulfillment of the promise meant that Torah could no longer be looked upon as a requirement (Gal. 3:19–29). Paul brands any attempt to require non-Jews to keep the Torah as a consequence of baptism as "Judaizing" (Gal. 2:14). That theology is obviously a precedent for the author of Hebrews, who proceeds to refer openly to a new covenant superseding the old (8:13). But for Paul "all Israel" was the object of God's salvation (Rom. 11:26), just as the covenant fulfilled by Jesus was nothing other than the covenant with Abraham (so Gal. 3:15–18). For that reason, Scripture in Paul's thought is a constant term of reference; from it derives the coherent narrative of a covenant revealed to Abraham, guarded under Moses and fulfilled in Christ. By contrast, Christ is the only coherent principle in Hebrews, and Scripture is a mine from which types may be quarried.

Hebrews' technique of argumentation is a logical extension of the allegorical and symbolic readings presented in the Synoptics and in John. But the Synoptics and John accept, in the manner of Philo of Alexandria, that Scripture is to be used—at least for some—to regulate behavior, as well as to uncover divine truth. When the Synoptics compare Jesus to Elijah (see Matt. 16:14; Mark 8:28; Luke 9:19), and when John presents him as Jacob (John 1:51), the assumption is that Elijah and Jacob have their own meaning, and that some people will live loyally within their understandings of Elijah's or Jacob's presentation of the God of Israel. In Hebrews, the past is of interest principally as a counterexample to the city which is to come (see Heb. 13:14), and old ways are to be left behind (Heb. 10:1–18).

It is possible to compare (provided one also contrasts) Peter to the Pharisees, James to the Essenes, Paul to Philo's allegorists, and Barnabas to Philo himself. The author of Hebrews resists such comparison, because in the Epistle nothing within Judaism has a value independent of Jesus. Of all the previous associations, the one with Philo is most viable, since the allegorical or symbolic interpretation of Scripture is clearly developed even further than in the Synoptics and John. Particularly, the theory of "types" is redolent of Philo's approach and vocabulary. But even when confronted with what he takes to be ethical lapses, the author of Hebrews does not rely on any argument on the basis of the authority of Scripture. The contrast with Philo could not be plainer.

Instead of invoking Scripture, or even an account (such as Paul's) of the covenantal meaning of Scripture, the author of Hebrews ties his ethical imperatives directly to the example of Jesus. The community is to overcome its fear of shedding blood (Heb. 12:4) by considering the perfection of Jesus (12:1–3). That perfection is held to exclude immoral or irreligious ways, because they are not compatible with the grace of God (12:15–17). The perspective upon social policy is strikingly more assured than anything else in the New Testament: the author of Hebrews can say precisely and without argument, when most of his predecessors could not, just how Jesus' example is to be followed and what behavior causes God to withdraw his grace.

The anticipated agreement in regard to mandated behavior is pursued in the next chapter of Hebrews. Urban virtues—hospitality as well as the care for prisoners and those who are mistreated (Heb. 13:1–3)—seem to reflect an awareness that Jesus had taught such duties (albeit in differing contexts; see Matt. 25:31–46; compare Luke 7:22–23 and Matt. 11:4–6). For the same reason, the honor of marriage (Heb. 13:4), the injunction not to love money (Heb. 13:5), the call to respect leaders and to beware false teaching (13:7, 9, 17), and the reminder to share and to pray (13:16, 18) can all follow as a matter of course.

Hebrews is written to a community that views the teaching of Jesus alone as regulative. Scripture (namely, the Old Testament, which was the only form of Scripture then available), is simply the foreshadowed truth of what Jesus the great high priest fully reveals. The community is addressed as a whole; most of its people have received baptism (6:1–3), and they know right from wrong in the light of Jesus' teaching. They need to be urged to continue meeting together (10:25) despite what is called "the custom of some." The impression of factions within a community in which there is general consensus is confirmed by the particular appeal to obey leaders (13:17).

In his commentary on Hebrews, William L. Lane relates the Epistle to the "Hellenists" described in the book of Acts (6:1; 9:29). The term refers to "Jews living in Jerusalem but originally connected with Diaspora Judaism and characterized by the use of Greek as their principle language, especially for worship and scripture." Lane suggests that those Hellenistic Jews who accepted baptism in Jesus' name became trenchant in their criticism of the Temple. Their position is reflected in the speech of Stephen (see Acts 7:2–53). But where Stephen in Acts assumes the continuing validity of the Torah because it is mediated by angels (7:53), Hebrews cites the mediation of angels to qualify the standing of the Torah in relation to the Son (2:2–4). On the whole, the sophistication of the Epistle marks it, as Lane argues, as a considerable advance in the position of Hellenistic Jews who had become Christians.[2]

The connection of the Hellenists to a form a Judaism in which the importance of the Temple was relativized is reminiscent of the people Philo (*The Migration of Abraham* 89–93) described as scrupulously pursuing the intellectual, symbolic meaning of the Mosaic laws while neglecting literal observance. But Hebrews takes a conceptual step beyond attributing an allegorical meaning to the Temple. Rather than portraying the cult as the direct counterpart of the heavenly sanctuary (which is Philo's conception), all Levitical regulations are dissolved in

---

2. William L. Lane, *Hebrews 1–8* (Word Biblical Commentary 47A; Dallas: Word, 1991), cxlvi–cl.

the single sacrifice of the great high priest. The Epistle to the Hebrews represents Hellenistic Judaism, as reflected by Philo, after its conversion into a form of Christian Judaism by means of a consciously symbolic interpretation of Scripture and of Scripture's contents.

Martin Luther had suggested that Apollos, described in Acts as an Alexandrian Jew who was learned and powerful in the Scriptures (see Acts 18:24–28), was the author of Hebrews. Neither Westcott nor Lane accords the suggestion much sympathy, probably because they both locate the community of the Epistle in Jerusalem prior to the destruction of the Temple. The advanced technique of interpretation, the formal denial of the efficacy of worship in Jerusalem, and the stilted description in chapter 9 of the arrangement of the sanctuary are all indications against a local knowledge of the Temple prior to 70. Luther's suggestion is probably incorrect because Apollos, a contemporary of Paul's, is too early a figure to have written Hebrews. The author and community were probably Alexandrian, but by the time the Epistle was written circumcision was not even an issue. It was assumed the readership had long known it was not a requirement. The period assumed is well after the council of 49 CE and the confrontation between Peter and Paul at Antioch.

The oldest form of the title of the Epistle, "To Hebrews," sums up the perspective which is represented. Westcott, with his usual skill, articulated the orientation succinctly:

> The arguments and reflection in their whole form and spirit, even more than in special details, are addressed to "Hebrews," men, that is, whose hearts were filled with the thoughts, the hopes, the consolations, of the Old Covenant. . . .[3]

The Epistle does not deal with circumcision, with a Temple which is standing, or in particular with any contemporary synagogue of Judaism. Its orientation is global. The author works out its Christian Judaism as a religion which replaces every major institution with Christ, their heavenly archetype, who now offers his perfection to humanity.

With Hebrews, a Christian Judaism becomes a closed system, Christianity complete within its own terms of reference. Primitive Christianity here becomes, before the reader's eyes, early Christianity. After Hebrews, it will be apparent to Christians that any loyalty to Judaism is a throwback, to be tolerated or not, but always off the center of the religious system. Before Hebrews, there were Christian Judaisms; after Hebrews, the appearance of any institution of Judaism within the church will be seen as a form of Jewish Christianity.

3. Westcott, *Epistle to the Hebrews*, xxviii.

The achievement of Hebrews is systemic, and the result of the intellectual effort of what appears to be a single author. The skill of the rhetoric, the relatively high level of the Greek, and the originality and coherence of the argument all suggest the contribution of a single mind. Westcott's conclusion, once again, is telling:

> On the one side we see how the Spirit of God uses special powers, tendencies and conditions, things personal and things social, for the expression of a particular aspect of the Truth; and on the other side we see how the enlightened consciousness of the Church was in due time led to recognise that teaching as authoritative which was at first least in harmony with prevailing forms of thought.[4]

What Westcott saw, and struggled to express, was that in Hebrews the ambient Christian Judaism of the author became a Christianity. It was not yet in the classical mode that emerged during the second century, within the terms of reference of popular philosophical discussion. Hebrews' Christianity is "early," not classical. Although it replaces the institutions of Israel with Christ, that replacement is taken to be complete in itself, without the addition of other forms of thought. Interpretation here makes an early Christianity out of the Christian Judaism of its community and offers the result to those who later wrestled in philosophical terms with this Son of God who also suffered for humanity as a whole.

The key to his victorious suffering, however, made Jesus unlike other human beings in one crucial respect. As compared to all other people, Jesus was "tempted in everything in the same way, apart from sin" (Heb. 4:15). Within the theology of Hebrews, this crucial qualification makes Jesus unique. Apart from this move, Jesus could not be presented as the blameless offering who takes the place of all sacrifice. The inevitable consequence of this presentation, however, is that people as a whole, unlike Jesus, need to be understood as inherently sinful. That is, they sin in their very being, not merely in particular acts. Hebrews did not argue, as St. Augustine later did,[5] that human beings are subject to original sin by virtue of sexual procreation, but Hebrews did imply that the difference between Jesus and everyone else is defined by the absence or the presence of sin. With or without Augustinian language, that has been the typical teaching of Christianity ever since.

4. Ibid., lxxxiv.
5. See Henry Chadwick, *The Early Church* (London: Penguin, 1993), 225–35.

Comparing Theologies

Judaism on Christianity

The most difficult conception of Christianity and at the same time the most critical is the notion that Christ died to atone for sins he did not commit. That Hebrews adopts the metaphor of Temple atonement to convey that conception does not make the matter any more accessible. A brief recapitulation will underscore the radical disjuncture between Christianity and Judaism with regard to atonement.

God lives forever, so it is in man's nature to surpass the grave. And how, God being just, does the sinner or criminal survive his sin or crime? It is by atonement, specifically, paying with his life in the here and now, so that at the resurrection he may regain life, along with all Israel. What then shall we make of the Israelite sinner or criminal? Specifically, does the sin or crime, which has estranged him from God, close the door to life eternal? If it does, then justice is implacable and perfect. If it does not, then God shows his mercy—but what of justice? We can understand the answer only if we keep in mind that the halakhah takes for granted the resurrection of the dead, the final judgment, and the life of the world to come beyond the grave. So this world's justice and consequent penalties do not complete the transaction of God with the sinner or criminal. Eden restored at the end of days awaits. From that perspective, death becomes an event in life but not the end of life. And, it must follow, the death penalty too does not mark the utter annihilation of the person of the sinner or criminal. On the contrary, because he pays for his crime or sin in this life, he situates himself with all of the rest of supernatural Israel, ready for the final judgment. Having been judged, he will "stand in judgment," meaning, he will find his way to the life of the world to come along with everyone else. Within the dialectics formed by those two facts—punishment now, eternal life later on—we identify within the halakhah of *Sanhedrin-Makkot* two critical passages: *m. Sanhedrin* 6:2 and 10:1.

In *m. Sanhedrin* 6:2 the rite of stoning involves an admonition that explicitly declares the death penalty the means of atoning for all crimes and sins, leaving the criminal blameless and welcome into the kingdom of heaven (I italicize the key language):

> A. [When] he was ten cubits from the place of stoning, they say to him, "Confess," for it is usual for those about to be put to death to confess.
> B. For whoever confesses has a share in the world to come.
> C. For so we find concerning Achan, to whom Joshua said, "My son, I pray you, give glory to the Lord, the God of Israel, and

confess to him, [and tell me now what you have done; hide it not from me.] And Achan answered Joshua and said, Truly have I sinned against the Lord, the God of Israel, and thus and thus I have done" [Josh. 7:19–20]. And how do we know that his confession achieved atonement for him? For it is said, "And Joshua said, Why have you troubled us? The Lord will trouble you this day" [Josh. 7:25]. —*This day you will be troubled, but you will not be troubled in the world to come.*

D. And if he does not know how to confess, they say to him, "Say as follows: 'Let my death be atonement for all of my transgressions.'"

m. Sanhedrin 6:2

So within the very center of the halakhic exposition comes the theological principle that the death penalty opens the way for life eternal. Just as Achan pays the supreme penalty but secures his place in the world to come, so all Israel, with only a few exceptions, is going to stand in judgment and enter the world to come, explicitly including all manner of criminals and sinners.

In the halakhic context, death achieves atonement of sin, leading to the resurrection at the end of days. It is an act of mercy, atoning for the sin that otherwise traps the sinner and criminal in death. In the context of the gospel narrative, with its stress on repentance at the end and atonement on the cross by a single unique man, representative of all humanity, for the sins of all humanity, we deal with no juridical transaction at all. It is an eschatological realization of the resurrection of humanity through that of Jesus Christ on Easter Sunday. Read in light of *m. Sanhedrin* and its halakhic theology with its climax, "All Israel has a portion in the world to come," the passion narrative coheres, each component in its right proportion and position, all details fitting together.

The Mishnah interprets the death penalty as a medium of atonement in preparation for judgment leading to resurrection, just as the theology of the passion narratives has always maintained. For both the Mishnah and the Gospels, the death penalty is a means to an end. It does not mark the end but the beginning. The trial and crucifixion of Christ for Christianity, like the trial and execution of the Israelite criminal or sinner for Judaism, form necessary steps toward the redemption of humanity from death, as both religions have maintained, each in its own idiom.

Christianity on Judaism

The theme of Jesus' sinfulness addresses the human condition, not his own personal condition. He is the perfect high priest and the perfect offering at one and the same time, because he manifests what it is to be human in the image and likeness of God. Hebrews may articulate this theme in its own idiom, but it does so for Christianity as a whole.

Christianity conceives of people as having a deep affinity with God, and at the same time it acknowledges that between God and humanity an unbridgeable chasm intrudes. That chasm is sin. As we have seen earlier, Paul explains in his letter to the Romans that while knowledge of God is available through observation of the created world, humanity tragically exchanges the worship of God for the worship of what God has made, and finally the idolatry of self (Rom. 1:21–32).[6] The tragedy—to express it as Augustine does in an argument the next chapter deals with—is that people become constitutionally sinful from the moment that they turn from the love of God to the love of self.

Christ extends the possibility that people might not only repent of their sins but also be transformed out of their sinfulness. Sins are more than acts, intentional or inadvertent: they betray a state of persistent human rebellion against God. That state is overcome, Paul tells us, when God's Son is revealed in the midst of one's being, a moment of revelation that is inextricably linked with the reception of the Spirit of God at baptism. Because the Spirit comes from God, the Spirit enables knowledge of God. Thus for Christianity Christ becomes mediator of a spiritual knowledge of God. This knowledge is of a God whose loving disposition is revealed in the acts of Jesus Christ himself (Phil. 2:5–8). Imitation of Christ is then not simply a series of actions but the concrete expression of one's willingness to accept union with the loving God.[7]

Christianity's anthropology directly reflects its call to humanity to enter into the vision of God and to be transformed by the divine Spirit. This is why Jesus by his death achieves the ultimate aim of sacrifice: a union with the divine that forever transcends any ritual act. In later centuries, when sacrifice was conceived of as a payment, rather than as an immediate engagement with God, some thinkers—most notably Origen and Anselm—described Jesus' death as a "ransom" in a transactional sense. Such theories are helpful as expressions of the magnitude of the achievement of Jesus' sacrifice, but they miss the point of Hebrews if they conceive of the aim of his sacrifice only as the transfer of punishment.

This emphasis upon union with God explains why, from the time of Jesus' teaching, repentance has emerged in a new light within Christian theology. Standard practice assumes that sinners are to repent (Matt. 18:15–18). But failing that, believers are in a position to offer preemptive forgiveness (Matt. 5:38–48) by imitating God's own compassion toward his erring children.

6. See above, pp. 52–54.
7. See pp. 55–56 above.

The conviction that what we are becoming determines who we are, rather than the reverse, caused Christianity to qualify the importance of repentance and everything connected with it. Psychologies of intention, inclination, obedience, attitude, and restitution have their place, but Christian thinkers have varied in their assessments within these domains, and have proven experimental. Finally, they have settled upon no single prescription for humanity's sin, because they place their trust in the divine capacity to match with grace all the varieties of human weakness.

7

Resurrection, Judgment, and Eternal Life

※

Philosophical monotheism, lacking an eschatology of judgment and the world to come, leaves unresolved the tensions inherent at the starting point: the omnipotent God is one, the one God is just. That is why the common starting point of the theology of classical Christianity and rabbinic Judaism dictates the conclusion that deeds done in this world bear consequences in the world to come. The merit attained through this-worldly deeds (e.g., of generosity) persists, and individuals retain their status as such through all eternity.

The mythic monotheism of Christianity and Judaism, with its doctrine of God's power and justice, precipitates the conflict between God's mercy and his justice. This conflict is resolved only with the doctrine of the resurrection of the dead: the judgment and the victory over the grave attained by those judged, in the balance, to be (in the language of the Torah) "Israel" and therefore worthy of "a portion in the world to come," or reversion to Eden and eternal life. Otherwise, as we have stressed, in their mythic statement commencing with creation and focused on the human condition, the monotheist systems cannot account for the suffering of the righteous and prosperity of the wicked. The absolute given, a logical necessity of a monotheist theology revealing God's justice, maintains that individual life goes forward from this world, past the grave, to the world to come, and people are both judged and promised eternal life. That is the required doctrine for a system that insists upon the rationality and order of the universe under God's rule. It is easy to explain the urgency of resurrection. It makes possible that act of judgment that restores the balance of creation. For without judgment and eternal life for the righteous, this world's imbalance cannot be righted, nor can God's justice be revealed.

The Theology of Classical Christianity

Jesus pictured life with God as involving such a radical change that ordinary human relationships would no longer prevail. Because that change, in all its comprehensiveness, was finally to the good, death—an intrinsic part of the way God changes our lives—was portrayed, deliberately and explicitly, as an opportunity, not a misfortune. To lose one's life, Jesus said, is to save it (see Matt. 16:25; Mark 8:35; Luke 9:24; John 12:25). That central assertion of Christianity is often treated as if it were poetic or paradoxical, but in fact it expresses a core element around which Jesus' teaching as a whole was constructed.

Jesus' profound confidence in God's will to change us radically brought with it a commitment to the language of eschatology, of the ultimate transformation which God both promised and threatened. Although Jesus' eschatology was sophisticated, there is no mistaking his emphasis on future transformation.[1] Some efforts have been made recently to discount the eschatological dimension of Jesus' teaching; they have not prevailed. Periodically, theologians in the West have attempted to convert Jesus' perspective into their own sense that the world is a static and changeless entity, but that appears to have been far from his own orientation.[2]

Eschatology and the Individual

Although the eschatological character of Jesus' thinking is widely recognized, consensus is elusive regarding Jesus' understanding of what will happen *to particular human beings* within God's disclosure of his

1. See Bruce Chilton, *Pure Kingdom: Jesus' Vision of God* (Studying the Historical Jesus 1; Grand Rapids: Eerdmans, 1996).
2. See Bruce Chilton, *The Kingdom of God in the Teaching of Jesus* (London: SPCK; Philadelphia: Fortress, 1984). For discussion since that time, and particularly the contribution of Marcus Borg, see *Pure Kingdom*.

kingdom. Resurrection, as usually defined, promises actual life to individual persons within God's global transformation of all things. Because Jesus, on a straightforward reading of the Gospels, does not say much about resurrection as such, there has been a lively dispute over whether he had any distinctive (or even emphatic) teaching in that regard.

Still, when Jesus does address the issue, what he says is in fact unequivocal. Sadducees are portrayed as asking a mocking question of Jesus, designed to disprove the possibility of resurrection.[3] Moses had commanded that were a man to die childless, his brother should raise up seed for him. Suppose then, they asked, that there were seven brothers, the first of whom was married. If they all died childless in sequence, whose wife would the woman be in the resurrection (see Matt. 22:23–28; Mark 12:18–23; Luke 20:27–33)? Jesus' response is categorical and direct:

> You completely deceive yourselves, knowing neither the Scriptures nor the power of God! Because when they arise from the dead, they neither marry nor are given in marriage, but are as angels in the heavens. But concerning the dead, that they rise, have you not read in the book of Moses, at the passage about the bush, when God said to him, I am the God of Abraham and the God of Isaac and the God or Jacob? He is not God of the dead but of the living. You deceive yourselves greatly. (Mark 12:24–27; cf. Matt. 22:29–32; Luke 20:34–38)

Two arguments are developed here, one from Scripture and one based on a comparison between angels and those who are resurrected. Of the two arguments, the one from Scripture is the more immediately fitting, an appeal both to the nature of God and to the evaluation of the patriarchs in early Judaism. If God identifies himself with Abraham, Isaac, and Jacob, it must be that in his sight, they live. And those three patriarchs—carefully chosen in Jesus' reflection—are indeed living principles of Judaism itself; they are Israel as chosen in the case of Abraham (see Gen. 15), as redeemed in the case of Isaac (see Gen. 22), and as struggling to identity in the case of Jacob (see Gen. 32). That evocation of patriarchal identity is implied, rather than demonstrated, but the assumption is that the hearer is able to make such

---

3. Acts 23:8 indicates that the Sadducees deny resurrection altogether, and that is also the judgment of Josephus. I have argued that, despite their unequivocal statements (or rather, precisely because they are so unequivocal), we should be cautious about what the Sadducees denied; see Bruce Chilton, *The Temple of Jesus: His Sacrificial Program within a Cultural History of Sacrifice* (University Park: Pennsylvania State University Press, 1992), 82. The Sadducees' position is attributed to them only by unsympathetic observers, such as Josephus (*War* 2 § 165–166) and various Christians (Mark 12:18–27; Matt. 22:23–33; Luke 20:27–38; Acts 23:6–8).

connections between the text of Scripture and the fulfillment of that Scripture within present experience.[4] Yet that implicit logic of the argument from Scripture makes the second argument seem all the bolder by comparison.

The direct comparison between people in the resurrection and angels is consonant with the thought that the patriarchs must live in the sight of God, since angels are normally associated with God's throne (so, for example, in Dan. 7:9–14). So once the patriarchs are held to be alive before God, the comparison with angels is feasible. But Jesus' statement is not only a theoretical assertion of the majesty of God, a majesty which includes the patriarchs (and, by extension, the patriarchs' comparability to the angels); it is also an emphatic claim of what we might call divine anthropology. Jesus asserts that what we know as the usual basis of human relations and social organization—namely sexual identity—is radically altered in the resurrection.[5]

That teaching of a radical alteration at the point of death underscores that Christianity's hope is not of a survival or a reincarnation of some remnant of our personalities. Rather, death is understood to be a watershed, such that the current configuration of relationships and of reality is wiped away. Part of the transformation of this world into the kingdom is that, as Paul put, "the form of this world is passing away" (1 Cor. 7:31). That is not in any sense a fatalistic statement. Rather, Paul is appropriating Jesus' hopeful teaching about the eschatological transformation of all things. From that perspective, the death of the individual, and the removal of the present form of the world, point toward the new thing God is about to do with all of us.

In strictly theological terms, then, it does not much matter how a person dies, except that the deliberate taking of one's own life or that

---

4. For Jesus' characteristic attitude towards Scripture, see Bruce Chilton, *A Galilean Rabbi and His Bible: Jesus' Use of the Interpreted Scripture of His Time* (Wilmington: Glazier, 1984); also published with the subtitle *Jesus' Own Interpretation of Isaiah* (London: SPCK, 1984).

5. It is commonly asserted that Jesus accorded with accepted understandings of resurrection within Judaism; see Pheme Perkins, *Resurrection: New Testament Witness and Contemporary Reflection* (London: Chapman, 1984), 75. That is an unobjectionable finding, but it leads to an odd conclusion: "Nor can one presume that Jesus makes any significant contribution to or elaboration of these common modes of speaking." Perkins is not clear about what she means here, or the basis of her assertion. Does warning the reader against presuming that Jesus had something original to say imply that he in fact said nothing original? Why speak of presumption at all, when there is an actual saying to hand? But the analysis of the saying is also confused, because Perkins speaks of it as invented by Mark when it has anything new to say, and as routine insofar as it may be attributed to Jesus. The discussion typifies the ill-defined program of trivializing the place of Jesus within the tradition of the New Testament by critics who once tended to exaggerate the literary aspirations of those who composed the documents.

of another would infringe on God's prerogative and so is prohibited. Otherwise death, regardless of how it comes (even death on a cross!), is from a Christian perspective not a punishment but an opportunity for resurrection. This reversal of the conventional perception accounts for the fact that Christianity does not advocate careful training for a peaceful departure as an ideal but emphasizes the stark fact of a fundamental interruption of life. Death is accepted because of the expectation of what comes after. Paul's statement in the letter to the Philippians is classic:

> Because to me to live is Christ, and to die is gain. Yet if to live in flesh is the harvest of my work, I do not know what I shall choose. But I am constrained between the two, having a desire to leave and to be with Christ, for that is very much better; but to remain in flesh is the more necessary for your sake. (Phil. 1:21–24)

Philippians was probably written after Paul's death, but on the basis of his companions' memories of his mature positions and attitudes. In the present case, there is an exceptional clarity in regard to the actual focus of ethical striving within Christianity. The measure of that struggle is the spiritual inheritance that awaits the follower of Jesus, rather than compensation in terms of this world. That is because the actual purpose of being alive is to achieve spirit, and on that basis to know a life that is no longer limited to the flesh and the self. Death is the closure of that limited existence and therefore holds out the prospect of a complete transformation into the realm of spirit.

Within the Christian emphasis upon spiritual transformation, the sense of Christianity's teaching in regard to sin becomes plain. Paul wrote in his letter to the Romans:

> For we know that the law is spiritual; but I am of flesh, sold under sin. For what I achieve I do not know: for what I want, this I do not accomplish, but what I hate is what I do. But if what I do not want is what I do, I agree that law is worthwhile. And now it is no longer I who achieve it, but sin dwelling in me. For I know that nothing good dwells in me, that is in my flesh, because to want lies within me, but to achieve the worthwhile does not. For I do not do the good I want, but the evil which I do not want, this I accomplish. But if what I do not want is what I do, I am no longer achieving it, but the sin dwelling in me. Therefore I find this law: when I wish to do the worthwhile, the bad lies within me. For I recognize the law of God by the inner man, but I see another law in my members, warring against the law of my mind and taking me prisoner by the law of sin which is in my members. I am a miserable person! Who will save me from the body of this death? Thanks to God through Christ Jesus our

Lord. So therefore: I serve God's law with the mind, but with flesh sin's law. (Rom. 7:14–25)

The fact of human limitation is there all our lives, written in our failed projects of improvement. Paul understands this condition not as the circumstance of an individual, tortured psychology but as inherently human. In the very act of aspiring to what is good, people provoke a resistance in their midst which assures their failure.

Finally, this teaching became known as that of original (in the sense of inherent) sin. Christianity is frequently charged with being too pessimistic in its assessment of people for that reason. A case can be made for the view that human history better accords with a teaching of inherent human sin than it does with faith in human progress. In fact, Augustine made out just that argument (among others) in his classic work, *The City of God*. In the end, however, the Christian doctrine of original sin is not grounded in the observation of human behavior. Its ground is rather the eschatological hope of the transformation which is to come. The promise of grace, sealed by the Spirit of God and anticipating a glorious fulfillment, makes it apparent by contrast that, just as the form of this world is passing away, so our human complicity in the failures of this world is also to be transcended.

Paul on Resurrection and New Creation

Paul's classic discussion of the issue of the resurrection in 1 Corinthians 15 clearly represents his continuing commitment to the categorical understanding of the resurrection which Jesus initiated. The particular occasion of his teaching is the apparent denial of the resurrection on the part of some people in Corinth (1 Cor. 15:12b): "How can some of you say that there is no resurrection of the dead?"[6] His address of that denial is first of all on the basis of the integrity of apostolic preaching. Indeed, Paul prefaces his question with the earliest extant catalog of the traditions regarding Jesus' resurrection (1 Cor. 15:1–11). That record makes it plain why so much variety was possible within

6. For a survey of attempts to explain this statement, see A. J. M. Wedderburn, *Baptism and Resurrection: Studies in Pauline Theology against Its Graeco-Roman Background* (Wissenschaftliche Untersuchungen zum Neuen Testament 44; Tübingen: Mohr Siebeck, 1987), 6–37. He comes to no finding regarding what view Paul meant to attribute to some Corinthians, but he seems correct in affirming that a simple denial on their part (despite the form of words Paul uses) is unlikely. More likely, Paul was dealing with people who did not agree with his teaching of a *bodily* resurrection.

stories of the appearance of the risen Jesus in the Gospels: reference is made to a separate appearance to Cephas, then to the Twelve, then to more than five hundred "brothers" (cf. Matt. 28:10!), then to James, then to "all the apostles," and then finally to Paul himself (vv. 5–8). The depth and range of that catalog is what enables Paul to press on to his first argument against the Corinthian denial of the resurrection (15:13–14): "But if there is no resurrection of the dead, neither has Christ been raised; and if Christ has not been raised, then our preaching is empty and your faith is empty!"

Paul expands on this argument in what follows (1 Cor. 15:15–19), but the gist of what he says in that section is as simple as what he says at first: faith in Jesus' resurrection logically requires our affirmation of the reality of resurrection generally. That may seem to be an argument entirely from hypothesis, until we remember that Paul sees the moment when belief in Jesus occurs as the occasion of our reception of the Spirit of God:

> When the fullness of time came, God sent forth his Son, born from woman, born under law, so that he might redeem those under law, in order that we might obtain Sonship. And because you are sons, God sent the Spirit of his Son into your hearts, crying, "Abba! Father!" (Gal. 4:4–6)

Because the Spirit in baptism is nothing other than the *living* Spirit of God's Son, Jesus' resurrection is attested by the very fact of the primordially Christian experience of faith. The availability of his Spirit shows that he has been raised from the dead. In addition, the preaching in his name formally claims his resurrection, so that to deny resurrection as a whole is to make the apostolic preaching into a lie: empty preaching, as Paul says, and therefore empty faith.

Paul's emphasis in this context on the spiritual integrity of the apostolic preaching, attested in baptismal experience, is coherent with Jesus' earlier claim that the Scriptures warrant the resurrection (since God is God of the living, rather than of the dead). Implicitly, Paul accords the apostolic preaching the same sort of authority which Jesus attributed to the Scriptures of Israel. Paul also proceeds—in a manner comparable to Jesus' argument—to an argument on the basis of *the category of humanity* which the resurrection involves: he portrays Jesus as the first of those raised from the dead. Where Jesus himself had compared those to be resurrected to angels, Paul compares them to Jesus. His resurrection is what provides hope for the resurrection of the dead as a whole (1 Cor. 15:20–28).

That hope, Paul goes on to argue, is what permits the Corinthians themselves to engage in the practice of being baptized on behalf of the dead (15:29).[7] The practice assumes that, when the dead come to be raised, even if they have not been baptized during life, baptism on their behalf after their death will confer benefit. Similarly, Paul takes his own courage as an example of the hopeful attitude which must assume the resurrection of the dead as its ground: why else would Christians encounter the dangers that they do (15:30–32a)?

The claim of resurrection, then, does not only involve a hope based upon a reception of Spirit and the promise of Scripture (whether in the form of the Scriptures of Israel or the apostolic preaching). Resurrection as an actual hope directly affects what we think becomes of persons as we presently know them after they have died. (And that, of course, will immediately influence our conception of people as they are now perceived and how we might engage with them.) Paul's argument therefore cannot and does not rest solely on assertions of the spiritual integrity of the biblical witness and the apostolic preaching. He must also spell out an anthropology of resurrection, such that the spiritual hope and the scriptural witness are worked out within the terms of reference of human experience.

Precisely when he does that in 1 Corinthians 15, Paul develops a Christian metaphysics. He does so by comparing people in the resurrection, not to angels, as Jesus himself had done, but—as we have seen—*to the resurrected Jesus*. And that comparison functions for Paul both because Jesus is preached as raised from the dead and because, within the experience of baptism, Jesus is known as the living source of the Spirit of God.[8] Jesus as raised from the dead is the point of departure for Paul's thinking about the resurrection, and because his focus is a particular human being, his analysis of the resurrection is much more systematic than Jesus'.

The metaphysics of both Christology and spirituality are the same: they relate Christ to creation and believers to God, because in each the principle is the eschatological transformation of human nature by means of Spirit. "Flesh" and "soul" become not ends in themselves but way stations on the course to "Spirit." Just as sin marks out the necessity of human transformation in the realm of ethics, so physical death marks out the necessity of human transformation in the realm of existence. When Paul describes that existential transformation, his thinking becomes openly and irreducibly metaphysical:

---

7. For a discussion of the practice in relation to Judaic custom (cf. 2 Macc. 12:40–45), see Ethelbert Stauffer, *New Testament Theology* (trans. J. Marsh; New York: Macmillan, 1955), 299 n. 544. C. K. Barrett also comes to the conclusion that the vicarious effect of baptism is at issue in *A Commentary on the First Epistle to the Corinthians* (London: Black, 1968), 362–64, although he is somewhat skeptical of Stauffer's analysis.

8. As Perkins puts it, "These associations make it clear that the resurrection of Jesus had been understood from an early time as the eschatological turning point of the ages and not merely as the reward for Jesus as a righteous individual" (*Resurrection*, 227).

But someone will say, How are the dead raised, and with what sort of body do they come? Fool, what you yourself sow does not become alive unless it dies! And what you sow, you sow not as the body which shall be, but as a bare seed, perhaps of wheat or of another grain. But God gives to it a body just as he wills, and to each of the seeds its own body. Not all flesh is the same flesh, but there is one of men, another flesh of animals, another flesh of birds, another of fish. And there are heavenly bodies and earthly bodies, but one is the glory of the heavenly and another of the earthly. One glory is the sun's and another the moon's, and another glory of stars, because star differs from star in glory. So also is the resurrection of the dead. Sown in corruption, it is raised in incorruption; sown in dishonor, it is raised in glory; sown in weakness, it is raised in power; sown a physical body, it is raised a spiritual body. (1 Cor. 15:35–44)

There is not a more exact statement of the process of resurrection in the whole of Christian literature, and Paul's words have had a firm place in Christian liturgies of burial. Their particular genius is the insight that resurrection involves a new creative act by God, what Paul elsewhere calls a "new creation" (2 Cor. 5:17; Gal. 6:15). But God's new creation is not simply an event which commences at death. Rather, a progressive transformation joins the realm of ethics together with the realm of metaphysics. Morally and existentially, the hope of the resurrection involves a fresh, fulfilled humanity.

Patristic Developments

The great third-century theologian Origen remained a controversial figure after his death (and until this day), to a large extent because he wrestled more profoundly than most thinkers with the consequences of Spirit's claim on the flesh. In his treatment of the resurrection, Origen shows himself a brilliant exegete and a profound theologian. He sees clearly that, in 1 Corinthians 15, Paul insists that the resurrection from the dead must be bodily. And Origen provides the logical grounding of Paul's claim:

If it is certain that we are to possess bodies, and if those bodies that have fallen are declared to rise again—and the expression 'rise again' could not properly be used except of that which had previously fallen—then there can be no doubt that these bodies rise again in order that at the resurrection we may once more be clothed with them. (Origen, *On First Principles* 2.10.1)[9]

9. Translations are from *Origen: On First Principles* (trans. G. W. Butterworth; London: SPCK, 1936).

But Origen equally insists upon Paul's assertion that "flesh and blood can not inherit the kingdom of God" (1 Cor. 15:50). There must be a radical transition from flesh to spirit, as God fashions a body which can dwell in the heavens (*On First Principles* 2.10.3).

Origen pursues the point of this transition into a debate with fellow Christians:

> We now direct the discussion to some of our own people, who either from want of intellect or from lack of instruction introduce an exceedingly low and mean idea of the resurrection of the body. We ask these men in what manner they think that the 'natural body' will, by the grace of the resurrection, be changed and become 'spiritual;' and in what manner they think that what is sown 'in weakness' will be 'raised in power', and what is sown 'in dishonor' is to 'rise in glory,' and what is sown 'in corruption' is to be transformed into 'incorruption.' Certainly if they believe the apostle, who says that the body, when it rises in glory and in power and in incorruptibility, has already become spiritual, it seems absurd and contrary to his meaning to say that it is still entangled in the passions of flesh and blood. (*On First Principles* 2.10.3)

Origen's emphatic denial of a physical understanding of the resurrection is especially interesting for two reasons.

First, his confidence in the assertion attests the strength of his conviction that such an understanding is "low and mean": the problem is not that physical resurrection is unbelievable, but that the conception is unworthy of the hope that faith relates to. Origen's argument presupposes, of course, that a physical understanding of the resurrection was current in Christian Alexandria. But he insists, again following Paul's analysis, that the body which is raised in resurrection is continuous with the physical body in principle, but different from it in substance:

> So we must suppose that our bodies, like a grain of corn, fall into the earth, but that implanted in them is the life-principle which contains the essence of the body; and although the bodies die and are corrupted and scattered, nevertheless by the word of God that same life principle which has all along been preserved in the essence of the body raises them up from the earth and restores and refashions them, just as the power which exists in a grain of wheat refashions and restores the grain, after its corruption and death, into a body with stalk and ear. And so in the case of those who shall be counted worthy of obtaining an inheritance in the kingdom of the heavens, the life-principle before mentioned, by which the body is refashioned, at the command of God refashions out of the earthly and natural body a spiritual body, which can dwell in the heavens. (*On First Principles* 2.10.3)

The direction and orientation of Origen's analysis is defined by his concern to describe what in humanity may be regarded as ultimately compatible with the divine. For that reason, physical survival is rejected as an adequate category for explaining the resurrection. Instead, he emphasizes the change of substance that must be involved.

Second, the force behind Origen's assertion is categorical. The resolution of the stated contradictions—psychic/spiritual, dishonor/glory, corruption/incorruption—involves taking Paul's language as directly applicable to the human condition. In the case of each contradiction, the first item in the pair needs to yield to the spiritual progression of the second item in the pair. That is the progressive logic of Origen's thought, now applied comprehensively to human experience.

In Origen's articulation, progressive thinking insists that resurrection involves radical transition. Although his discussion is a brilliant exegesis of Paul's argument, Origen also elevates the progressive principle above any other consideration that Paul introduces. Paul had used this kind of method for understanding Scripture (see Gal. 4:21–31) but in Origen's thought that approach is turned into the fundamental principle of global spiritual revolution. Only that, in his mind, can do justice to the promise of being raised from the dead.

For all that the transition from flesh to spirit is radical, Origen is also clear that personal continuity is involved. To put the matter positively, one is clothed bodily with one's own body, as we have already seen. To put the matter negatively, sins borne by the body of flesh may be thought of as visited upon the body that is raised from the dead:

> Just as the saints will receive back the very bodies in which they have lived in holiness and purity during their stay in this life, but bright and glorious as a result of the resurrection, so, too, the impious, who in this life have loved the darkness of error and the night of ignorance, will after the resurrection be clothed with murky and black bodies, in order that this very gloom of ignorance, which in the present world has taken possession of the inner parts of their mind, may in the world to come be revealed through the garment of their outward body. (*On First Principles* 2.10.8)

Although Origen is quite consciously engaging in speculation at this point, he firmly rejects the notion that the flesh is involved in the resurrection, even when biblical promises appear to envisage earthly joys:

> Now some men, who reject the labour of thinking and seek after the outward and literal meaning of the law, or rather give way to their own desires and lusts, disciples of the mere letter, consider that the promises of the future are to be looked for in the form of pleasure and bodily luxury. And chiefly on this account they desire after the resurrection to have flesh

of such a sort that they will never lack the power to eat and drink and to
do all things that pertain to flesh and blood, not following the teaching
of the Apostle Paul about the resurrection of a 'spiritual body.' (*On First
Principles* 2.11.2)

His reasons for rejecting such a millenarian view are both exegetical
and theological. Paul is the ground of the apostolic authority he invokes,
in a reading we have already seen. He uses that perspective to consider
the Scriptures generally (*On First Principles* 2.11.3). But Origen deepens
his argument from biblical interpretation with a profoundly theological
argument. He maintains that the most urgent longing is the desire "to
learn the design of those things which we perceive to have been made
by God." This longing is as basic to our minds as the eye's longing for
light or the body's longing for food: constitutionally, we long for the
vision of God (*On First Principles* 2.11.4).

The manner in which Origen develops his own thought is complex,
involving a notion of education in paradise prior to one's entry into the
realm of heaven proper:

> I think that the saints when they depart from this life will remain in some
> place situated on the earth, which the divine Scripture calls 'paradise.' This
> will be a place of instruction and, so to speak, a lecture room or school for
> souls, in which they may be taught about all that they had seen on earth
> and may also receive some indications of what is to follow in the future;
> just as when placed in this life they had obtained certain indications of
> the future, seen indeed 'through a glass darkly', and yet truly seen 'in
> part', which are revealed more clearly and brightly to the saints in their
> proper times and places. If anyone is 'pure in heart' and of unpolluted
> mind and well-trained understanding he will make swifter progress and
> quickly ascend to the region of the air,[10] until he reaches the kingdom of
> the heavens, passing through the series of those 'abiding places,'[11] if I may
> so call them, which the Greeks have termed spheres, that is, globes, but
> which the divine scripture calls heavens. (*On First Principles* 2.11.6)

Even this brief excerpt from a convoluted description represents the
complexity of Origen's vision, but two factors remain plain and simple.
First, the vision of God is the moving element through the entire discussion. Second, Origen clearly represents and develops a construction of
the Christian faith in which eschatology has been swallowed up in an

---

10. At this point, Origen is reading 1 Thessalonians 4 through the lens of 1 Corinthians 15,
just as later in the passage he incorporates the language of "mansions" from John 14:2.

11. Here Origen uses the word that the King James Bible translates "mansions" in
John 14:2.

emphasis upon transcendence. The only time that truly matters is that time until one's death, which determines one's experience in paradise and in the resurrection. "Heaven" as cosmographic place now occupies the central position once occupied by the eschatological kingdom of God in Jesus' teaching. That, too, occurs on the authority of progressive dialectics, the refinement of Pauline metaphysics.[12]

Augustine discussed the resurrection in a different context from Origen's, namely, his rejection of the Manichaean philosophy that he accepted prior to his conversion to Christianity. In Manichaeism (named after Mani, a Persian teacher of the third century), light and darkness are two eternal substances that struggle against one another, warring over the creation they have both participated in making.[13] As in the case of gnosticism, on which it was dependent, Manichaeism counseled denial of the flesh. By his insistence on the resurrection of the flesh, Augustine revives the strong assertion of the extent of God's embrace of his own creation (in the tradition of Irenaeus, the great millenarian thinker of the second century).[14]

At the same time, Augustine sets a limit on the extent to which one might have recourse to Plato. Augustine had insisted with Plato against the Manichaeans that God was not a material substance, but transcendent. Consequently, evil became in his mind the denial of what proceeds from God (see *Confessions* 5.10.20). When it came to the creation of people, however, Augustine insisted against Platonic thought that no division between soul and flesh could be made (so *City of God* 22.12). Enfleshed humanity was the only genuine humanity, and God in Christ was engaged to raised those who were of the city of God. Moreover, Augustine specifically refuted the contention of Porphyry (and Origen) that cycles of creation could be included within the entire scheme of salvation. For Augustine, the power of the resurrection within the world as it is was already confirmed by the miracles wrought by Christ and his martyrs. He gives the example of the healings connected with the relics of St. Stephen, recently transferred to Hippo (*City of God* 22.8).

Even now, in the power of the catholic church, God is represented on earth, and the present, Christian epoch (*Christiana tempora*) corresponds

12. For more on Origen's eschatology, see Brian E. Daley, *The Hope of the Early Church: A Handbook of Patristic Eschatology* (Cambridge: Cambridge University Press, 1992; repr., Peabody, Mass.: Hendrickson, 2003), 47–60.

13. See Stanley Romaine Hopper, "The Anti-Manichean Writings," in *A Companion to the Study of St. Augustine* (ed. R. W. Battenhouse; New York: Oxford University Press, 1969), 148–74.

14. See Jaroslav Pelikan, *The Christian Tradition: A History of the Development of Doctrine*, vol. 1: *The Emergence of the Catholic Tradition, 100–600* (Chicago: University of Chicago Press, 1971), 123–32.

to the millennium promised in Revelation 20 (*City of God* 20.9). This age of dawning power, released in flesh by Jesus and conveyed by the church, simply awaits the full transition into the city of God, complete with flesh itself. It is telling that, where Origen could cite a saying of Jesus to confirm his view of the resurrection (see Matt. 22:30; Mark 12:25; Luke 20:36), Augustine has to qualify the meaning of the same saying:

> They will be equal to angels in immortality and happiness, not in flesh, nor indeed in resurrection, which the angels had no need of, since they could not die. So the Lord said that there would be no marriage in the resurrection, not that there would be no women. (*City of God* 22.17)

In all of this, Augustine is straining in his insistence that the resurrection is a matter of "flesh," a category that Jesus' saying never invokes, although he is usually a less convoluted interpreter of Scripture. But he is committed literally to what the Old Roman Creed promises: "the resurrection of the flesh" and all that implies. He therefore cannot follow Origen's exegesis.

There is a double irony here. First, Origen the sophisticated allegorist seems much simpler to follow in his exegesis of Jesus' teaching than Augustine, the incomparable preacher. Second, Augustine's discussion of such issues as the fate of nail clippings (!) in the resurrection sounds remarkably like the Sadducees' hypothesis that Jesus argues against in the relevant passage from the Synoptic Gospels.

Augustine is well aware, as was Origen before him, that Paul speaks of a "spiritual body," and acknowledges that "I suspect that all utterance published concerning it is rash." And yet he can be quite categorical that flesh must be involved somehow: "The spiritual flesh will be subject to spirit, but it will still be flesh, not spirit; just as the carnal spirit was subject to the flesh, but was still spirit, not flesh" (*City of God* 22.21). Such is Augustine's conviction that flesh has become the medium of salvation now and hereafter.[15]

Not only within the New Testament, but through the centuries of discussion which the key figures cited here reflect, Christianity represents itself as a religion of human regeneration. Humanity is regarded not simply as a quality which God values but as the very center of being in the image of God. God created everything; to humanity alone he gave the patent of divine creativity. That center is so precious to God that it is the basis upon which it is possible for human beings to enter the kingdom of God, both now and eschatologically.

15. For more on Augustine's eschatology, see Daley, *Hope of the Early Church*, 131–50.

The medium in which that ultimate transformation is to take place is a matter of debate. Regenerated people might be compared to angels (so Jesus), to Jesus in his resurrection (so Paul), to spiritual bodies (so Origen), and to spiritualized flesh (so Augustine). But in all of these analyses of how we are to be transformed into the image of Christ so as to apprehend that humanity which is in the image and likeness of God (see Gen. 1:27), there is a fundamental consensus. Jesus is claimed as the agency by which this transformation is accomplished.

The Theology of Rabbinic Judaism

Throughout the oral Torah the main point of the theological eschatology—the theory of last things—registers both negatively and affirmatively. Death does not mark the end of the individual human life, nor exile the last stop in the journey of Holy Israel. Israelites will live in the age of the world to come, all Israel in the Land of Israel; and Israel will comprehend all who know the one true God. The restoration of world order that completes the demonstration of God's justice encompasses both private life and the domain of all Israel. For both, restorationist theology provides eternal life; to be Israel means to live beyond the grave. So far as the individual is concerned, beyond the grave, at a determinate moment, man (1) rises from the grave in resurrection, (2) is judged, and (3) enjoys the world to come. For the entirety of Israel, congruently: all Israel participates in the resurrection, which takes place in the Land of Israel, and enters the world to come.

The restorationist eschatology flows from the same cogent logic that has dictated theological doctrine from the beginning of this systematic account. The last things are to be known from the first. In the just plan of creation man was meant to live in Eden, and Israel in the Land of Israel, in time without end. The restoration will bring about the perfection of the world order that was initiated on the first Sabbath but tragically postponed, an act sealing the demonstration of the justice of God's plan for creation. Risen from the dead, having atoned through death, man will be judged in accord with his deeds. Corresponding to man, Israel for its part, when it repents and conforms its will to God's, recovers its Eden, which is the land. So the consequences of rebellion and sin having been overcome, the struggle of man's will and God's word having been resolved, God's original plan will be realized at the last. The simple, global logic of the system, with its focus on the world order of justice established by God but disrupted by man, leads inexorably to this eschatology of restoration, the restoration of balance, order, and proportion for eternity.

Atonement through Death

The integrity of rabbinic theology is evident in the interconnection of the doctrine of resurrection with the doctrine of sin and atonement, including specific provisions for criminal justice, in tractates *Sanhedrin* and *Makkot*. The rabbinic sages believe that since man is created in God's image, and God lives forever, it is in man's nature to surpass the grave. Hence their conviction that all Israel possesses a share in the world to come (meaning, nearly everybody will rise from the grave). But being in God's image also means possessing the autonomous and free will that makes possible rebellion against God—sin and crime—and another essential conviction of the sages is that all creatures are answerable to their Creator. Thus the criminal justice system encompasses deep thought on the interplay of God's justice and God's mercy: how are these reconciled in the case of sinners and criminals? Specifically, does the sin or crime that has estranged them from God close the door to life eternal? If it does, then justice is implacable and perfect. If it does not, then God shows his mercy—but what of justice?

We can understand the answer only if we keep in mind that the halakhah takes for granted the resurrection of the dead, the final judgment, and the life of the world to come beyond the grave. So this world's justice and consequent penalties do not complete the transaction of God with the sinner or criminal. Eden restored at the end of days awaits. Death becomes an event in life but not the end of life, so the death penalty does not mark the utter annihilation of the person of the sinner or criminal. On the contrary, because he pays for his crime or sin in this life, he situates himself with all of the rest of supernatural Israel, ready for the final judgment. Having been judged, he will "stand in judgment," meaning, he will find his way to the life of the world to come along with everyone else. That is why the climactic moment in the halakhah comes at the end of the long catalogue of those sins and crimes penalized with capital punishment. With ample reason the Bavli places at the conclusion and climax of its version the ringing declaration, "all Israel has a portion in the world to come, except . . ."—and the exceptions pointedly do not include any of those listed in the long catalogues of persons executed for sins or crimes. Thus an entirely abstract theological problem, the fate of man after death, is reasoned through to its conclusion in the halakhah pertaining to the criminal justice system.

Within the dialectics formed by those two facts—punishment now, eternal life later on—we identify as two critical passages in the halakhah of *Sanhedrin-Makkot*, namely, *m. Sanhedrin* 6:2 and 11:1. The former elaborates the theological principle that the death penalty opens the way for life eternal. Just as Achan pays the supreme penalty but secures his place in the world to come, so all Israel—explicitly including all manner of criminals and sinners, with only a few exceptions—is going to stand in judgment and enter the world to come.[16] And the latter passage states explicitly that all Israel, with specified exceptions, inherit the world to come:

A. All Israelites have a share in the world to come, as it is said, "your people also shall be all righteous, they shall inherit the land forever; the branch of my planting, the work of my hands, that I may be glorified" [Isa. 60:21].
B. And these are the ones who have no portion in the world to come: He who says, the resurrection of the dead is a teaching which does not derive from the Torah, and the Torah does not come from heaven; and an Epicurean.

m. Sanhedrin 11:1

The executed criminal does not figure among these exceptions, only those who willfully defy God in matters of eternity.

What the halakhah wishes to explore, then, is how the Israelite sinner or criminal may be rehabilitated through the criminal justice system so as to rejoin Israel in all its eternity. The answer is, the criminal or sinner remains Israelite, regardless of what he does—even though he sins—and in spite of the death penalty exacted by the earthly court. So the halakhah of Sanhedrin embodies these religious principles: (1) Israel—man "in our image"—endures for ever, encompassing (nearly) all Israelites; (2) sinners or criminals are able to retain their position within that eternal Israel by reason of the penalties that expiate the specific sins or crimes spelled out by the halakhah; (3) it is an act of merciful justice that is done when the sinner or criminal is put to death, for at that point, he is assured of eternity along with everyone else. God's justice comes to full expression in the penalty, which is instrumental and contingent; God's mercy endures forever in the forgiveness that follows expiation of guilt through the imposition of the penalty.

That explains why the governing religious principle of *Sanhedrin-Makkot* is the perfect, merciful justice of God, and it accounts for the detailed exposition of the correct form of the capital penalty for each capital sin or crime. The punishment must fit the crime within the context of the Torah in particular so that, at the resurrection and the judgment, the crime will have been correctly expiated. Because the halakhah rests on the premise that God is just and that God has made man in his image, after his likeness, the halakhah cannot deem sufficient that

16. See pp. 219–20 above.

the punishment fit the crime. Rather, given its premises, the halakhah must pursue the issue of the sinner's fate beyond punishment. And the entire construction of the continuous exposition of *Sanhedrin-Makkot* aims at making this simple statement: the criminal, in God's image, after God's likeness, pays the penalty for his crime in this world but like the rest of Israel will stand in justice and, rehabilitated, will enjoy the world to come. That is what I mean when I insist that the criminal justice system explores in highly abstract terms the concrete meaning of incarnate man.

Where then is the limit to God's mercy? It is at the rejection of the Torah, the constitution of a collectivity—an "Israel"—that stands against God. Israel is made up of all those who look forward to a portion in the world to come: who will stand in justice and transcend death. In humanity, idolaters will not stand in judgment, and entire generations who sinned collectively as well as Israelites who broke off from the body of Israel and formed their own Israel do not enjoy that merciful justice that reaches full expression in the fate of Achan: he stole from God but shared the world to come. And so will all those who have done the dreadful deeds catalogued here. The theological principle expressed here—God's perfect, merciful justice, correlated with the conviction of the eternity of holy Israel—could not have come to systematic statement in any other area of the halakhah. It is only in the present context that the sages could link God's perfect, merciful justice to the concrete life of ordinary Israel, and it is only here that they could invoke the certainty of eternal life to explain the workings of merciful justice.

Resurrection, Judgment, and Messiah

Let us now address the resurrection of the dead in its own terms as the aggadic exposition defines it. That conviction is stated in so many words: in the end of days, death will die. The certainty of resurrection derives from a simple fact of restorationist theology: God has already shown that he can do it, so *Genesis Rabbah* LXXVII:I.1: "You find that everything that the Holy One, blessed be he, is destined to do in the age to come he has already gone ahead and done through the righteous in this world. The Holy One, blessed be he, will raise the dead, and Elijah raised the dead."

The first component of the doctrine of the resurrection of the dead—belief both that the resurrection of the dead will take place and that it is the Torah that reveals that the dead will rise—is fully exposed in the fundamental composition devoted by the framers of the Mishnah to that subject. The components of the doctrine fit together, in that statement, in a logical order. (1) In a predictable application of the governing principle of measure for measure, those who do not believe in the resurrection of the dead will be punished by being denied what they do not accept. Some few others bear the same fate. (2) But to be Israel means to rise from the grave, and that applies to all Israelites. That is to say, the given of the condition of Israel is that the entire holy people will enter the world to come, which is to say, will enjoy the resurrection of the dead and eternal life. "Israel" then is anticipated to be the people of eternity. (3) Excluded from the category of resurrection and the world to come, then, are only those who by their own sins have denied themselves that benefit. These are those who deny that the teaching of the world to come derives from the Torah, or who deny that the Torah comes from God, or hedonists.

Exegesis of Scripture also yields the names of three kings who will not be resurrected, as well as four commoners, and specified generations: the flood, the dispersion, and Sodom, the generation of the wilderness, the party of Korah, and the Ten Tribes. To resume the passage cited above:

> A. All Israelites have a share in the world to come, as it is said,
> "Your people also shall be all righteous, they shall inherit the
> land forever; the branch of my planting, the work of my hands,
> that I may be glorified" [Isa. 60:21].
>
> *m. Sanhedrin* 10:1 [*b. Sanhedrin* 11:1]

That single statement serves better than any other to define Israel in the oral Torah. Now we forthwith take up exceptions:

> B. And these are the ones who have no portion in the world to come:
> C. He who says, the resurrection of the dead is a teaching which
> does not derive from the Torah, and the Torah does not come
> from heaven; and an Epicurean.
> D. R. Aqiba says, "Also: He who reads in heretical books,
> E. "and he who whispers over a wound and says, 'I will put none of
> the diseases upon you which I have put on the Egyptians, for I
> am the Lord who heals you' [Exod. 15:26]."
> F. Abba Saul says, "Also: He who pronounces the divine Name as it
> is spelled out."

From classes of persons, we turn to specified individuals who are denied a place within Israel and entry in the world to come; all but one are Israelites, and the exception, Balaam, has a special relation to Israel, as the gentile prophet who came to curse but ended with a blessing:

> A. Three kings and four ordinary folk have no portion in the world
> to come.

B. Three kings: Jeroboam, Ahab, and Manasseh.
C. R. Judah says, "Manasseh has a portion in the world to come,
D. "since it is said, 'And he prayed to him and he was entreated of him and heard his supplication and brought him again to Jerusalem into his kingdom' [2 Chron. 33:13]."
E. They said to him, "To his kingdom he brought him back, but to the life of the world to come he did not bring him back."
F. Four ordinary folk: Balaam, Doeg, Ahithophel, and Gehazi.

m. Sanhedrin 10:2

Then come entire generations of gentiles before Abraham, who might have been considered for eternal life outside of the framework of God's self-manifestation first to Abraham, then in the Torah. These are the standard sets, the Generation of the Flood, the Generation of the Dispersion, and the Men of Sodom:

A. The generation of the flood has no share in the world to come,
B. and they shall not stand in the judgment,
C. since it is written, "My spirit shall not judge with man forever" [Gen. 6:3]—
D. neither judgment nor spirit.
E. The generation of the dispersion has no share in the world to come,
F. since it is said, "So the Lord scattered them abroad from there upon the face of the whole earth" [Gen. 11:8].
G. "So the Lord scattered them abroad"—in this world,
H. "and the Lord scattered them from there"—in the world to come.
I. The men of Sodom have no portion in the world to come,
J. since it is said, "Now the men of Sodom were wicked and sinners against the Lord exceedingly" [Gen. 13:13].
K. "Wicked"—in this world,
L. "And sinners"—in the world to come.
M. But they will stand in judgment.
N. R. Nehemiah says, "Both these and those will not stand in judgment,
O. "for it is said, 'Therefore the wicked shall not stand in judgment [108A], nor sinners in the congregation of the righteous' [Ps. 1:5].
P. "'Therefore the wicked shall not stand in judgment'—this refers to the generation of the flood.
Q. "'Nor sinners in the congregation of the righteous'—this refers to the men of Sodom."
R. They said to him, "They will not stand in the congregation of the righteous, but they will stand in the congregation of the sinners."
S. The spies have no portion in the world to come,
T. as it is said, "Even those men who brought up an evil report of the land died by the plague before the Lord" [Num. 14:37].

U. "Died"—in this world.

V. "By the plague"—in the world to come.

m. Sanhedrin 10:3

What about counterparts in Israel, from the Torah forward? The issue concerns the Generation of the Wilderness, which rejected the Land; the party of Korah; and the Ten Tribes. These match the gentile contingents. But here there is a dispute, and no normative judgment emerges from the Mishnah's treatment of the matter:

A. "The generation of the wilderness has no portion in the world to come and will not stand in judgment,

B. "for it is written, 'In this wilderness they shall be consumed and there they shall die' [Num. 14:35]," the words of R. Aqiba.

C. R. Eliezer says, "Concerning them it says, 'Gather my saints together to me, those who have made a covenant with me by sacrifice' [Ps. 50:5]."

D. "The party of Korah is not destined to rise up,

E. "for it is written, 'And the earth closed upon them'—in this world.

F. "'And they perished from among the assembly'—in the world to come," the words of R. Aqiba.

G. And R. Eliezer says, "Concerning them it says, 'The Lord kills and resurrects, brings down to Sheol and brings up again' [1 Sam. 2:6]."

m. Sanhedrin 10:4

A. "The ten tribes [of northern Israel, exiled by the Assyrians] are not destined to return [with Israel at the time of the resurrection of the dead],

B. "since it is said, 'And he cast them into another land, as on this day' [Deut. 29:28]. Just as the day passes and does not return, so they have gone their way and will not return," the words of R. Aqiba.

C. R. Eliezer says, "Just as this day is dark and then grows light, so the ten tribes for whom it now is dark—thus in the future it is destined to grow light for them."

m. Sanhedrin 10:5

Scripture thus contributes the details that refine the basic proposition; the framer has found the appropriate exclusions. But the prophet, in Scripture, also has provided the basic allegation on which all else rests, that is, "Israel will be entirely righteous and inherit the Land forever." Denying the stated dogmas removes a person from the status of "Israel," in line with the opening statement, so to be Israel means to rise from the dead, and Israel as a collectivity is defined as those persons in humanity who are destined to eternal life, a supernatural community, as we saw in chapter 3. So much for the initial statement of the eschatological doctrine in the oral Torah.

The details of judgment following resurrection prove less ample. The basic account stresses that God will judge with great mercy. But the rabbinic corpus presents no fully articulated story of judgment. Within the documents of the oral Torah, we have little narrative to tell us how the judgment will be carried on. Even the detail that through repentance and death man has already atoned plays no role that I can discern in discussions of the last judgment. What we do know concerns two matters: When does the judgment take place? And by what criteria does God decide who inherits the world to come? As to the former: The judgment is comparable to the annual judgment for man's fate in the following year. It will happen either at the beginning of the New Year on the first of Tishri, when man is judged annually, or on the fifteenth of Nisan, when Israel celebrates its freedom from Egyptian bondage and begins its pilgrimage to Sinai.

How to stand in judgment? Through proper conduct and study of Torah one can go through the process of divine review of one's life and actions and emerge in the world to come, restored to the Land that is Eden. What is striking is the appeal to Eden for just this message about reentry into the Land.

1. A. Said R. Abba b. Eliashib, "[The reference at Lev. 26:3 to statutes is to] statutes which bring a person into the life of the world to come.
    B. "That is in line with the following verse of Scripture: 'And he who is left in Zion and remains in Jerusalem will be called holy, everyone who has been recorded for life in Jerusalem' [Isa. 4:3]—for he is devoted to [study of] Torah, which is called the tree of life."

Now comes the reference to Eden in the context of the world to come, a matter to which we return:

2. A. It has been taught in the name of R. Eliezer, "A sword and a scroll wrapped together were handed down from heaven, as if to say to them, 'If you keep what is written in this [scroll], you will be saved from the sword,
    B. "'and if not, in the end [the sword] will kill you.'
    C. "Whence is that proposition to be inferred? 'He drove out the man, and at the east of the Garden of Eden he placed the cheru-

bim, and a flaming sword which turned every way, to guard the
way to the tree of life' [Gen. 3:4].

D. "The [first] reference to 'the way' refers to the rules of proper
conduct, and the second reference, '[the way to] the tree of life'
refers to the Torah."

The same message is given in a different framework:

3. A. It was taught in the name of R. Simeon b. Yohai, "A loaf and a rod
wrapped together were given from heaven.

B. "It was as if to say to them, 'If you keep the Torah, lo, here is bread
to eat, and if not, lo, here is a staff with which to be smitten.'

C. "Whence is that proposition to be inferred? 'If you are willing
and obedient, you shall eat the good of the land; but if you refuse
and rebel, you shall be devoured by the sword' [Isa. 1:19–20]."

Leviticus Rabbah XXXV:VI:1f

The world to come, involving resurrection and judgment, will be attained
through the Torah, which teaches proper conduct. That simple doctrine
yields the proposition here.

The final subtopic of the theme of resurrection as of the world to
come, already encountered, now has to be addressed systematically:
what of the Messiah? The Messiah figures at every point in the categorical structure of the oral Torah's eschatological thinking: (1) troubles
attendant upon the coming of the Messiah, which either do or do not
bring about (2) Israelite repentance, leading to (3) resurrection, as we
shall see here, and a task then to be performed (4) in the world to come.
But while the Messiah theme is critical, the Messiah as a particular
person is not. That fact is born out by the first and most important element of theological thinking about the Messiah theme: the multiplicity
of Messiahs, even in the eschatological setting. One Messiah comes out
of the line of Joseph, another out of the line of David. Both Messiahs
(and others in that same classification, for example, the Messiah who
is anointed to be high priest in charge of the army [Deut. 20:2–7,
m. Sotah 8]), are mortal and subject to the human condition. One
Messiah is murdered, replaced by another. The Messiah, moreover,
is subject to the impulse to do evil, like any other man. Furthermore,
the Messiah's role is transient. Like Elijah, the Messiah is forerunner
and precursor, but he is hardly an enduring player in the eschatological drama. Only God is. Time and again we shall see that the Messiah
refers back to God for instructions on what he is to do. People want
the Messiah to come—that is the premise of the stories told in connection with repentance—but that is only because he will inaugurate

the eschatological drama, not because, on his own, he will bring the drama to its conclusion. Only God will.

Most strikingly, the Messiah theme plays itself out not only in the eschatological categories but also in those that concern sin and the evil inclination. This presentation of the theme is accomplished through a complex composite at *b. Sukkah* 5:1D–5:4. Here the Mishnah passage evokes from the framers of the Talmud's composite some comments on the "evil inclination," which in this context refers to libido in particular. Thus we have a rather substantial discussion of sexuality. But a second look shows us that the focus of the composite is not really illicit sexual behavior or desire but the Messiah theme. Here we find the allegation that the Messiah son of Joseph was killed because of the evil inclination; the Messiah son of David will be saved by God; the evil inclination then is made the counterweight to the Messiah and a threat to his survival. It is overcome, however, by study of the Torah. The composite is hardly coherent in detail, but its thematic program—Torah, Messiah, in the context of the Festival of Tabernacles—imposes upon the topic of the Mishnah paragraph a quite different perspective from that set forth in the Mishnah itself. The pertinent part is as follows:

> 3. A. [With regard to "And the land shall mourn, every family apart; the family of the house of David apart, and their wives apart" (Zech. 12:12),] What was the reason for the mourning [to which reference is made in Zechariah's statement]?
> B. R. Dosa and rabbis differed on this matter.
> C. One said, "It is on account of the Messiah, the son of Joseph, who was killed."
> D. And the other said, "It is on account of the evil inclination, which was killed."

The dispute balances the death of the Messiah against the death of the inclination to do evil, though these surely are opposites, and that leads to the inquiry, why should the land mourn at the death of the latter?

> E. Now in the view of him who said, "It is on account of the Messiah, the son of Joseph, who was killed," we can make sense of the following verse of Scripture: "And they shall look on me because they have thrust him through, and they shall mourn for him as one mourns for his only son" [Zech. 12:10].
> F. But in the view of him who has said, "It is on account of the evil inclination, which was killed," should this be an occasion for mourning? It should be an occasion for rejoicing. Why then should [the people] have wept?

The eschatological drama now comes into play: the disposition of the inclination to do evil at the end of days, which is to say, the key action in the restoration of Eden. God himself intervenes, slaying the evil inclination and thus securing for man the capacity to carry out God's will without obstacle.[17]

So much for the Messiah son of Joseph. Now what of the Messiah son of David, and how does he relate to the events just now portrayed?

> 5. A. Our rabbis have taught on Tannaite authority:
>   B. To the Messiah, son of David, who is destined to be revealed—speedily, in our days!—the Holy One, blessed be he, will say, "Ask something from me, and I shall give it to you."
>   C. So it is said, "I will tell of the decree . . . this day have I begotten you, ask of me and I will give the nations for your inheritance" [Ps. 2:7–8].
>   D. When [the Messiah, son of David] sees the Messiah, son of Joseph, killed, he will say before [God], "Lord of the Age, I ask of you only life."
>   E. He will say to him, "Life? Before you spoke of it, David your father had already prophesied about you, as it is said, 'He asked life of you, you gave it to him, [even length of days forever and ever'] [Ps. 21:5]."
>
> *b. Sukkah* 5:1D–5:4 II.3ff./52a–b

Here the Messiah theme works itself out in the story of two Messiahs, one who was killed, the other not. This latter Messiah is the one who will participate in the process of the end of time, beginning with the resurrection—a matter more clearly expressed in sources we shall consider in a moment.

First, let us ask about the place, within the composite to which reference has just now been made, of the Messiah and the message that is conveyed by introducing that figure. A rapid recapitulation of the propositions in the large composite tells us what the Talmud has added to the Mishnah's topic, which is the Festival of Tabernacles.

> 1. God created the impulse to do evil but regrets it: there are four things that the Holy One, blessed be he, regrets he created, and these are they: exile, the Chaldeans, the Ishmaelites, and the inclination to do evil.
> 2. The impulse to do evil is weak at the outset but powerful when it becomes habitual. The inclination to do evil to begin with is like

---

17. See the quotation from *b. Sukkah* 5:1 on p. 191 above.

a spider's thread and in the end like cart ropes. In the beginning one calls the evil inclination a passerby, then a guest, and finally a man of the household. The impulse to do evil affects one's status in the world to come.

Now the integral character of the insertion about the Messiah becomes clear:

3. The Messiah was killed on account of the impulse to do evil. That is why the Messiah, son of David, asked God to spare his life and not allow him to be killed the way the Messiah son of Joseph was killed.
4. The impulse to do evil is stronger for sages than for others. But they possess the antidote in the Torah: "For it has done great things" (Joel 2:20): "And against disciples of sages more than against all the others." A man's inclination [to do evil] overcomes him every day. A man's inclination to do evil prevails over him every day and seeks to kill him. If that vile one meets you, drag it to the house of study. If it is a stone, it will dissolve. If it is iron, it will be pulverized.

Here is where the self-evident connection proves revealing. If we did not know that the Festival of Tabernacles was not only associated with an autumnal celebration of the advent of rain and the fructifying of the fields but also identified as the occasion for the coming of the Messiah, then on the strength of this extrinsic composite we should have formed the theory that those two protean conceptions governed. Nowhere do I see a claim that the Messiah is the one who raises the dead. The language used always simply says that when he has come the dead will rise or live; but God is the one who gives them breath. But does the Messiah bear responsibility for raising the dead? I do not identify that claim in so many words. Who then bears responsibility for doing so? It is Israel. That point is made time and again when pertinent. Israel's own repentance will provide the occasion, and God will do the rest. It is when Israel has repented that the Messiah will come. It follows that the Messiah's advent and activity depend upon Israel, not on the Messiah's own autonomous decision, character, and behavior. Israel decides issues of its own attitude toward God and repents, and God decides to respond to the change in will. The Messiah responds to Israel's decision as to when he should appear to signal the change in the condition of mankind, and the Messiah responds to God's decision, taking a part within the sequence that comes to an end with Elijah.

The Restoration Paradigm

What of the world to come? The theology of the oral Torah sets forth a thought world in which at stake are not beginnings and endings in an ordinal or (other) temporal sense. At issue, rather, are balances and proportions, the match of this to that, start to finish, Eden and world to come. Specifically, when sages speak of the world to come, their language signifies a final change in relationship between God and man, a model of how God and man relate that marks the utter restoration of the world order originally contemplated. That is the way man and God conduct the cosmic transaction that God had intended from the beginning and for eternity—time having no place in his category-formation for ordering creation. The point, specifically, is that Israel enjoys a set of relationships with God that are not differentiated temporally and not organized in causative sequence through time.

How then are these relationships classified in this governing model? They are either rebellious or obedient, selfish and arrogant or selfless and humble, and so on, as we have seen at great length. Since at issue are patterns of relationship, the circumstance and context, whether temporal or singular in some other way, make no impact. That is because they make no difference, the relationship transcending circumstance. Therefore it is entirely reasonable that the world to come should match the world that has been—why not? The one, like the other, will find its definition in how God and man relate. But the sages did not have in mind a "cyclical" pattern of human existence. They did not contemplate a recurring cycle of existence, beginnings and endings and new beginnings, such as nature presents. Cyclical thinking is as alien to the sages as historical thinking, because it presupposes an eternal return, an endless recapitulation of the pattern. But that is not what the sages have in mind. They anticipate a one-time return, then an eternity of perfection.

The perfection of world order leaves no alternative. Once man has repented and conformed his will to God's, that relationship, embodying measure for measure in a most just and merciful realization, attains perfection. Man's will and God's meet, producing finality, complementarity, utter correspondence. That is why there is no room in the sages' system for an endless cycle of sin, punishment, atonement, reconciliation. I see, within the system, three embodiments:

1. Adam loses Eden, and Israel (the new Adam), loses the Land.
2. Israel repents, and the dead are raised,
3. Israel is restored to the Land, and eternal life follows.

Now, in that model, with its stress on eternal life with God, no logical place opens up for the cyclical replay of the pattern. Paradigmatic thinking then finds its place between historical-linear and ahistorical-cyclical thinking.

So here the story comes full circle that commences with God's creation of a perfect world defined by a just order. That world exhibits flaws; it is not perfect by reason of the character of man. But the world will be restored to perfection (requiring, then, eternity), man to Eden, and Israel to the Land of Israel through man's, and Israel's, act of repentance and reconciliation with God. That act of reconciliation, prepared for in countless lives of virtue and acts of merit, is realized in the world or age to come. Through its account of that world or age, therefore, that theology writes the last, but unending, chapter in the story of how God's justice establishes and ultimately restores the world order of perfection and equity.

The world to come concludes the eschatological series comprised of sequenced paradigms that cover (1) past, (2) present, (3) Israel's collective repentance, (4) the age (days) of the Messiah, (5) days of the war of Gog and Magog, (6) the resurrection of the dead, (7) the judgment, and onward to the last things at (8) the world to come. If resurrection concerns the individual Israelite, with some further implications for the whole of Israel, the world to come that follows encompasses all Israel. The one embodies salvation for the private person, the other, redemption for the entire holy people, now at the end encompassing all of mankind within Israel. But what, exactly, when the sages set forth their theological eschatology, do they mean by *olam habba*, the world or the age that is coming? (Hebrew *olam* may sustain either the locative or the temporal-ordinal meaning.) The world or the age to come completes, and necessarily forms the final chapter of, the theology of the oral Torah. The age that is coming will find Adam's successor in Eden's replacement, that is, resurrected, judged, and justified Israel—comprising nearly all Israelites who ever lived—now eternally rooted in the Land of Israel.

As we have seen, the governing theology sets forth its main components in a simple narrative, and very often a single sentence captures the story. Here is such a version of the complete tale of the world to come in one short sentence: "When Israel returns to God, God will restore their fortunes." The sentence remains brief enough with the added phrase "after the model of Adam and Eve in Eden." Everything else amplifies details. That simple sentence is explicitly built on the verb root for return, encompassing *shuv* (restore), yielding *teshuvah* (repentance), as well as the causative form of the verb, *hashiv* (return or restore). It thereby defines the condition, (intransitive) returning or repenting, for the advent of the age to come, which encompasses the action of (transitively) returning matters to their original condition.

The upshot is that "last" does not define a temporal category or even an ordinal one in the exact sense. By "last things" the sages' theology means the model of things that applies at the last, from now on, for eternity: *the last, the final realization or recapitulation of the ever-present and enduring paradigm(s),* creation and Exodus. In concrete terms, that means intense interest will focus on how the redemption of Israel from Egypt compares with the advent of the world to come. This point is made explicitly. The fall of the oppressor at the start of Israel's history and the fall of the nations at the end, characteristic of the redemption of that time and of the coming time, will be matched by the fall of the other at the end and the traits of the redemption that is coming. To see how this is made concrete is to enter into the theological workshop of the sages. No passage more clearly exposes the character of their thought—both its method and its message—than the one that requires them to select paradigmatic moments out of the detritus of history:

> 2. A. R. Levi, son-in-law of R. Zechariah, in the name of R. Berekhiah said, "As at the news concerning Egypt, so they shall be startled at the fall of the adversary" [Isa. 23:5].
>   B. Said R. Eliezer, "Whenever the name of Tyre is written in Scripture, if it is written out [with all of the letters], then it refers to the province of Tyre. Where it is written without all of its letters [and so appears identical to the word for adversary, the reference of Scripture is to Rome. [So the sense of the verse is that Rome will receive its appropriate reward.]"

Now the fall of Egypt is matched by the fall of Rome, which, we surely should anticipate, is a precondition for the advent of the world to come, at which point, at a minimum, the subjugation of Israel to the pagan empire ceases:

> 3. A. R. Levi in the name of R. Hama bar Hanina: "He who exacted vengeance from the former [oppressor] will exact vengeance from the latter."

Now the first redemption, from Egypt, is shown to match point by point the final redemption, from Edom/Rome. Each detail finds its counterpart in an amazing selection of consequential facts, properly aligned—ten in all:

> B. "Just as in Egypt it was with blood, so with Edom [= Rome] it will be the same: 'I will show wonders in the heavens and in the earth, blood, and fire, and pillars of smoke' [Joel 3:3].

C. "Just as in Egypt it was with frogs, so with Edom it will be the same: 'The sound of an uproar from the city, an uproar because of the palace, an uproar of the Lord who renders recompense to his enemies' [Isa. 66:6].

D. "Just as in Egypt it was with lice, so with Edom it will be the same: 'The streams of Bosrah will be turned into pitch, and the dust thereof into brimstone, and the land thereof shall become burning pitch [Isa. 34:9]. Smite the dust of the earth that it may become lice' [Exod. 8:12].

E. "Just as in Egypt it was with swarms of wild beasts, so with Edom it will be the same: 'The pelican and the bittern shall possess it' [Isa. 34:11].

F. "Just as in Egypt it was with pestilence, so with Edom it will be the same: 'I will plead against Gog with pestilence and with blood' [Ezek. 38:22].

G. "Just as in Egypt it was with boils, so with Edom it will be the same: 'This shall be the plague wherewith the Lord will smite all the peoples that have warred against Jerusalem: their flesh shall consume away while they stand upon their feet' [Zech. 14:12].

H. "Just as in Egypt it was with great stones, so with Edom it will be the same: 'I will cause to rain upon Gog . . . an overflowing shower and great hailstones' [Ezek. 38:22].

I. "Just as in Egypt it was with locusts, so with Edom it will be the same: 'And you, son of man, thus says the Lord God: Speak to birds of every sort . . . the flesh of the mighty shall you eat . . . blood shall you drink . . . you shall eat fat until you are full and drink blood until you are drunk' [Ezek. 39:17–19].

J. "Just as in Egypt it was with darkness, so with Edom it will be the same: 'He shall stretch over Edom the line of chaos and the plummet of emptiness' [Isa. 34:11].

K. "Just as in Egypt he took out their greatest figure and killed him, so with Edom it will be the same: 'A great slaughter in the land of Edom, among them to come down shall be the wild oxen' [Isa. 34:6–7]."

Pesiqta de Rab Kahana VII:XI.3

Merely juxtaposing "Egypt" and "Edom" suffices to establish that we shall compare the one and the other, and the paradigm of redemption emerges. The known, Egypt, bears the distinguishing trait of marking Israel's initial redemption; then the unknown can be illuminated. Therefore, say "Edom" (= Rome) and no one can miss the point. The stakes are sufficiently identified through the combination of the native categories, and all the rest spells out what is clear at the very outset. The redemption that is coming replicates the redemption that is past in a world that conforms to enduring paradigms. And that must encompass also the return to Eden that we have many times considered. The world to come marks the final condition of world order. It signifies the realization of correct and perfect relationships between God and man, God and Israel in particular. Once those who reject God have been disposed of, the age to come finds its definition in the time of total reconciliation between God and man. It is the age when man loves God, accepts his dominion, and completes the work of repentance and atonement for acts of rebellion. Clearly that reconciliation of God and man takes place in individual life, so that we may use the language of salvation.

The theology of the oral Torah accordingly reaches its climactic statement as it turns from the transcendent situation of Israel in the age to come to Israel at this time and there finds grounds for sublime hope. The theology contains the promise that while now Israel grieves, in the end of days God will give them grounds for rejoicing, and that will be in a measure commensurate to the loyalty and patience shown in the interim. How do we know, and how long? The perfect justice of the one God comes to realization in the promises that have been kept, surety and guarantee of the promises that will be kept. A homely story captures the promise:

> A. Said R. Aqiba, "Simeon b. Luga told me, 'A certain child of the sons of their sons and I were gathering grass in the field. Then I saw him laugh and cry.
> B. "'I said to him, "Why did you cry?"
> C. "'He said to me, "Because of the glory of father's house, which has gone into exile."
> D. "'I said to him, "Then why did you laugh?"
> E. "'He said, "At the end of it all, in time to come, the Holy One, blessed be He, is going to make his descendants rejoice."'"

The exile guarantees the return, one promise kept, another is sure to be carried out. Now the story winds its way onward:

> F. "'I said to him, "Why?" [What did you see to make you think of this?]
> G. "'He said to me, "A smoke-raiser in front of me [made me laugh]."
> H. "'I said to him, "Show it to me."
> I. "'He said to me, "We are subject to an oath not to show it to anyone at all."'"
> J. Said R. Yohanan b. Nuri, "One time I was going along the way and an old man came across me and said to me, 'I am a member of the house of Abtinas.

K. "'At the beginning, when the house of father was discreet, they would give their scrolls [containing the prescriptions for frankincense only] to one another.

L. "'Now take it, but be careful about it, since it is a scroll containing a recipe for spices.'

M. "And when I came and reported the matter before R. Aqiba, he said to me, 'From now on it is forbidden to speak ill of these people again.'"

N. On the basis of this story, Ben Azzai said, "Yours will they give you,

O. "by your own name will they call you,

P. "in your place will they seat you.

Q. "There is no forgetfulness before the Omnipresent.

R. "No man can touch what is designated for his fellow."

t. Kippurim 2:7

Israel finds itself subjugated to the gentiles in a world flawed by the prosperity of the wicked and the suffering of the righteous. So it is a time of mourning—but one of remembrance of the future, which the past promises out of the pathos of the present. Given the condition of the world and of Israel in it, it is right to mourn—beginning after all with mourning for Israel's own failures. But those who mourn properly now will rejoice in time to come, the one serving as an act of faith for what is to be. Whoever mourns for Jerusalem now will merit rejoicing with her in the world to come.

Comparing Theologies

Christianity on Judaism

Christianity can only endorse the insight that humanity is created in the image and likeness of God (Gen. 1:26). The affinity between divine and human identity is pursued in the ethical realm, when Jesus links two quite disparate commands in the Torah, to love God (Deut. 6:4) and love one's neighbor (Lev. 19:18), by his careful insistence that they are like one another (Matt. 22:34–40; Mark 12:28–34). The Scriptures of Israel had discovered within the vision of the divine Throne that an image of humanity was present (see Ezek. 1:26; Dan. 7:13), and Jesus joined himself to that vision (see, for example, Luke 12:8–9). In the Revelation of John, the crucified Jesus is himself part of the Throne (see chapters 4–5 especially), and that signals an essential aspect of the teaching of his resurrection: even when he was put to death, and particularly when he was experienced alive after his death, Jesus was the inherent image of divine humanity.

The defect of the primordial man and woman as the emblem of who we are does not seal our fate but is part of the master plan of the restoration of humanity to God's image and likeness. That is a hope Christianity also shares with Judaism, but Israel's return to the Land of Israel is no longer seen as a necessary part of that hope. As Paul expresses the matter, "Just as through one person's disobedience many were caused to be sinners, so also through one's obedience many shall be caused to be righteous" (Rom. 5:19). Human salvation is no longer here a matter of place but of the medium of life itself; the first Adam was a living being, the last Adam a life-giving spirit (1 Cor. 15:45). Christianity's anthropology is of a new, restored humanity in Christ, attested both by Jesus' resurrection and by the promptings of the Holy Spirit within us.

Spelling out how the case of Jesus can resonate with humanity as such involves a detailed analysis of how humans are connected to one another, as well as to God. Philo of Alexandria, an older contemporary of Jesus, developed just such a theology in his treatise *On the Creation of the World*. In his exposition, the pattern of divine creation (the "word," *logos*) corresponds to the model of humanity, so that we all share a correspondence with the creative ideal in God's mind, with the natural world around us, and with one another. *Avot de Rabbi Nathan* XXXI:III.1 expounds that analysis from a rabbinic point of view as does John 1:1–18 from the point of view of Christianity. What is immediately striking, when one sets the two texts side by side, is that the terms of reference are as categorically cosmographic in the rabbinic application as they are soteriological in the Christian application. Both aspects are present in Philo (and neither is excluded in Judaism or Christianity), but the difference of emphasis is notable. John's Gospel itself adumbrates this distinction at the close of its famous prologue regarding the word of God: "Because from his fullness we all received, even grace in place of grace, because the law was given through Moses; grace and truth occurred through Christ Jesus" (1:17).

The principle of *zekhut* or grace undergirds our lives, because only divine generosity gave us being, and the uncoerced mirroring of that generosity by humanity is among heaven's greatest joys. As in every case of divine pleasure, this embrace of grace results in a new creation: the restored humanity promised in Christ and first effected in his resurrection. His Spirit becomes accessible to all, which is why, in Christianity, the single unforgivable sin is not against the Torah, but against the Spirit of God (see Matt. 12:31–32; Mark 3:28–30).

Judaism on Christianity

Here is where Judaism and Christianity come together: the belief in the resurrection of the dead. That is not broadly grasped. Recently a prominent biologist reported that "a scholar at a religious conference" told him that "what little Judaism has to say about the afterlife is only there because Christians asked them."[18] Far from the truth. Secular Jews deny that and much else, but Judaic faithful know better. On its own, not in dialogue with any other religious tradition, Judaism has a great deal to say about eschatology, including afterlife, and what it says is integral to its normative theology, law, and liturgy. It is not invented just to please the Christians. Judaic eschatological doctrine has its roots deep in pre-Christian times. It is a matter not only of theologians' doctrines but also of the living faith embodied in obligatory prayer. The obligatory liturgy of the prayerbook of Judaism, in all versions down to our own times and in most versions today (including Orthodox, Reform, and Conservative), holds explicitly that God raises the dead; that belief is repeated in the prayer recited three times every day of the year and some days four times. One will easily find it in the prayer known as the Amidah: it is the second of the eighteen benedictions. The Christians didn't provoke the Jews to develop an eschatology involving the resurrection of the dead at the end of days. The resurrection doctrine was there before Christianity came into being.

Two creedal hymns sung in Judaic worship on a great many public occasions, *Yigdal* and *Adon Olam*, both refer to the resurrection of the dead as principles of the faith.

We have already seen that the Mishnah (the authoritative code of law, and foundation of the two Talmuds, and basis for the law of Judaism) explicitly states: "All Israel has a portion in the world to come" (*m. Sanhedrin* 10:1; *b. Sanhedrin* 11:1). Those who deny that principle of the faith are denied a portion in the world to come, that is, do not undergo resurrection out of the grave.

Every formulation of the principles of the faith, Judaism, whether Maimonides, whether rabbinical councils, until nearly our own times, and most, though not all, of those adopted in our own times, affirm the resurrection of the dead and the eschatological narratives that convey that principle. The wording varies, but there is no Judaic system, no community of Judaism, that lacks an eschatology encompassing afterlife in some language or other.

18. Natalie Angier, "The Origin of Religions, from a Distinctly Darwinian View," *New York Times*, December 24, 2002, quoting biologist David Sloan Wilson.

True, there is diverse opinion in contemporary Judaisms on eschatology. But the Judaism represented today by Orthodox, Conservative, and Reform Judaisms is explicit on having an eschatological doctrine conforming to, or deriving from, the classical authoritative Torah. Reform interprets resurrection in a more this-worldly framework, but its liturgy renders the same blessing as the received prayer book, which says, "Who keeps faith with those who lie in the dust . . . blessed are you . . . who resurrects the dead." I don't see how eschatology can be more explicit than that.

Epilogue

Comparing Theologies

Why Judaism Is True

Judaism is true because it accurately translates the law and theology of the Torah into the design of the kingdom of priests and the holy people that God commands humanity to bring into being. By the criterion of Scripture, Judaism is true. That is the sole basis on which Judaism lays claim to truth.

Judaism and Christianity sustain theological comparison because they share a common Scripture and its narrative. They produce theological contrasts because each brings to Scripture a distinctive perspective. Judaism receives Scripture as the written record of revelation, along with the oral components of the same act of revelation at Sinai ultimately transcribed in the rabbinic canon of the first six centuries CE. Scripture and tradition, formed into a systematic theology realized in the laws that set the norms of the Israelite social order, all together define Judaism. They embody its claim to truth: God's will for humanity.

That claim points for justification to the character of the Torah, beginning with the written component thereof. Judaism follows the narrative of Scripture from the beginning to the eschatological present, while Christianity reads from present to past. Judaism finds in Scripture the story of holy Israel, the community called into being by God through

259

Abraham and Sarah and realized at Sinai with the covenant of the Torah: "We shall do and we shall obey." That yields a community with no counterpart in humanity: not a race, not an ethnic group, not an extended family, but a social entity formed by a common affirmation, a shared response to God. That response takes the form of covenantal nomism: keeping the law of the Torah as the realization of Israel's covenant to be God's people. Christianity, coming after so much has happened and been learned, starts fresh and rewrites Scripture, imposing its story upon the eternal tale of the Torah. While concurring with Judaism in many details, Christianity misses the main point of Sinai: the regeneration of all humanity through the discipline of the Torah.

Christianity misses the point because it substitutes the individual for the community, Christ for Israel, the world to come that is attained through faith for this world that we know and endure in patience. It consequently centers on the notional and personal instead of on the public and the perpetual. And it imposes upon this world, in all its unredemption, the dimension of a now-realized salvation, as though the time had come, although it has manifestly not come. For the criteria set forth by the Torah for the realization of God's kingdom can be met only with the advent of the Messiah to raise the dead. Then comes the last judgment, and those who "stand in judgment" (having atoned for sin through death) will enter the world to come and live for eternity in Eden. That represents the restoration of humanity to the condition God intended from the beginning.

Judaism and Christianity tell a story beginning in the same place—Eden—and ending in the same place—the resurrection of the dead. But while Judaism tells that story to the holy community, Israel, and about Israel, defined as those who take shelter under the wings of God's presence in the world and accept the Torah as God's will, Christianity stresses the individual relationship between God and man. To be sure, Judaism teaches that God wants the heart, that the religious duties or commandments were given only to purify the heart of man. And for its part Christianity acknowledges the social dimension. But the focus of the one—on that unique individual, Jesus Christ—differs in essence from the focus of the other on God's people, the community of those who know God in the Torah. On that point of difference Judaism takes its stand. For Christianity the Torah prepares the way; for Judaism the Torah *is* the way. True, as chapter 3 has shown—in answering the question, What is to be done about man?—the two traditions of ancient Scripture address the same problem, with different results. And the differences are many and complex. But they keep doubling back to the same point: Torah versus Christ.

Both traditions invoke the conception of a kingdom of God, but differ on when that comes about and how it is conceived. Judaism expects God's kingdom to come at the end of days and views with astonishment the notion, not sustained in the everyday world, of a kingdom realized in the advent of Jesus. Easter has not yet come, and when it does it will encompass the entirety of humanity that knows God and seeks reconciliation with him. "All Israel has a portion in the world to come" promises resurrection and eternal life to those who have atoned through death and arisen from the grave, have been justified, and have entered into Eden. What are the halakhah's media for the reformation, regeneration, and renewal of man? Judaism legislates not for Eden but for the kingdom of God, in the here and now—and therefore in the future.

Sinai's answer to Eden's question both encompasses and transcends the matter of sin and atonement. After the reconciliation, what? That is the question that the halakhic structure addresses: the conduct of the ordinary, everyday life lived under God's rule. That is because the normative deals with the normal, not just the exceptional: the life made up of not only sinful, but also obedient, moments. Christianity for its part makes no provision for the present tense of time, but only for that entry into God's intangible kingdom. There is no here and now. And, as our examination of the corresponding doctrines of sin and atonement has shown, there also is no sacred community, only an individuated humanity, each person by himself before God. But that is not how life is lived. That explains, also, why Christianity produces no coherent doctrine of resurrection, only a set of incoherent promises.

If I had to specify the three points at which I believe Christianity in all its complexity has taken leave of God's truth as revealed in the Torah, therefore, I should point to these fundamentals: (1) Christianity picks and chooses among the details of Scripture (its "Old Testament") without addressing its main point and principal message, namely, that God yearns for the love of humanity, expressed in willing obedience to God's will *in the Torah*. (2) Christianity removes the individual from the social order and conceives of humanity one by one, not formed into a moral entity, a community called to form God's portion, God's kingdom here and now. That is the message of the Prophets: God responds to the moral entity formed by the entire society, not just to individual attitudes and actions. (3) Christianity posits a radical break between history and eschatology, deferring to a time yet to be seen the consolidation of messy human reality into a theologically coherent world. The Writings, with their diverse and sage readings of events, both personal (as in Job) and public (as in Proverbs and Qohelet), achieve that kind of synthesis in the present.

If I had to specify the three points at which Judaism, for all its imperfections in realizing its sacred calling, accomplishes God's purpose in his self-manifestation to humanity through the Torah, they correspond: (1) Judaism finds its definition in the Torah of Sinai. (2) It focuses on the social order as the medium for serving God: the community as the arena of responsibility. (3) It grasps the realities of history and understands its meaning. Scripture is thereby replicated: the Torah, the Prophets, the Writings all fulfilled in the practicalities of a world not yet redeemed but susceptible of sanctification.

To Christianity, Judaism must say: Not yet, not thus, not that one in particular. That is because Judaism affirms: Yes to the Torah, yes to the Prophets, yes to the Writings—to which the Christian message is asymmetrical and awry.

Some would then ask, has Christianity accomplished God's purpose? Does it not bring Israel's Scriptures to humanity? I find it difficult to share the view of some contemporary rabbis that Christianity forms the preparation for the Torah. That is not its intent, that is not its record. It is a different religion from Judaism, and to the extent of the difference, it diverges from what God has instructed us to receive as his will. Scripture—"the Old Testament" for Christianity, "the written part of the Torah" for Judaism—forms the arena for conflict between the competing heirs of Sinai—*sola Scriptura*. That conflict was joined at the very outset, in the language, "You have heard it said . . . but I say to you . . . ," and persists even in the pages of this labor of comparison and contrast. It would demean Christianity for Judaism to say less in response to Christianity's "Why not?" than Judaism's "Why yes?"

Why Christianity Is True

Christians endorse the claim of Judaism to the Torah in calling the Scriptures of Israel "the Old Testament." Those writings are cited as documents with a previous ownership. Christians believe in the durability of the covenant with Israel and locate themselves within that covenant's history.

But that history's importance derives from the opportunity it offers; Christianity understands that the human condition transcends history. Where one might see present reality as determined by the past, the church sees it as defined by the future we are heading for. So—in the case of defining the people of God—the only Israel that matters is the Israel we are all becoming, not the Israel that has been. Descent does not matter; heritage does not matter; the past is interesting but ultimately beside the point. Everything depends on where you are going.

Every single person who believes in the way that Abraham believed in God becomes a child of Abraham (Gal. 3:6–9) and therefore an Israelite. Paul said that, but in doing so he articulated a consensus of theology. Faith alone was Abraham's righteousness (Gen. 15:6), and that is a prophetic truth for us as well. The whole issue of affiliation with Abraham and Sarah is set aside, because Jew and Greek, slave and free, male and female are explicitly rejected as yesterday's divisions, which are to be dissolved in the future glory of God's kingdom (Gal. 3:28).

As the *Epistle to Diognetus* (5.6) puts the matter, if the world is to be carved up between the race of the Greeks and the race of the Jews, then Christians are a third race, foreigners in every country and patriots of every land. Boundaries of race, class, and country are artificial structures of a corrupt world that is now in the process of passing away. "Israel" is the integer of salvation that emerges when the Spirit of God moves over you, a reality the Old Testament points to without mapping precisely.

So the Old Testament is every Christian's story, whether "Jew or Greek" because it is the record of how faith came to fruition, how it grew and developed like a plant, bobbed and weaved like a boxer, and broke through to the promise of a new heaven and a new earth in the poetry of vision that scholars call apocalyptic. That faith is the promise Christ fulfills, and for us the patriarchs and prophets and psalmists equally sing our song—and sing it in our words. But the melody, Christianity insists against Judaism, is that of prophecy rather than Torah.

In the Transfiguration Jesus appears to his disciples as he converses with Moses and Elijah; at the close of that discussion, a divine echo identifies him alone as God's own "child" (see Mark 9:2–8). Here we come to the heart of the matter. For the church, what Moses and Elijah and Jesus talk about is not the Torah, but the revelation of this special relationship to God.

The ways of fathers and sons, parents and their children, are remarkably constant. Many elemental features travel over time and across cultures. One stands out vividly in the memory of any first-time parent: children talk back. They interrupt. They get upset at you for no good reason. Remember that when the prophet Hosea (11:1) said, "Out of Egypt I called my son," he was talking about the Israelites, and in the same breath complaining graphically and bitterly about their lack of constancy. Simon ben Shetah said something similar about Honi called the Circler, a worker of wonders (*b. Ta'anit* 23a): God listened to his prayers because he spoiled him like a child. Children behave like children, Jesus included.

The Spirit of God in his case brought a life of rigor and passion and vision and commitment, but also of doubt, anger, suffering, and loneliness. The Gospels do not conceal any of that; in fact they celebrate Jesus' weakness, although the celebration is too much for many pseudo-orthodox in the modern period. Tertullian went so far as to describe Jesus as short, squat, and ugly (*De carne Christi*). Why? This genuine humanity means that the sonship of Jesus, his intimacy with Spirit, is a model for our receiving of the Spirit, for all our own ugliness. At baptism, Paul says, the Spirit within us cries out to God, "Abba, Father" (Gal. 4:4–7; Rom. 8:14–17) as happened when Jesus was immersed by John the Baptist. Sonship is ours; it comes to us with our own immersion in the Spirit, our own crosses to bear, our own transformation into eternal life.

Sonship belongs to us because it belongs to Jesus, and vice versa. Sonship is the central theme of the story of God's ways with his people. For Paul, it is the first and best of Israel's gifts to all believers—well ahead of the law (Rom. 9:5). Christians believe the real content of revelation is the story of God's ceaseless longing to bring home his vagrant children in every time and place. As St. Augustine, bishop of Hippo, wrote in his longest treatise, *The City of God*, the whole of human history takes place in the dreadful caesura written in humanity's catastrophic confusion between passion and self-indulgence, between love of God and love of self:

> So two loves have constituted two cities—the earthly is formed by love of self even to contempt of God, the heavenly by love of God even to contempt of self. For the one glories in herself, the other in the Lord. The one seeks glory from man; for the other God, the witness of the conscience, is the greatest glory. . . . In the one the lust for power prevails, both in her own rulers and in the nations she subdues; in the other all serve each other in charity, governors by taking thought for all and subjects by obeying. (*City of God* 14.28)

By book 18, Augustine arrives at his own time and repeats that the two cities "alike enjoy temporal goods or suffer temporal ills, but differ in faith, in hope, in love, until they be separated by the final judgment and each receive its end, of which there is no end" (*City of God* 18.54). That, for us, is the context of Scripture, its story of all time.

Augustine wrote while *Genesis Rabbah* was being compiled, and like the sages of that Midrash, Augustine synthesized Scripture with his view of the world and salvation as a whole. Unlike the sages, his perspective was not one of a repeated pattern. Augustine teaches us something about Christianity that Christians themselves often have trouble seeing, so I am not surprised when those looking at our faith from outside miss the point. To the naked eye, it can seem that Judaism and Christianity are fighting over words: you say the Scripture is about Torah, I say it is about Christ. As Margaret Thatcher once said of her opponents, "They would say that, wouldn't they?" At some level, our disputation has to come down to that. But Augustine shows us plainly why the issue here is not merely a matter of words.

Jesus' sonship leads not to restoration but to resurrection. This is not just a matter of afterlife somehow sometime, a wish for the pleasant parts of the status quo to keep on going or a return to nostalgia as it used to be. Rather, Jesus in the most ancient creed of the church was raised to a new order of spiritual being at *God's right hand*, such that believers also strive for a transformation into life in the Spirit, rather than the flesh. The focus of the Christian orientation expressed in the Apostles Creed is precisely that resurrection of the spiritual bodies of believers (so Paul in 1 Cor. 15:12–54), a new and transformed life that the world has glimpsed before only in the case of Jesus.

So Christians must of necessity read the Bible backward. When you are moving forward at great speed into unmapped territory, maps tell you where you have been and provide only an inkling of where you are going. The heavenly Jerusalem that is our true home is not objectively there in the text at all; our intimacy with that Jerusalem, she who is our mother (Gal. 4:26), comes only with the Spirit that the Scriptures attest and awaken. We search not for patterns that always have been and will be, nor for any city ever on earth, but for directions to that city whose constitution is a kingdom not of this world.

Perhaps Professor Neusner and I have canceled each other out, convincing you that neither Judaism nor Christianity owns the Bible. That would be productive, because any ownership is God's. Scripture is divine property. We have really been arguing over the lease we hold on the property. That lease has run longer then either side anticipated, so it may seem we own the Bible, but we don't.

What is the key provision of the lease? Is it that the form of the revealed Torah should never be altered? Or is it that the prophetic visions fulfilled by Jesus should never be abandoned? There are some issues only an owner can decide. Christianity is true because it pleads its case on the basis of the Spirit of the God who will judge us all, just as he made us all and longs to reconcile us to himself.

Index of Subjects

Index of Ancient Sources

Apocrypha and Septuagint

2 Maccabees

Wisdom

Targumic Texts

Targum of Isaiah

Classical Writings

Livy

Ab urbe condita

Plato

Republic

Seneca

De clementia

Postbiblical Hellenistic Jewish Writings

Josephus

War

Philo

De specialibus legibus

The Migration of Abraham

Postbiblical Christian Writings

Augustine

City of God